Augmented Reality

Jon Peddie

Augmented Reality

Where We Will All Live

 Springer

Jon Peddie
Jon Peddie Research Inc.
Tiburon, CA, USA

ISBN 978-3-319-85409-0   ISBN 978-3-319-54502-8   (eBook)
DOI 10.1007/978-3-319-54502-8

This Springer imprint is published by Springer Nature
The registered company is Springer International Publishing AG
The registered company address is: Gewerbestrasse 11, 6330 Cham, Switzerland

*To Kathleen Maher, my best friend,
supporter, nudger, editor, and wife—couldn't
have done it without you darling*

Foreword by Thomas A. Furness III

During the mid-80s there was rush of media exposure related to the Super Cockpit[1] project I was working on at Wright-Patterson Air Force Base, Ohio. I was inundated by people out of the blue asking me about the possibility for applications of virtual interfaces beyond the military. One such individual was a golf pro from Australia. He wanted to create a better way to instruct novice golfers how to swing the golf club. He told me that he had tried everything. He started by saying to these novices, "watch me" and "do as I do" then demonstrating how to stand, hold the club and swing the club. He would show them videos of their own swings and point out corrections. He attempted to stand behind them as they were gripping the club…but the students still didn't get it. Finally, in frustration he asked me, is there any way you can use this virtual interface stuff to put me inside the student…like a ghost. So that when the students wear a headset they see my arms and feet coming out of their own bodies and, in turn, just position their real feet, hands and club where I position and move mine in the ghost image. This way they have a 'personal' or 'inside-out' view rather that the typical 'outside-in'. The golf pro's problem with novice golfers was clearly one of perspective…that is, switching from a third person, or 'outside-in' perspective to that of a first person perspective.

This question opened a flood of ideas for other applications of virtual interfaces beyond the military ones that I was pursuing. I thought of the notion of virtual embedded experts, for training, remote operation and physical therapy. For example, an embedded expert cohabiting a person's body could show them how to repair a jet engine, perform brain surgery, or go through a physical therapy session ("put your arm where mine is" or "put you hand *in* mine"). My wife suggested, "let me show you how to knit from my perspective or learn American Sign Language." Interestingly, this cohabitation can all be done equally well in a remote setting where the 'co-inhabitor' and 'co-inhabitee' are not physically present in the same location. In this way a remote surgeon could, in real time, show a medical corpsman in the battlefield how to perform a life saving procedure while looking through the corpsman's point of view and then saying: "follow my hands and do what I am showing you to do."

---

[1] The Super Cockpit is a virtual cockpit that the pilot wears. Using devices embedded into the pilots helmet, flight suit and gloves, the super cockpit creates a circumambience of visual, acoustic, and haptic information that can be superimposed over the real world.

Wow, the implications of this switch in perspective are enormous!

I began my journey in developing and applying virtual interfaces in 1966 when I was assigned as an Air Force Engineering officer to what is now known as the Air Force Research Laboratory at Wright-Patterson Air Force Base. My job was to research, design, build and test better fighter aircraft cockpit interfaces that would improve system performance of both pilots and their machines in military operations. But it was clear that this wasn't going to be easy. The most daunting constraints were the small cockpit space into which we needed to place a myriad of instruments and controls (maybe 300 switches and 75 instrument displays). This made addition of sensor image displays (so that the pilot could see at night) darn near impossible. That is when I turned to virtual interfaces[2] as a means to better couple the pilot's sensory capability to the complexity of the machine. Virtual images, when tied to the pilot's helmet, allowed us to create sensor displays with sufficient size and resolution that better matched the pilot's eyes. The addition of helmet tracking then allowed us to position those sensors in synchrony with pilot head movement so as to create a moving portal or 'picture window' to see through the cockpit and at night. Furthermore, these virtual displays could be populated with other relevant information in the form of graphics that related to threats and aircraft dynamics, such as orientation, navigation, airspeed, altitude and other parameters. The helmet tracking also allowed the pilot to aim various weapon systems to line of sight. Significantly, all of these crucial features would be added without taking up any cockpit space!

I was not the first to think about these issues[3]. Much of the initial thinking about advanced cockpit concepts using virtual interfaces such as helmet-mounted display and graphical displays overlaid over the outside world evolved in the early Army Navy Instrumentation program that began in 1953. The motivation of the program was to take a user-centered approach for cockpit design, starting with the pilot and working toward the machine rather than the traditional way of working from the machine to the pilot. It was this program that established the platform for inspiring my further work in virtual interfaces, visual coupling aids, and eventually the Super Cockpit.

Certainly another part of my willingness to go down the virtual path was inspired by my interest in science fiction. I have been a sci-fi junkie and dreamer since my childhood, beginning in the 40s. One of my favorites was: *They Shall Have Stars*, by James Blish. It was the first of his novel series: Cities in Flight. Interestingly, when published in 1956 its original title was: *Year 2018*. In the novel there was a vivid description of construction workers building an unusual bridge on the planet Jupiter using blocks of frozen ammonia. Because of the harsh environment on

---

[2] By virtual interfaces I mean the *appearance* of virtual, acoustic and haptic images or interfaces in a location in three dimensional space surrounding the pilot, without the object creating the image actually being there.

[3] Even though I seem to have inherited the moniker "the grandfather of virtual reality", I was not the first to begin thinking about these approaches. But to my credit I am probably among the few that have worked continuously in the field of virtual interfaces since 1966.

Jupiter, the workers were physically located on a moon orbiting Jupiter but were telepresent on the 'surface' of Jupiter. This was made possible by using sensors and displays at both ends to transport the eyes and hands of the construction workers to the construction equipment at some distance. Other novels in the same genre extended these notions, such as Heinlein's *Waldo* and *Starship Troopers*. The *Lensman* space opera series by Edward Elmer 'Doc' Smith opened my mind to the use of virtual interfaces for command and control applications using virtual image projection and gestures to control remote entities.

But now these dreams and early developments have evolved and become the new tools of our age. I liken their advent to 'splitting the atom' in terms of unleashing enormous power to unlock and link minds. This unlocking comes from the unprecedented shift in perspective that augmented, virtual and mixed reality gives us…like the golf pro. It is like breaking the glass of the display and going inside and being there. We can augment the real world or share and collaborate in a virtual world. Our research has shown the amazing results of doing so, especially in education and training. Somehow, 'breaking the glass' unlocks spatial memory. It allows us to take the real or virtual world and superimpose or imbed artifacts in the form of graphics or images that 'attach' themselves to that space…and gives us a better way to relate to those items. In a way this awakens our long term memory. It is akin to what the Greeks called the method of loci; that is, to remember things by associating them to spatial locations. The key idea is that we often remember things better when they are spatially associated with locations in 3D spaces rather than as abstract ideas.

For many years we have been adding artificial things to real world things; for example, like adding the laugh tracks to TV sitcoms or showing the first down line superimposed (or embedded) on the playing field (appearing under the players) during televised football games. Why do we want to do this? Think about head-up displays in military cockpits that enable pilots to associate abstract graphical information to the real world such as navigation waypoints and landing projections. This combination of the real and virtual adds to our knowledge and understanding, and helps us to do things better and more efficiently. But at the same time, we need to be careful so as not to obscure important images from the real world.

When I asked Jon Peddie what was his motivation for writing this book, he said: "I genuinely and truly believe we will all use AR and that it will alter forever our lives…" I share Jon's enthusiasm and predictions. But while I am excited about what is happening in the virtual space, I throw out the caution that we don't want to become *intoxicated* by our technology. Technology tools are not an end in themselves, but a means to an end. We should ask not only what, but so what! This means a shift in our perspective from just pushing technology because we can do it, to a mode of developing technology because it helps solve problems and provide new avenues for emergence. Let me explain this further.

I feel we need application 'pulls' that we haven't had in the past. In my half-century journey in this work, I have been as guilty as others in overhyping what is possible with virtual interface technology. It is not as much an issue of developing this technology so much as the question, do we really need to do it. Certainly we can anticipate vertical market applications in military, medicine, design, training and education, but what good is it going to do for the everyday person not affiliated with these specialties. We are all aware of the outcome of the Google Glass experience where promoters had a substantial pushback from the social experience of people's wariness of interacting with people wearing these virtual gadgets. So the solution is to tap the 'pull'…or those applications that can benefit from having virtual augmentation. Combined, the 'push' of technology and the 'pull' of solving problems can propel the development and uptake of this technology.

Certainly we are not finished with the hardware development of augmented reality or virtual reality or mixed reality depending on what you call it. There is a lot of work to do on the technology to make the devices comfortable, useful and successful. Tracking and luminance are big issues when overlaying virtual images on the real world. But most importantly we need to address human factors, and not just the ergonomics of comfort. We need to remember that we are deeply coupling to the human senses, and we don't want to do any harm. That should be our mantra: DO NO HARM! There is a substantial portion of this book that Jon has dedicated to these issues.

As Jon also reports in this book, the augmented reality industry is forecasted to be big…really big, far eclipsing the virtual reality industry. That is why this book is important. For some time we have needed a definitive work on AR to parallel all that has been written about VR, such as the excellent *The VR Book*, written by Dr. Jason Jerald. Dr. Jon Peddie is a pioneer himself in digital media and graphics. From his early work he has taken the approach to understand the trees but to elevate beyond that to view the forest in the context of the industry landscape. His current work is to guide thrusts in our industry with his substantial insights into the complex dynamics of our workplaces especially with this new emergence of augmenting reality.

What you are going to experience as you turn the next pages of this book is an authoritative, comprehensive and modern treatment of the subject of augmented reality. The author says that this is for the layman…that is true, but it is more than that. It also contributes to the hardware and software development community, building upon the scholarly work of many pioneers such as the seminal work by Ronald T. Azuma[4]. In this book, Jon Peddie has amassed and integrated a corpus of material that is finally in one place. This, in itself, is a grand launching platform for achieving the billions in this growing industry that has been forecasted.

Jon's book is also fun, peppered with quips and sarcasm. This is probably how the author kept himself entertained. It has brought back a lot of memories for me, but more importantly, it gets me excited again about the possibilities of this great tool of our age.

Seattle   Thomas A. Furness III
WA, USA
January 28, 2017

---

[4] See for example: http://ronaldazuma.com/publications.html

Foreword by Steve Mann

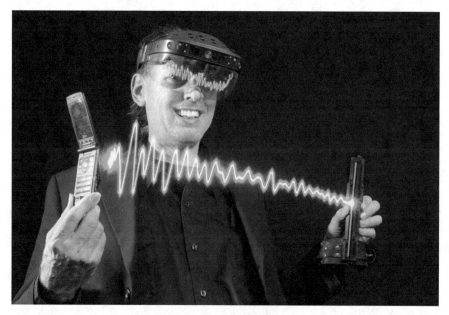

Real Augmented Reality: Steve Mann with SWIM (Sequential Wave Imprinting Machine) and Meta2 that visualizes electromagnetic radio waves from his modified smartphone

Since childhood, for more than 40 years, I've been living my life in a computer-mediated universe called "augmented reality" where I see otherwise invisible radio waves, sound waves, and electrical signals traveling through neurons.

In the next few years, this is the universe "where we will all live."

The father of the field of AI (artificial intelligence), Marvin Minsky, together with the world's foremost futurist, Ray Kurzweil, and myself, put forth a view that AI and machine learning are turning the world into a one-sided control system that's evolving toward total sensing of all aspects of our lives, while at the same time, it remains completely opaque to us [Minsky, Kurzweil, Mann 2013]. We argued for a different kind of intelligence, called HI (humanistic intelligence), as the fundamental basis for augmented reality.

HI is intelligence that makes itself visible and understandable to humans through something we call "sousveillance," or inverse surveillance. Rather than only having the machines watch us, we get to also watch and understand them. HI is intelligence that keeps humans in the loop.

This very principle is what was at the heart of my childhood fascination with being able to see and lay bare the otherwise hidden world of machines and their otherwise secret world of sensory modalities.

There were three fundamental problems I solved in my childhood, through the creation of a wearable computer augmented reality device:

1. Space. The shining light of augmentation must align in space with what it represents. When your eyes focus and converge on reality, the shining light needs to appear at the same focus and convergence.
2. Time. The shining light of augmentation must align in time with what it represents. Feedback delayed is feedback denied.
3. Tonality. The light itself needs to be correct in terms of tonality (i.e., contrast), so that the shining light of augmentation matches what it is supposed to represent.

These three criteria are like a tripod that supports the experience. If one is not met, the experience falls over. And yet so many companies fail to meet all three.

And that's one of the reasons why I've been involved in the founding of a number of institutions in this space.

I believe that, rather than building a carceral world of AI and machine learning, what we need to do is to build a world of HI and AR—a world in which we will live and in which we will thrive as humans.

During my lifetime of living in a computer-mediated reality, I have dreamed of the day when we can all live better, safer, healthier lives through a new form of existential technology.

Today, with the publishing of Jon's book, a large number of people will be gaining access to a deeper and broader understanding of the amazing benefits AR can offer to all industry and individuals. The book wonderfully identifies the benefits and opportunities of AR, as well as the obstacles that could delay its design and realization. The book shows how AR will make people more healthy and self-confident and not just secure but "suicure" (self-care) as well: AR is not so much a device for surveillance (security) but, more importantly, a device for sousveillance ("suicurity"). In this sense, your eyeglass will serve as your personal life recorder and record keeper, such that your most up-to-date medical record will be the one on your body. It will also be your real-time health, fitness, and wellness advisor and personal trainer/assistant.

AR is as important as electric light and may well be the most important invention over the last 5000 years, since the days when "elÄ"krÅ • n" is said to have meant "shining light."

The world of sousveillance is a world where we won't have to fear the police nor honest police fear us.

It will take many years to master all the challenges required to make a socially acceptable-looking device that meets the three fundamental criteria (space, time, tonality), but the path is clear, and we are well on our way to doing it. This book will help us on that journey.

Chief Scientist, Meta Company   Steve Mann

Preface

Abstract The goal of this book is to explain the many nuances of augmented reality and what augmented reality is. Often confused with virtual reality and mixed reality, it is the objective of the book to establish clear delineation between those other technologies whose only common element is a display, but not the content, proximity, or problems.

Augmented reality holds the promise of forever altering, and improving our lives. It will give us freedom from oppression, unlimited sources of information in real time, and new ways to communicate and understand one another. We will be able to help and get help from each other at great distances, and increase the quality of service, health and welfare, maintenance, design, and education. We will also have more fun. This is not science-fiction, although the concepts have their roots in such fiction.

This is not a science fiction book, well, not exactly. But it is about the future, or at least one possible future.

Philosophers, scientists, futurists, and other have speculated about the moment in time when computers will match, and quickly exceed, human processing speed, memory access, and ultimately supposition. The conceit is when machines can process data in enormous volumes, and at lightning speeds, our innate inferiority complex predicts those machines will find us irrelevant, feebly competitive, and a misuse of resources. There is no analog, or metaphor for such an analysis, after all, despite our irresponsible coexistence and husbandry of other animals, fowl, and aquatic species, we never deliberately, or maliciously (with a few notable exceptions) sought their genocide. Insects are another story.

So why then would super intelligent machines, based (grown up you might suggest), on our morals, culture, and history behave any differently? Logic is the typical answer. Super smart machines, whose basic DNA is logic, would assess, adjudicate, and execute on cold, uncompromising logic; and logic is not conducive to human behavior or vice-versa. Therefore, the popular notion is the computer, would simply eliminate us.

Another possibility is as machines develop seemingly sentient capabilities, they will become companions. And lacking (and never able to fully obtain) imagination, will rely on us to come up with the next idea, the next goal, the next artistic expression, and the next interpretation of current events or characters' behaviors.

So how does augmented reality fit into all of this? As we are more conveniently, and comfortably able to access information in real time, we will literally and figuratively become augmented, though not physical—at least for a while. We will have greater access to information, and more quickly. And as we learn how to assimilate, process, and use this enhanced capability, we will become more creative, imaginative, and interesting. And as we do, emerging, or even nouveau-sentient machines will be confounded by us, always a step behind so to speak despite their astronomical processing speeds and memory access.

However, for us to be so augmented and in touch with the databases and the data analysis tools, we must have real-time, inconspicuous localized information, information about where we are, and all the things around us.

To be in touch with the databases and analytical tools requires wireless communications and real-time updating. To have inconspicuous capture of localized information in real-time, we will have smart contact lenses, and ultimately implants.

So the science fiction scenario is we will have augmented reality contact lenses while the computers approach or perhaps reach sentience, and rather than dismiss, or kill us because we would be irrelevant and unnecessary resource usages, they will rely on us for insight, imagination, and challenges; cynically perhaps a necessary evil.

This book will provide insight for technologists, marketing and management people, educators, academics, and the public who are interested in the field of augmented reality concepts, history, and practice, and the visual and sensory science behind the improvements in advanced display systems. From the explanation of the human-machine interaction issues, through the detailing of visual display and informational access systems, this book provides the reader an understanding of the issues related to defining, building, and using (with respect to our senses), our perception of what is represented, and ultimately how we assimilate and react to this information (Fig. 1).

Fig. 1 Renowned AR artist Zenka's depiction of the joy of augmented reality (Image curiosity artist)

The artist Zenka[1], is an artistic and curator-historian of augmented and virtual reality headsets says that augmented reality catapults us from the information age to the knowledge age.

What Are We Doing Here?

Augmented reality is such a complex, wide ranging topic, it's difficult to organize all it encompasses in a logical outlined way. But one has no choice, so this book is organized into ten sections: The beginning chapter introduces the benefits and potential dangers of augmented reality, an overview of the applications, some proposed rules or law for augmented reality, the definitions, and augmented reality's place in the metaverse. In the second chapter a taxonomy is presented, and the ways in which augmented reality can be delivered is presented. This is followed by an overview of how augmented reality has the potential to make all of us experts with information at our eyeballs.

In the next chapter, some of the technical aspects of seeing things in augmented reality are discussed, and the challenges of describing technology. That is followed with a brief historical overview of when augmented reality started (earlier than most people think).

Next some of the applications are examined, and the distinction is made between commercial, and consumer. However, there is overlap in some of the applications for example, the use of augmented reality in real estate can be commercial (the real estate agent) or it can be consumer (the house buyer searching for homes) That chapter is one of the largest and still it can't cover all of the existing, or future applications of augmented reality—augmented reality isn't going to be a big thing—it's going to be everything.

The following chapter gets technical and delves into the physiology of the eye, on to the types and technology of displays, and ends with brand waves and implants—you've been warned.

Finally, there is a brief discussion on some of the suppliers, take note—there are too many and then last but not least conclusions and a very brief vision of the future.

Augmented reality will touch all parts of our lives, our society, and the subsequent rules we live by. As we adapt to the new capabilities, and power that augmented reality bestows on us, we will have to think about things differently and give up some cherished ideas and fantasies. It will change social mores and rules, and challenge those who hold power arbitrarily.

Studying augmented reality is like spiraling down a Mandelbrot that reveals progressively ever-finer recursive detail. Down and down I go into the never-ending rabbit hole, finding one thing, only to learn about three others and on and on it goes.

Tiburon   Jon Peddie
CA, USA

---

[1] http://www.zenka.org/

Acknowledgements

No book was ever written in isolation or without help. A book is joint effort, a team effort, a massive body of work contributed to, edited by, and at times painfully read by friends, colleagues, relatives, and underpaid editors. Listing all their names alone would fill pages, their contributions would require even more pages, it would appear as the credits of a major movie.

And yet I try, for to do otherwise would at the least be rude, and at the most make me the most unappreciative person to walk the earth. (Egotistical and selfish also come to mind).

The second problem is how to list? By order of appearance, by number of hours invested, alphabetically, topically? I took the easy route—alphabetically. I did that for two reasons, A-so they could find themselves and make sure I didn't forget them (as I have sadly done in other books), and B-so I could easily add them when their contribution was realized.

So here are some of the folks who helped make this book possible. If you know any of them, give them a pat on the back, and tell them, Jon thanks you.

Beverley Ford, my sponsor at Springer a good friend with questionable judgement.
Bob Raikes, a tireless writer and editor of all things display, and dear old friend.
Douglass (Doug) Magyari, king of FOV, great engineer and good friend.
James Robinson, editorial assistant, protector, and sometimes pain in the butt friend at Springer.
Karl Guttag, inventor of VRAM and other amazing graphics devices, a tremendous help with display section, and great friend.
Kathleen Maher, my mentor, partner, muse, and best friend.
Khaled Sarayeddine, CTO of Lumus Optical.
Mark Fihn, author, publisher, display expert, and good friend.
Michael Burney, entrepreneur, technologist, who's willing to read what I write.
Robert Dow, my researcher, reader, and good friend.
Ron Padzensky, an AR blogger excellent, and helpful critic, great help with the taxonomy.
Soulaiman Itani, an amazing augmented reality scientist with a great sense of humor.

Steve Mann, The father of AR, and a tremendous help and guide with this book.
Ted Pollak, my collogue in gaming, opinionated and surprising sounding board.
Tom Furness, the grandfather of AR, and most generous advisor.
Tracey McSheery, an augmented reality scientist, friend, and font of great ideas.
And so many others like Dr. Garth Webb, Ori Inbar, Jay Wright, Tom Defanti, Oliver
    Ktrylos, Jean-François Chianetta, Khaled Sarayeddine, Christine Perey, and
    Neal Leavitt, to name a few.

Contents

List of Figures

List of Tables

Introduction

1

Abstract

Augmented reality will do more than just give us directions, and visualizations of products. In time, Augmented Reality will integrate with body sensors to monitor our temperature, oxygen level, glucose level, heartrate, EEG, and other important parameters. We will in effect be wearing the equivalent of the tricorder.

Augmented Reality evolved from a laboratory experiment to the military and then industrial applications. The military, industrial, and scientific users, with specific and urgent needs and budget constraints were able to tolerate the limitations in comfort and performance of early systems.

Science fiction has long been a predictor of future technologies and there are many examples of augmented reality imagined by artists, writers and scientists before the technology to realize such devices, environments, and oblique ideas where not widely available (or available at all), but work was going on to make augmented reality practical.

Augmented reality is thought of as a visual system, augmented what we see with information and graphics. However, one's auditory senses can also benefit from augmented reality, with special location clues, and can be very helpful if one is blind, or partially blind.

1.1 Introduction

In 1956, Philip K Dick (1928–1982) wrote *The Minority Report* [1] and created the reality of augmented reality, information literally at our finger tips. Since then augmented reality has become—a reality.

From Pepper's Ghost to contact lenses: Augmented Reality—is where we all will live

© Springer International Publishing AG 2017

J. Peddie, *Augmented Reality*, DOI 10.1007/978-3-319-54502-8_1

However, as prolific and prescient as Dick was, the first example of augmented reality was the concept of Pepper's Ghost used in the teleprompter developed in 1950 by Hubert Schiafly [2] (1919–2011).

We have spent the last century and half learning how to communicate with our computers, with each generation getting more natural. Starting with banks of switches, which evolved to punch cards and tape and typewriter-like keyboard, to graphics user interfaces and mice, touch panels, voice, and gesture recognition.

Augmented reality systems take us to the next phase in computer interfaces, and are unlike any interface we may be familiar with from the past. Prior to augmented reality our communications with the computer were via 2D, a flat, interface. Although amazingly effective in almost all situations, they are nonetheless limiting. Imagine seeing a tea pot floating in space in front of you, and having the desire to rotate it, to see how light bounces off it at various angles, or to see the manufacturer's or artist's name on the bottom. It can be done with a flat display, but how much more natural would it be if you could reach out to the image, turn it directly, and immediately with your fingers, and then pass it on to a companion or discard it?

Wearable augmented reality displays that overlay virtual data and images into the real world combined with new operating systems that enable a new kind of spatial computing will demand a new user interface. However, augmented reality systems are extremely complicated and complex, combined with the challenge of being lightweight, portable, and inconspicuous, and of course affordable (Fig. 1.1).

With an augmented reality system, we become part of the computer environment, rather than just an external, detached observer with limited interaction. Some commenters have said we will become the interface. This represents a revolution in computer interfaces and interaction. And because it's a revolution all the nuances and opportunities are not yet understood, nor will they be for a long time as developers and users experiment with this new way of communicating with a computer.

Now, with augmented reality, our bodies become a critical component in the process. Where are our eyes looking, where are our hands, what are we saying, and potentially what is our EEG saying?

Augmented reality mixes the completely real with the simulated or synthetic and projects images and information in the wearer's line of vision.

Almost everyone has seen the image of Princes Leia in *Star Wars* as a hologram projected from R2D2 onto some imaginary light field. As fantastic as that imagery was in 1977, we are now able to realize it with augmented reality. But instead of a science fiction light field, the ghost-like image can be seen with augmented reality.

The idea of having reams of concurrent and timely information immediately, or constantly available to you is a dream we have shared for a long time. The miracle of augmented reality is that we've taken our pocket computers and magically connected them to the enormous quantities of information stored in data clouds while feeding them our movements and locations in real-time, and accessing what we need from them. Augmented reality is also paradoxically about the efficiency of human action in relation to usable data and the avoidance of reality in the form of pictures and graphics. So, it could also evolve to a situation of "be careful what you wish for". If you have too many labels in a scene, or too many objects, it gets

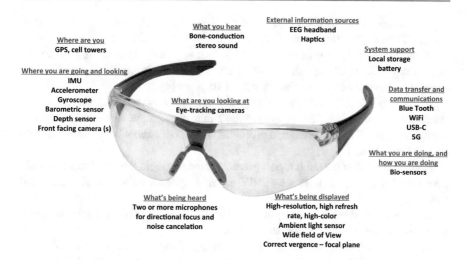

Fig. 1.1 The many things an augmented reality smart glasses must accommodate (Suggested by Steve Mann)

confusing and is difficult to read. Without limits, and privacy protection (if there ever was such a thing), your augmented reality device could be inundated with unwanted and overwhelming information, advertisements, correspondence, reminders, and intrusions.

In 2006, Vernor Vinge (1944–) wrote his Hugo award winning science fiction novel, *Rainbows End*, a story about augmented reality and its moral implications and consequences. In Vinge's book, the concept of security in such an increasingly digital/virtual world with ubiquitous computing is imagined. He explores the implications of rapid technological change that empowers both the disgruntled individuals who would threaten to disrupt society and those that would seek to stop them, and the implications for the age-old "who watches the watchers" issue at the interplay between surveillance (oversight) and sousveillance (undersight). Later in 2013, augmented reality pioneer Steven Mann (1962–) gave a presentation (at TEDex) on his personal confrontations with surveillance and sousveillance [3].

Therefore, augmented reality is also paradoxically about the efficiency of human action in relation to usable data and the avoidance of reality in the form of pictures and graphics, and the balance with societal norms, expectations, tolerances, and regulatory agencies and their agents. That's a big job.

This book will identify the many aspects of Augmented Reality (AR), and will, when appropriate or necessary, refer to Virtual Reality (VR), but it should be clear to the reader that the two are quite dramatically different technologies and experiences.

Trying to describe virtual or alternate reality is tricky because it is interpretive, we all see it, and think of it a little differently from each other. Defining it in terms of the hardware used is inadequate because the hardware will change.

Augmented reality is not a thing, it is a concept that can be used by many things, and it will be a ubiquitous part of our lives just like electricity.

According to a report released in 2015 by the non-profit organization, Augmented Reality.org., Smart Glasses sales will reach one billion shipments near 2020, and surpass shipments of mobile phones within 10 years [4].

Augmented reality will completely disrupt the way we conduct our lives. Augmented reality is a new medium rather than just a new technology that will change people's lives in varied and profound ways, so it cannot be dismissed as just a topic for fiction.

A Gartner market research report predicted that the Field Service Industry could save about one billion dollars by 2017 as smart glasses enhances diagnosis and repair [5].

And, one size does not fit all, nor does one type of so-called immersive reality satisfy all markets, users, needs, or expectations.

There is no main feature to augmented reality. There are many benefits that we will get from this. I can't emphasize it too much; the name of this technology truly depicts what it is. It will generally (and greatly) augment us, and by augment that means expand, be better, be more. We will literally be capable of doing more things than we have before. Augmented reality will help (it won't completely do it, but it will greatly help) reduce the friction in our lives. We encounter friction as we go through life. Imagine you are going to go to the store. When you get to the store you find it's very crowded and you just want to get a loaf of bread. You ask your smart glasses, "Where can I get a loaf of bread where it's not crowded?" And then, up on your glasses, comes some information that says go left here and so forth. Imagine you're driving around downtown and you can't find a parking lot that's not full, your glasses will tell you where to park.

These are functions that can somewhat be done today on a smartphone, except that you have to pick up the phone and look at it. That's friction. Because now you're interfering with your normal travel, your normal communications, etc. You've got to stop some process in order to look at the phone. With augmented reality, you don't have to stop—the data will be right in front of you while you are going to where you are trying to get to; these are benefits.

That's for the consumer. It's different for the industrial applications, because industrial applications, with the exception of first responders, don't move around that much. Typically, with augmented reality in an industrial application, you go to the thing (the airplane, car, production line, pump, etc.) without the glasses on and then you put them on and you take care of the job. If you're a designer, for example, and you go into the design studio, and then you put the glasses on and you do your design, take the glasses off and you go home. Consumers will wear the glasses more often because they'll use them for everyday stuff.

Head-up displays in automobiles and buses, helmets with displays, and augmented reality glasses will be commonplace and make us uncomfortable when not available. First responders will be able to see and anticipate obstacles. Educational aspects from sports training to remedial education will be assisted by augmented reality. Entertainment will evolve to new exciting, immersive, and amazing heights.

Real time visual translations will be used daily. Game playing will reach across the world and throughout it, and military battlefield operations will be even more deadly and effective. Surgeons will operate and diagnose remotely, and we will visit museums, potential new homes, and wondrous travel vistas that had been out of our reach.

1.2 The Promise of Augmented Reality

Augmented reality headsets will do more than just give us directions and visualizations of products, they will integrate with body sensors to monitor our temperature, oxygen level, glucose level, heartrate, EEG, and other important parameters. We will in effect be wearing the equivalent of the tricorder from StarTrek, and that information will be available to us, and people/organizations we authorize (such as family physicians, or trainers).

And not just our bodies, but our environment as well. Augmented reality helmets for first responders will measure oxygen, methane, Co_2, as well as other gases and pollutants we can't see, and give early warning to explosive or poisonous situations. In pollution-heavy areas an individual's augmented reality glasses can alert the wearer of conditions that can be dangerous for people with respiratory conditions. That includes dosimeters that will measure the amount of radiation absorbed by the wearer, as well as detect radon and other harmful sources.

Augmented reality will be like having X-ray vision

These augmented devices will amplify us, make us feel like a super hero, enable and empower us as never before, and free us from tyranny and fear.

And we will use it without being aware of it, it will become invisible. As I and others have pointed out over time:

Technology works when its invisible

And books will continue to be written about it as new ideas and capabilities continue to emerge. Aren't we there yet? No, not for a while, but we can enjoy and benefit from augmented reality now.

1.3 The Dangers of Augmented Reality

Ericsson ConsumerLab has been conducting consumer surveys for over 20 years studying people's behaviors and values, including the way they act and think about information-and-communications-technology (ICT) products and services, and as a result have provided unique insights on market and consumer trends. Ericsson ConsumerLab consumer research program is based on interviews with 100,000 individuals each year, in more than 40 countries—statistically representing the views of 1.1 billion people.

In October 2016, Ericsson ConsumerLab conducted a survey and used the data to produce their *10 Hot Consumer Trends 2017* report [6]. In that study, they found three out of five smartphone users think their phone makes them safer, and therefore take more risks.

These days, we take our phones everywhere we go. If we get lost we can call, text, look up information on the internet or navigate using GPS—all with our phones. For example, more than half of smartphone users already use emergency alarms, tracking or notifications on their smartphones. Another three in five have emergency contacts stored in their phone. But what happens if you lose your phone while still looking for your destination? Or you have an accident in a remote area of town while your phone is not charged? In many ways, the basic features of your smartphone can make you safer—and around two in five citizens in five major cities surveyed agree. But here's the paradox: three in five of those who say so take more risks because they rely on their phone to keep them safe.

As consumers learn to rely on their augmented reality glasses, the same risk of over confidence will likely develop.

The fact that more than half of advanced internet users would like to use augmented reality glasses to light up dark surroundings in order to highlight potentially dangerous objects, and/or people approaching may not be surprising. But more than one in three would also like to edit out disturbing elements around them, such as graffiti, garbage, or even badly dressed people. They would like to modify surroundings by adding birds, flowers, or to mimic their favorite movie or TV show.

At least as many would like to erase street signs, uninteresting shop windows and billboards. Although this could be a nightmare to brands that do not manage to capture consumer imaginations (they might simply be wiped from view for good) it also creates the risk that the wearers of augmented reality glasses may become blasé' and lackadaisical about urban dangers—losing their "street smarts" so to speak.

Consumers want to use augmented reality glasses to change the world into something that reflects their own personal moods. Around two in five want to change the way their surroundings look and even how people appear to them.

Almost as many would like to have augmented reality glasses that let you find and pick up digital game items, like in an augmented reality game such as Pokémon GO. It is very likely that this will not be the only game to become integrated in people's physical reality. They would like to make people look like aliens, elves or even characters from their favorite movie.

As augmented reality glasses become popular and commonplace, people are going to have to learn how to use them, just as they are learning how to use (or not use) a smartphone.

1.4   Augmented Reality Skills

To design, build, manufacture, and support an augmented reality device a company
has to have an extensive and bewildering range of experts: engineers, scientist, technicians, doctors, mathematicians and managers. They have to understand and know
how to integrate:

- Audio technology
- Camera technology
- Display technology
- Ergonomics and user interfaces
- Geometric and trigonometric mathematics
- Image processing techniques and processes
- Manufacturing engineering
- Optics and optometry
- Physiology
- Positional, tracking, and location methodology
- Power management
- Processors (CPUs. GPUs, DSPs, FPGAs, and special purpose) and memory
- Semiconductor technology
- Software engineering, operating systems, APIs, drivers, computer graphics,
  game engines

More than one augmented reality supplier has told me this was the most difficult
thing he had ever done.

It's difficult just to explain it because there are so many aspects to it. Nonetheless,
the rest of this book will attempt to do just that. You won't be able to design an
augmented reality system after reading this book, but you will know how they work,
what they can, and cannot do, and why you and I can't wait to get our own.

1.5   Seeing Augmented Reality

There are three ways to visually present an augmented reality.

Visual see-through   is the primary method of creating an augmented reality view.
This is the design Sutherland developed in the early 1960s, a see-through lens (such
as glasses, or a helmet's faceplate) which leaves the user's perception of the real-
world   unmodified   (or   restricted)   and   displays   the   information   and/or
graphics-augmented reality as an overlay by means of transparent displays, or mirrors and lenses or miniature projectors.

Within visual see-through augmented reality systems, there are several classes:

- Contact lens
- Helmet

- Head-up Display (HUD)
- Smart-glasses
  - Integrated
  - Add-on display and system for convential, sun, or safety glasses
- Specialized and other

These classes of augmented reality see-through systems are discussed further in Chap. 2 "Types of Augmented Reality Systems", Sect. 2.1.

Obstructed view, where the user wears a head-mounted display (HMD) that blocks the real world, and displays in the HMD are fed a view of the world from a front facing camera in the HMD. This is the closest model to mixed reality and is also referred to as video see-through. The augmented information or graphics is overlaid or blended into the video feed. This technique restricts the field of view of the user, and can restrict it to just a flat 2D view if only one camera is used.

Projected augmented reality is a technique where the augmented reality overlay of information and/or graphics, is projected from the headset or HMD out onto the real world and objects within it resulting in projective displays.

The three techniques may be applied at varying distance from the viewer: head-mounted, hand-held and spatial.

Visual perception is the key to understanding, information transfer, and memory. Edgar Dale (1900–1985) was an American educator who developed the Cone of Experience. He postulated that we remember 10% of what we read, and 50% of what we see and hear (Fig. 1.2).

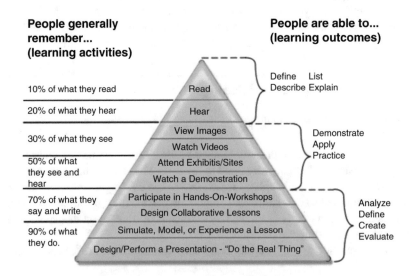

Fig. 1.2 Edgar Dale's Cone of Learning does not contain percentages as listed here. It relates to abstraction vs. concrete and the greater use of senses (Credit: Jeffrey Anderson)

Dale's "Cone of Experience," which he intended to provide an intuitive model of the concreteness of various kinds of audio-visual media, has been widely misrepresented. Often referred to as the "Cone of Learning," it purports to inform viewers of how much people remember based on how they encounter information. However, Dale included no numbers and did not base his cone on scientific research, and he also warned readers not to take the cone too seriously [7]. The numbers originated from 1967, when a Mobile oil company employee named D. G. Treichler published a non-scholarly article in an audio magazine titled Film and Audio-Visual Communications.

However, academic, and pedantic issues aside, it is pretty well accepted (if not fully understood or quantified) that we take in the majority of our information through our eyes, and augmented reality devices enhance that information level. And then as they learn and gain experience, the information is turned into wisdom.

1.6   The Realities

Immersive reality is a multidiscipline multi-labeled and massively confusing collection of technologies, applications, and opportunities. It, or they, go by many labels (Table 1.1).

And whatever modality is used to describe the holodeck.

Table 1.1   Reality has many names

Alternate	Interactive	Spatial-augmented
Another	Magic	Super vision
Artificial	Mediated	Synthetic
Augmented	Merged	Trans
Blended	Mirrored	Vicarious
Cognitive	Mixed	Virtual augmented
Digital	Modulated	reality
Digitally mediated	Perceptive	Virtual Environment
Dimensional	Projected	Visual
Diminished	Previsualization	Window-on-the-world
Extended	Spatial augmented reality (SAR)	
External	Second	
False	Simulated	
Hybrid		
Immersive (Tactical, Strategic, Narrative, and Spatial)		

1.7   Augmented Reality's Place in the Metaverse

There are so many technologies with conflicting names and purpose it's helpful to sort them out and label them for ease of conversation and commination, and in so doing take steps toward constructing a taxonomy and definition.

The Metaverse is a collective virtual shared space, created by the convergence of virtually enhanced physical reality and physically persistent virtual space, and is a fusion of both, while allowing users to experience it as either. The term came from Neal Stephenson's (1959–) science fiction novel *Snow Crash* [8], (1992) where humans, as avatars, interact with each other and software agents, in a three-dimensional space that uses the metaphor of the real world.

Industry, investors, governments, and consumers alike recognize there's something special about augmented reality, virtual reality and mixed reality head-mounted displays, but many wonder if it's something they would actually use in everyday life. That means we're not quite there yet, but we're getting there faster than ever before.

The way we interact with our devices has evolved. Every advancement in computing technology has required a new method of input: from keyboard, to mouse, to touch. Yet, next-generation devices are using limited methods of control, like head, hands, and voice, which are carried over from the generations of devices before them. These interactions must evolve as well. Augmented reality systems are going to break those paradigms, and invite new natural user interfaces such as voice, and eye-tracking, abandoning earlier approaches borrowed from touch screens, and virtual reality gesturing. Proponents of natural eye-tracking say it transforms intent into action through your eyes.

1.7.1   Translating the World

Humans see, and for the most part think in 3D. We can imagine the back side of an object, and grasp the size relative to its place in the environment. It's one of the advantages of having stereoscopic vision, and cognition.

However, we have had to deal with projections of 3D objects on to flat 2D surfaces in the form of drawings on paper, maps, and illustrations of people.

Illustrations and maps on paper, or a monitor or smartphone screens are cognitively limiting, challenging, and often confusing. They are difficult to understand. For one thing, they must be simplified, to accommodate the medium, and very often that makes it difficult for our brains to process and understand; and/or translate into necessary actions.

Translating 2D spatial information really works the brain as it tries to move from one dimension to another and back and forth until the 2D representation is fully understood—sometimes it never is.

And if there are a series of 2D images and you are required to remember their sequence in order to perform some task, there's a very good chance you won't and you will have to repeat the steps to refresh your memory.

Table 1.2 The seven mass media vehicles

1. Print (books, pamphlets, newspapers, magazines, etc.) from the late 1400s
2. Recordings (records, tapes, cassettes, cartridges, CD's, DVD's) from the late 1800s
3. Cinema from about 1900
4. Radio from about 1910
5. Television from about 1950
6. Internet from about 1990
7. Mobile phones from about 2000

Augmented Reality systems overcome this cognitive dimensional challenge by providing 3D information superimposed and correctly aligned with the environment. Metavision and Accenture conducted a survey in 2016 which they presented at the 2106 International Symposium on Mixed and Augmented Reality (ISMAR), on this subject, titled, "What Works Better: 2D or 3D Instructions?" [9].

This creates a knowledge-based augmented reality system which can be used to explain how to perform 3D spatial tasks, such as assembly of furniture or the repair of equipment.

In 2006 former telecoms executive and tech author Tomi Ahonen (1943–) developed the list of the seven mass media vehicles or experiences (Table 1.2).

The 8th mass media will be augmented reality predicted Raimo van der Klein, founder of Layer (see Sect. 6.1.3.1).

1.7.2 Consumers vs. Industrial, Military, and Scientific

Augmented Reality evolved from a laboratory experiment to the military and then industrial applications. The military, industrial, and scientific users, with specific and urgent needs, and the necessary budget we are able to tolerate the limitations in comfort and performance the early systems had because of the desired result. Later in this book I identify several, but far from all, Augmented Reality applications and use cases for the military, industrial and scientific/medical fields.

The consumer applications are just as far reaching, but only slowly being realized due to prices, applications, and appearance/comfort. Also, consumers are not as aware of Augmented Reality, although that is changing rapidly. Once there was a clearer understand of the broad applications of Augmented Reality, interest and excitement spiked.

However, in all consumer studies it was pointed out that glasses must be lightweight and look "normal", especially for those who don't wear glasses. Almost everyone wears sunglasses, and that has become the metaphor in most consumer's minds for how they will engage with Augmented Reality for an extended period. Smartphones and head-up displays in automobiles were the second use model.

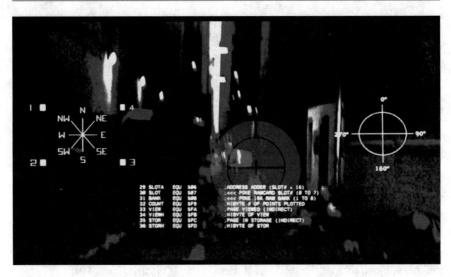

Fig. 1.3 The augmented reality eye of The Terminator evaluates the situation and provides suggestions for action (Source: Orion Pictures)

Consumers quickly extrapolated the use of augmented reality beyond games like Pokémon GO to use augmented reality in cases such as shopping, fitness tracking and health monitoring, museums and travel information, video calls and social media interchanges, education and training, collaboration and virtual assistance, and a teleprompter to name a few. The idea of being able to have the web and your phone instantly visible and interactive any time, and all the time, truly lit up the imagination of consumers.

1.7.3   Movie Metaphors and Predictors

Science fiction has long been a predictor of future technologies. One reason the concepts developed by artists, writers and scientists, and the flights of imagination and extrapolation are prescient is because at the time they were writing we lacked the technology to realize such devices, environments, and oblique ideas.

Two such persistent and compelling concepts and images are the *Star Trek*'s Holodeck (1974) [10] and *The Matrix* (1999) [11], a thematic concept proposed by Philip K. Dick in 1977 [12]. In the case of augmented reality, there is frequent reference to the *Minority Report* (2002) [13], and for devotees of the genre, John Carpenter's (1948–), *They Live* (1988) [14], and several others. (Interestingly, the *Minority report* was based on a book by Philip K. Dick) [15] . And in 1984 the movie, *The Terminator*, written and directed by James Cameron (1954–), depicted a menacing robot from the future with an augmented reality eye (Fig. 1.3).

According to Ori Inbar (1965–) of Games Alfresco [16], the use of augmented reality in movies can be traced back as far as 1907 when French magician and

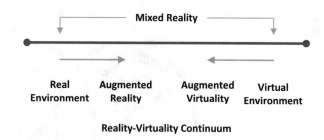

Fig. 1.4   Simplified representation of an metaverse continuum (Milgram 1994)

moviemaker George Melies (1861–1938) created his *Hilarious Posters*. Characters in the posters came to life and interacted on screen [17].

Augmented Reality is one part of the metaverse. Paul Milgram (1938–) and Fumio Kishino, defined augmented reality in 1994 as part of the continuum middle ground between virtual reality (completely synthetic) and telepresence (completely real) (Fig. 1.4) [18].

Telepresence is the experience of "being there," and is commonly implemented in the form of a remote control and display device for teleoperation, and called "virtual presence" in the case of computer-generated simulation. You may have seen examples of a computer screen on a stand that is eye height, with a motorized platform at the bottom.

Steve Mann (1962–) took the concept further and added mediated reality based on the fact that no matter what we do, the technology modifies our world in some way, and doesn't merely add (augment) to it. Sometimes this modification is deliberate (e.g., Mann's augmented reality welding helmet that darkens the image in areas of excessive light) or accidental (the way that a smartphone, for example, changes our view of the world when looking through it while using an augmented reality app.). Mediated Reality takes place anywhere that one's perception of the world is mediated (modified) by the apparatus being worn i.e., augmented reality glasses [19, 20]. Video cameras are used both to warp the visual input (mediated reality) and to sense the user's world for graphical overlay (Fig. 1.5).

Through the use of such artificial modification of human perception by way of devices for augmenting, the wearer could deliberately diminish, and alter sensory input (Fig. 1.6).

The origin R denotes unmodified reality. The x-axis connotes the Virtuality axis V which is the continuum from reality augmented with graphics (Augmented Reality), as well as graphics augmented by reality (Augmented Virtuality). However, the taxonomy also includes modification of reality or virtuality or any combination of these.

The y-axis is the mediality continuum, which includes diminished reality and generalizes the concepts of mixed reality, etc. It includes the virtuality reality continuum (mixing) but also, in addition to additive effects, also includes multiplicative effects (modulation) of (sometimes deliberately) diminished reality.

Fig. 1.5 Mixed reality
with mediated reality

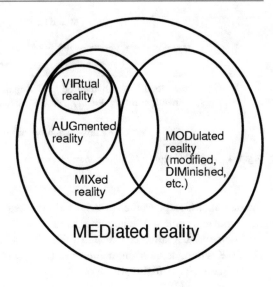

Fig. 1.6 Mann's
taxonomy of reality

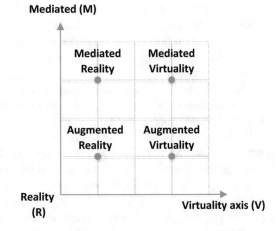

Mann extended the concept to include Augmented Reality devices that could block out advertising or replace real-world ads with useful information) [21].

Augmented reality mixes the completely real with the simulated or synthetic. The idea of having reams of concurrent and timely information immediately or constantly available to you, is (as mentioned above) a dream we have shared for a long time. But it could also evolve to a situation of "be careful what you wish for." If you have too many labels in a scene, or too many objects, it gets confusing and difficult to read. Without limits, and privacy protection, your augmented reality device could be inundated with unwanted and overwhelming information, advertisements, correspondence, reminders, and intrusions.

Animator and futurist Keiichi Matsuda (1984–) made a video in 2015 depicting the potential world of hyper-reality that we may face [22] (Fig. 1.7).

Fig. 1.7 Keiichi Matsuda vision of riding a busy while using a smartphone to play a game, get alerts, be inundated with advertisements, and get a phone call (Source: Keiichi Matsuda)

Matsuda's vision is funny, and frightening, and one which will no doubt find its way to regulators and privacy organizations, as the nascent industry develops standards and codes of ethics. Will the user of augmented reality smart glasses have the option of blocking such messaging?

Another short film, *Sight*, creates a scenario of augmented reality using contact lenses (and can be seen at: https://vimeo.com/46304267).

The problem with wearing augmented reality glasses, as unobtrusive as they might be, is that they will probably distract your gaze from whomever you are speaking. I can envision a scene where the other person, who may be your superior, or the police, say, "Take off your glasses when you talk to me." In the case of it being the police, that would put you at risk for not being able to record the incident. So now we have a new freedom of speech issue.

Then there is the possibility of augmented reality contact lenses, will they overcome the gaze issue and let you look normally at people while viewing data? Samsung, Google and others have filed patents for such devices. Issues of powering and connecting to them are challenges, but also a concept originating in science fiction stories, so it would seem it's just a matter of time for the technology to catch up with the concept.

Another scenario might include an interviewer asking to tap into the feed of the eye-tracking in your glasses to see if you are lying, and look at the recent history to see if your questions or comments are legitimate.

However, the more positive visions of the use of augmented reality smart-glasses is people will no longer bump into each other or objects as they do now while looking down at their smartphone while walking.

And Matsuda's vision of an over cluttered barrage of adverts and information will be mitigated by machine learning and training so your smartglasses only deliver the information you want, and don't interrupt you when you are with someone else.

It does however suggest some regulation and code of ethics needs to be instilled, just as Asimov proposed for robots. Steve Mann has suggested a code of ethics for augmented reality, and John Rousseau has proposed laws for mixed reality.

1.7.4 The Code of Ethics on Human Augmentation

In 2004, Steve Mann introduced the "Code of Ethics on Human Augmentation" in his Keynote Address at Transvision 2004, Second annual conference of the World Transhumanism Association.

This code was further developed at the IEEE International Symposium on Technology and Society [23].

As we augment our bodies and our societies with ever more pervasive and possibly invasive sensing, computation, and communication, there comes a point when we ourselves become these technologies [24]. This sensory intelligence augmentation technology is already developed enough to be dangerous in the wrong hands, e.g., as a way for a corrupt government or corporation to further augment its power and use it unjustly. Accordingly, Mann has spent a number of years developing a Code of Ethics on Human Augmentation, resulting in three fundamental "laws".

These three "Laws" represent a philosophical ideal (like the laws of physics, or like Asimov's Laws of Robotics, not an enforcement (legal) paradigm:

1. (Metaveillance/Sensory-Auditability) Humans have a basic right to know when and how they're being surveilled, monitored, or sensed, whether in the real or virtual world.
2. (Equality/Fairness/Justice) Humans must (a) not be forbidden or discouraged from monitoring or sensing people, systems, or entities that are monitoring or sensing them, and (b) have the power to create their own "digital identities" and express themselves (e.g., to document their own lives, or to defend against false accusations), using data about them, whether in the real or virtual world. Humans have a right to defend themselves using information they have collected, and a responsibility not to falsify that information.
3. Rights and responsibilities
   (a) (Aletheia/Unconcealedness/TechnologicalAuditability) With few exceptions, humans have an affirmative right to trace, verify, examine, and understand any information that has been recorded about them, and such information shall be provided immediately: feedback delayed is feedback denied. In order to carry out the justice requirement of the Second Law, humans must have a right to access and use of the information collected about them. Accordingly, we hold that Subjectrights [6] prevail over Copyright, e.g., the subject of a photograph or video recording enjoys some reasonable access to, and use of it. Similarly, machines that augment the

human intellect must be held to the same ethical standard. We accept that old-fashioned, hierarchical institutions (e.g., law enforcement) still have need for occasional asymmetries of surveillance, in order to apply accountability to harmful or dangerous forces, on our behalf. However, such institutions must bear an ongoing and perpetual burden of proof that their functions and services justify secrecy of anything more than minimal duration or scope. Application of accountability upon such elites—even through renewably trusted surrogates, must be paramount, and a trend toward ever-increasing openness not thwarted.

(b) Humans must not design machines of malice. Moreover, all human augmentation technologies shall be developed and used in a spirit of truth, openness, and unconcealedness, providing comprehensibility through immediate feedback. (Again, feedback delayed is feedback denied.) Unconcealedness must also apply to a system's internal state, i.e. system designers shall design for immediate feedback, minimal latency, and take reasonable precautions to protect users from the negative effects (e.g., nausea and neural pathway overshoot formation) of delayed feedback.

(c) Systems of artificial intelligence and of human augmentation shall be produced as openly as possible and with diversity of implementation, so that mistakes and/or unsavory effects can be caught, not only by other humans but also by diversely completive and reciprocally critical AI (Artificial Intelligence) and HI (Humanistic Intelligence).

A metalaw states that the Code itself will be created in an open and transparent manner, i.e. with instant feedback and not written in secret. In this meta-ethics (ethics of ethics) spirit, continual rough drafts were posted (e.g., on social media such as Twitter #HACode), and members of the community were invited to give their input and even become co-authors.

1.7.5 Laws of Mixed Reality

In 2016, John Rousseau proposed three "laws of mixed reality [25]" to ensure that augmented and virtual technology positively impacts society.

Rousseau said, "The future of human consciousness will be a hybrid affair. We will live and work in a ubiquitous computing environment, where physical reality and a pervasive digital layer mix seamlessly according to the logic of software and the richness of highly contextual data. This is mixed reality."

We're not there yet, though this vision is far from science fiction.

Rousseau, citing Isaac Asimov's "Law of Robotics [26]," suggested three "Laws of Mixed Reality" that will help us shape the discourse and future development of mixed reality with an emphasis on preferable outcomes. The Laws are aligned to three significant problem areas, covering the individual, society and economics.

1. Mixed reality must enhance our capacity for mindful attention.
2. Mixed reality must embody a shared human experience.
3. Mixed reality must respect boundaries between commerce and data.

Rousseau noted in a blog post that as mixed reality starts to take over, "data will become more valuable and easily manipulated to serve other interests."

1.7.6   Augmented Reality Can Help and Monitor

With an always on augmented reality system, in your smartphone, or smart-glasses, that has a camera, geo-location sensors, and motion sensors, the augmented reality device can call for help if you fall, record the fall, and possibly offer live saving information when help arrives.

The augmented reality device can make almost anything appear in the display. It could be monsters in game, or, directions to your dinner date. The direction can be a map, or explicit instructions consisting of bright yellow arrows along the roads of your travel. You will be able to shop at home and see how a piece of furniture you are interested in looks in your living room, and be able to walk around it, see how it looks in the evening or bight daytime. We will all be experts now, and without any special training repair or install home appliances, or repair or service our automobiles, with interactive instructions highlighting exactly which part needs to be replaced and alerting you if you're doing it wrong. And some companies offering either cloud service, or devices, will be positioned to profit from every interaction: not just from the hardware and software it will sell but also from the flow of data the device and/or cloud services provider will collect, analyze–and resell.

We will all be big brother

Augmented reality will be an aid, a monitor, a snitch, and sadly a spy. How we and government restrictions mitigate and manage this flow of information will be discussed and worked on for decades. Not only will big brother be watching us, but we will be big brother.

1.7.7   Augmented Reality in Games

Augmented Reality is anchored on practical use, but can cross over to fun. In the popular (and sometimes intense) first-person shooter (FPS) games, the protagonist (you) often has a augmented reality head-up display (HUD) to show the status of life support, weapons, nearby enemies, etc.

One such popular game of 2016–2017, and longer (because it keeps getting upgraded), is *Fallout4*, a post-apocalyptic story where the world has suffered a massive nuclear war, everything is left in ruin. The player has an Augmented Reality

Fig. 1.8 Augmented reality head-up display in a first-person shooter game, Fallout 4 (Source:Bethesda Softworks)

device strapped to his or her wrist and it provides information on the player's health, location and destination, supplies, and condition of clothing or armament (Fig. 1.8).

Generations of game players have had this kind of experience without having a name for it, although the term HUD has been used in FPS games since the late 1990s, beginning with just a few characters of text at the bottom of the screen. That was due to the level of technology at that time. Today PCs and mobile devices have processors thousands of times more powerful with thousands of times the memory, running hundreds, if not thousands of times faster, making the issue of displaying more robust head-up display images and data almost trivial. So almost by osmosis, game players have been involved with augmented reality for decades and take it for granted. Those generations of users will adopt to augmented reality without hesitancy when comfortable, non-obtrusive devices are available. If anything, they represent a pent-up demand for the technology.

1.7.8 Auditory Augmented Reality

Augmented reality is thought of as a visual system, augmenting what we see with information and graphics. However, one's auditory senses can also benefit from augmented reality, with special location clues, and can be very helpful if one is blind, or partially blind.

For location assistance audible instructions, such as directions, can be helpful for the sighted as well as for people with limited or no vision. For athletes and people active in sports such as running, bicycling, and skiing, getting information on your distance from your destination, rate of speed, as well as your body functions such as heart rate in real time is extremely useful.

Audible translation of street signs, notices, and restaurant menus for the sighted or limited sighted person will be greatly empowering and offer new levels of engagement, exploration, and enrichment.

1.8   Definitions

In this section, we will define the most commonly used terms in this book, and the ones that are critical to understanding the issues and opportunities in augmented reality. An expanded glossary of terms can be found in the appendix.

1.8.1   What Is Augmented Reality?

Augmented reality, not to be confused with virtual reality, superimposes digital content (text, images, animations, etc.) on a user's view of the real world. Augmented reality and virtual reality devices, also known as head mounted-displays (HMDs), share similar problems around mobility and power consumption.

Encyclopedia Britannica gives the following definition for augmented reality: "Augmented reality, in computer programming, a process of combining or 'augmenting' video or photographic displays by overlaying the images with useful computer-generated data" [27].

Augmented reality is a real-time view of information overlaid on a view of the real world. The information is generated by a local processor and data source, as well as a remote data source/data base, and is augmented by sensory input such as sound, video, or positional, and location data. By contrast, virtual reality (virtual reality) replaces the real world with a simulated one.

The technological requirements of augmented reality are much greater than those for virtual reality, which is why the development of augmented reality took longer than that of virtual reality. However, the key components needed to build an augmented reality system have remained the same since Ivan Sutherland's pioneering work of the 1960s. Displays, trackers, and graphics computers and software remain essential in many augmented reality experiences.

Various technologies are used in augmented reality rendering including optical projection systems, displays, mobile devices (such as tablets and smartphones), and display systems worn on one's person in the form of glasses or a helmet. Augmented reality devices are also characterized as a wearable device (Fig. 1.9).

Augmented reality devices (glasses, helmets, HUDs, etc.) employ several technologies:

- A GPU to drive the display(s).
- Display/projection device(s) to create images.
  - Optics to route the images to your field of view.

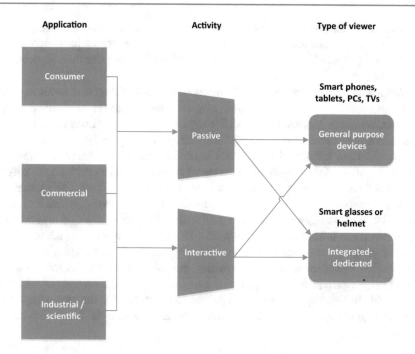

Fig. 1.9 Augmented reality uses various devices and is used in various applications

- Sensors:
  - Forward-looking to see the world you are looking at (i.e., the camera)
  - Real-world position to map the world in 3D
  - Motion sensor(s)
  - Elevation sensor
  - Eye sensors to track where you are looking.
- Audio systems (microphones, processing and speakers) for communications and augmentation of the real world. (A microphone is another sensor).
- Object identification and categorization systems that recognizes what your glasses are looking at (table, chair, floor, walls, windows, glasses, etc.) to position virtual images on top of or near them (some systems use markers for object identifications).
- An operating system to control the virtual images with voice, eyes, hands and body motions.
- Wireless communications to a server-like device (could be your smartphone).

Augmented reality allows for every type of digital information—videos, photos, links, games, etc.—to be displayed on top of real world items when viewed through the lens of a mobile or wearable device.

The concept of a wearable computer or personal computer interface has been discussed since the late 1950s, first in science-fiction, later as a technological development. Through micro-miniature electronics, sensors and displays, always connected communication, and modern manufacturing techniques, appliances, wearable, connected, and augmenting devices are changing our lives forever, and for the better.

Augmented reality can employ 3D models of the world around us from previously generated data sets and/or from scanning sensors in the augmented reality headset, helmet or glasses. It is possible to generate extensive 3D representations of data sets that can lead to remarkable discoveries of complex relationships.

Visualization technologies with easy to use interfaces have introduced new and innovative ways of viewing and interacting with big data sets through portable lightweight devices; devices that look like normal sun glasses, or corrective glasses.

Augmented reality is often associated with visual discovery, which in turn is defined as a technology that fulfills a user's curiosity about the world around them by giving them information and relevant content when objects and images in the field of view are selected. Visual discovery requires an initial display or layer of information to appear instantly, by pulling the most relevant links related to the object being examined. The information can come from local storage, or via a link to the web. In some applications with AI and neural networks, the more people that use the application, the smarter it becomes by anticipating the user's requests or needs.

1.8.2   Internet of Things

The Internet of Things (IoT) is a system of interrelated computing devices, mechanical and digital machines, objects, animals or people that are provided with unique identifiers and the ability to transfer and receive data over a network without requiring human-to-human or human-to-computer interaction.

1.8.2.1 Wearables
Wearables are portable devices that collect and/or deliver information to the person wearing it. Smart watches, and activity trackers are examples. Body cameras and personal GPS devices are other examples. Wearables that have a Wi-Fi or internet connection capability are part of the IoT universe.

Smart Glasses and Augmented Reality
Smart glasses and augmented reality devices that are connected to a network or Wi-Fi, or even blue ray to another device (which in may be connected to some network) are connected-wearables, and therefore a subject of wearables which in turn are a subset of IoT.

Therefore, one can describe augmented reality devices as an IoT device, and/or a connected-wearable device Augmented reality actually was initially called wearable computing by pioneers like Steve Mann, Jaron Lanier, and others in the early 1980s and wasn't labeled augmented reality till 1990 by Thomas P. Caudell, and David Mizella while at Boeing.

1.8.2.2 Augmenting Reality

Augmented reality devices that superimpose information on your view of your surroundings are different from using a device like a smartphone to give you information about your location or surroundings, or even your destination. Your phone gives you your location, directions and/or information on where you want to go and will give you images of your destination. That is not augmented reality, that is just a sophisticated 2D map. Granted, places of interest and other information may also be available, and that is augmenting the overall informational content of the map. And since your phone can locate you, the information about your destination, and points of interest will change as you move.

1.8.3 Types of Augmented Reality

The difference between mixed reality versus augmented reality and cognitive reality, is mostly a semantics issue, but deeply critical to some people working in the field. In the broadest definition, augmented reality can have data overlaid on the real world from any digital source, video, games, 3D models, or locally captured information. Mixed reality has a specific knowledge of your world and where things are. Cognitive reality can employ artificial intelligence, analysis from deep learning processes, and neural networks.

1.8.3.1 Mixed Reality

Mixed reality (MR) in the virtual reality or simulation world refers to the combination or merging of a virtual environment together with a real environment where both of them can co-exist. Sometimes people also refer to it as "Hybrid reality".

In mixed reality, a user can navigate through the real world and a virtual environment seamlessly, and simultaneously. The virtual objects are accurately positioned in the real-world space. If one moves towards an object it will get larger and vice versa. And when one moves around it, the virtual objects are seen from different angles and perspectives—just like the behavior of real objects. Some people describe the experience to that of viewing holographic objects.

Users are able to manipulate the virtual objects in mixed reality. Users can interact with their concepts in virtual object form as if they existed in front of them.

Like augmented reality, mixed reality employs several technologies (see Sect. 1.8.1). To build a mixed reality system, you have to substitute the open real world view one gets with augmented reality smart glasses or helmet (or HUD) with a camera view since the display (typically a smartphone) screen occludes your view. And in order to overcome the feeling of looking through a toilet paper tube, you need to broaden the FOV of devices camera. Therefore, developers add a fish-eye lens to the assembly in front of the high-resolution front-facing camera of the smartphone.

Some examples of the mixed reality technology are Microsoft's HoloLens, Magic Leap, Occipital, and Canon's MREAL System. Some contend that HoloLens is under the augmented reality category, Microsoft, possibly for marketing and product differentiation reasons, insists it should fall under the mixed reality domain.

Another approach to mixed reality is the projected augmented reality approach taken by CastAR, where a pair of 3D shutter glasses with polarized lenses are combined with a forward facing, head mounted 720p pico-projectors. The projector casts 3D images on the viewer's surrounding environment.

The system creates a hologram-like image, that can be unique to each viewer in what the company calls "Projected Reality". A tiny camera is placed between the projectors to scan for infrared identification markers placed on a special retro-reflecting surface. The image bounces off a retro-reflective surface back to the wearer's eyes.

This approach keeps the viewer's eyes focused naturally (no eye strain or near-eye optics needed). It allows multiple people to see the surface simultaneously. The glasses have a camera sensor that tracks infrared light-emitting diodes (LED) points in the physical world into point data (AKA a point-cloud).

There's a radio frequency identification (RFID) tag that sits underneath the reflective surface. Any object also equipped with an RFID tag can be tracked across the surface with centimeter-level accuracy and uniquely identified.

1.8.4   Difference Between Virtual Reality and Augmented Reality

Often used interchangeably, Virtual Reality and Augmented Reality are not the same thing. Also, one is not a subset of the other, and the only attribute they share in common is the term "reality." They do share some underlying technologies, but offer distinctly different experiences.

Virtual reality takes you into a completely isolated computer generated world, typically with only three-degrees of freedom (3DOF), while augmented reality gives you additional visual information overlaid on the world around you, and six-degrees of freedom (6DOF).

From a graphics perspective, augmented reality is functionally similar to virtual reality, with the main difference being a transparent screen to allow the wearer to see both the actual view and the computer rendered overlay. Therefore, the hardware to display the graphics and software tools are similar. However, augmented reality has additional requirements in optics and tracking that make it a more difficult task to do well. Augmented Reality as described above superimposes computer-generated data and objects on the real worldview of the user. Virtual Reality creates an artificial environment and totally obscures the real world.

Virtual reality takes you totally out of actual reality, whereas augmented reality enhances your actual reality.

Virtual reality and augmented reality are used for training, education, and entertainment, but augmented reality has capabilities to allow you to see data superimposed on objects, diagrams, and instructions overlaid on equipment needing repair or maintenance, or locating a proposed change of the kitchen on top of the existing walls and room. Most agree that this additional capability will command a greater market share once the technical details are resolved.

In Augmented Reality, the computer uses location, motion, and orientation sensors and algorithms to determine the position and orientation of a camera. Augmented reality technology then renders the 3D graphics as they would appear from the viewpoint of the camera, superimposing the computer-generated images over a user's view of the real world. As mentioned above, augmented reality is possible with a smartphone, helmet, tablet, PC or glasses. Virtual reality only uses a head-mounted display, and one that does not provide any direct view of the real world; however, the head-mounted display can be a simple as Google's Cardboard.

Because the wearer of an augmented reality headset can see real objects, tracking and positional information is more critical. Consider looking at a table with an augmented reality generated vase on it. A vase that moves in and out of the table, or vibrates when the table is still is distracting and ruins the effect. As you walk closer to the table, you expect everything to match in terms of perspective, scaling and changes in occlusion as if the computer-generated objects were actually on top of the real object. This requires smooth tracking, awareness of the positions of real objects and the ability to compete with ambient lighting and extremely fast and accurate image generation. Otherwise the optical distortion mapping, rendering of objects, and geospatial attributes of computer imagery are functionally identical for virtual reality and augmented reality.

The optical solution is critical to the success of fusing virtual and real scenes. If the eye focuses at the virtual screen image, then looks at an object four meters away, there will be a mis-match between the focus. That will throw the user out of the illusion. That problem is what is hoped will be managed by the so-called light field displays that match the apparent focal lengths.

While most people aren't technical enough to explain why various augmented reality solutions don't work, they are capable of deciding if it isn't working for them in seconds of viewing.

That is another major difference between augmented reality and virtual reality—the focal length. In virtual reality, there basically isn't one. In augmented reality, it is absolutely critical.

One other thing about the difference between augmented reality and virtual reality—in augmented reality you can always see your hands, feet, and other parts of your body. And although not completely impossible, no one has complained of augmented reality sickness.

Commentators [28, 29] have observed that the most exciting thing about virtual reality is that it is the stepping stone to augmented reality—the real revolutionary tech.

1.8.4.1 Dual Modality

Some suppliers and industry observers have suggested a headset with dual modality, that is it could be an augmented reality headset in one case, and a virtual reality in another.

The closest you can come to such a dual modality, is a virtual reality headset with a camera, but this fails because it blocks your peripheral vision.

A planetarium is a (passive) virtual reality experience, a CAVE (Cave Automatic Virtual Environment) is an interactive virtual reality experience. I tell audiences, and clients, a virtual reality headset is a CAVE on your face.

A well-designed simulator is a virtual reality experience, and interactive.

iMAX approaches a passive virtual reality experience.

It's about immersion, and presence.

As for 360 video, it is indeed virtual reality. The difference is the type of content. 360 video is passive, whereas a game is interactive. If you engage either one in a totally obscuring viewer environment, it is virtual reality.

1.8.5   AR Preferred over VR if Forced to Choose

In late 2016 Qualcomm conducted a survey of consumers in focus groups in the US and China to assess their attitude and awareness of augmented and virtual reality. The focus groups felt augmented reality is anchored on practical use, but can cross over to fun.

The consumers generally had less awareness of augmented reality (unlike virtual reality). However, augmented reality is considered a cool technology. Initial perceptions and value center on practical daily life and learning.

Once the focus groups were made aware of augmented reality their eyes were opened, and they commented thatthe "possibilities are endless" and the versatility feels "limitless". Once there was a clearer understanding of the broad applications of augmented reality, interest and excitement spiked.

In China, augmented reality is perceived as a 3D Baidu (China's search engine like Google) which can reduce the need to search for things.

Mainstream users felt more comfortable with augmented reality and see it as an introduction to learn VR.

Because the focus groups saw a role for both augmented reality and virtual reality in their lives, they would like to combine VR & augmented reality into one device.

However, the glasses must be lightweight and look "normal", especially for those who don't wear glasses.

1.9   Summary

Augmented reality will completely disrupt the education sector from training for sports to remedial education. Head-up displays (HUDs) in automobiles, buses, and motorcycle helmets will be commonplace, and make us uncomfortable when not available. First responders will be able to see and anticipate obstacles. Entertainment will evolve to new exciting, immersive, and amazing heights. Real time visual translations will be used daily. Game playing will reach across the world and throughout it, and military battlefield operations will be even more deadly and effective. Surgeons will operate and diagnose remotely, and we will visit museums, potential new homes, and wondrous travel vistas that had been out of our reach.

References

1. *The Minority Report*, originally published in "Fantastic Universe," (1956).
2. http://www.smithsonianmag.com/history-archaeology/A-Brief-History-of-the--Teleprompter-175411341.html
3. *Wearable Computing and the Veillance Contract*: Steve Mann at TEDxToronto. https://www.youtube.com/watch?v=z82Zavh-NhI
4. http://www.augmentedreality.org/smart-glasses-report
5. http://www.gartner.com/newsroom/id/2618415
6. https://www.ericsson.com/assets/local/networked-society/consumerlab/reports/ten-hot-consumer-trends-2017-ericsson-consumerlab.pdf
7. Lawrence, W. K. (2015, January 1). *Learning and personality: The experience of introverted reflective learners in a world of extroverts*. Newcastle upon Tyne: Cambridge Scholars Publishing. ISBN 9781443878074.
8. Stephenson, N. (1992, June). *Snow crash*. New York: Bantam Books.
9. https://blog.metavision.com/how-neuroscience-based-ar-can-improve-workplace-performance
10. http://www.startrek.com/database_article/star-trek-the-animated-series-synopsis
11. https://en.wikipedia.org/wiki/The_Matrix
12. http://www.openculture.com/2014/02/philip-k-dick-theorizes-the-matrix-in-1977-declares-that-we-live-in-a-computer-programmed-reality.html
13. https://en.wikipedia.org/wiki/Minority_Report_%28film%29
14. https://en.wikipedia.org/wiki/They_Live
15. https://en.wikipedia.org/wiki/Philip_K._Dick
16. https://gamesalfresco.com/about/
17. https://gamesalfresco.com/2008/12/04/9-movies-that-will-inspire-your-next-augmented-reality-experience/
18. Milgram, P. Takemura, H., Utsumi, A., Kishino, F. (1994). *"Augmented reality: A class of displays on the reality-virtuality continuum" (pdf)*. Proceedings of Telemanipulator and Telepresence Technologies (pp. 2351–34).
19. Mann, S. (1999, March). Mediated reality: university of Toronto RWM project. *Linux Journal*, 59.
20. Mann, S. (1994). *Mediated reality* (Technical Report 260). Cambridge, MA: MIT Media Lab, Perceptual Computing Group.
21. Mann, S., & Fung, J. (2001, March 14–15). *Videoorbits on EyeTap devices for deliberately diminished reality or altering the visual perception of rigid planar patches of a real world scene*. Proceedings of the Second IEEE International Symposium on Mixed Reality (pp. 48–55).
22. https://vimeo.com/166807261

23. Keynote—Steve Mann: *Code of Ethics: Virtuality, Robotics & Human Augmentation*, (VRTO) Virtual & Augmented Reality World Conference & Expo 2016, Pages 1 and 9–13, http://wearcam.org/vrto/vrto2016.pdf
24. Minsky, Kurzweil, & Mann. (2001 June). *Sensory Singularity*. The Society of Intelligent Veillance, IEEE.
25. https://www.artefactgroup.com/articles/mixed-reality-without-rose-colored-glasses/
26. Asimov, I. (1950). *I, Robot*. New York: Doubleday & Company.
27. Augmented reality in: Encyclopedia Britannica 2010. http://www.britannica.com/technology/augmented-reality [13 May 2016].
28. Landgrebe, M. (2016, October 12). *The future looks bright (and pretty augmented)*. Study Breaks Texas State University. http://studybreaks.com/2016/10/12/augmented-reality-isnt-future-stepping-stone/
29. Niu, E. (2016, October 14). *Apple, Inc. Is more interested in augmented reality than virtual reality*. The Motely Fool. http://www.fool.com/investing/2016/10/14/apple-inc-is-more-interested-in-augmented-reality.aspx

Types of Augmented Reality

2

Abstract

One of the most important parts of augmented reality is the ability of the user to see his or her environment. However, the augmented reality device also has to "see" it, and that involves a computer-based vision system. Augmented reality is an amazingly diverse, robust, and complicated field, and if ever there was an industry where one size does not fit all, it is the augmented reality arena.

There are seven classes of augmented reality systems: helmet, head-up display smart-glasses (Integrated, and add-on), projection, specialized and other.

Some of the glasses use audio as the information presentation (including navigation). Others, again designating themselves as offering augmented reality smart-glasses merely offer an embedded camera in a glasses frame.

2.1 Types of Augmented Reality Systems

One of the most important parts of augmented reality is the ability of the user to see his or her environment. However, the augmented reality device also has to "see" it, and that involves a computer-based vision system (Fig. 2.1).

A camera combined with a display is an appealing configuration. Such a setup provides vision-based feedback that effectively closes the loop between the localization process and the display. This also reduces the need for heavy calibration procedure.

But, what should, or will be the display device. We have several choices, as described in the following sections.

All the displays used in wearable augmented reality systems (which excluded by definition mobile devices such as smart phones, tablets, and notebooks) are commonly referred to see-through, near-to-the-eye displays, or NEDs.

© Springer International Publishing AG 2017
J. Peddie, *Augmented Reality*, DOI 10.1007/978-3-319-54502-8_2

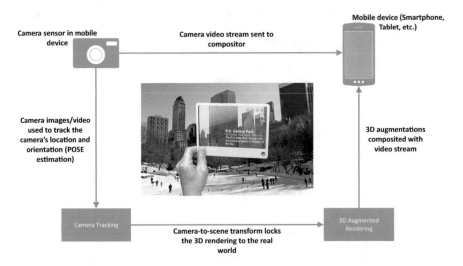

Fig. 2.1 Vision-based augmented reality

2.2 The Taxonomy of Augmented Reality

Augmented reality is an amazingly diverse, robust, and complicated field, and if ever there was an industry where one size does not fit all, it is the augmented reality arena.

At high level, it starts with two main categories: wearable and non-wearable (portable or stationary devices).

Wearable includes headsets, helmets, and one day, contact lenses.

Non-wearable includes mobile devices (smartphone, tablets, notebooks, weapons, etc.), stationary devices (TVs, PCs, plays, etc.), and head-up displays (integrated or retrofitted).

The diagram in Fig. 2.2 (Sect. 2.2) outlines the taxonomy of the augmented reality field.

I will attempt to define and give examples of the various devices for these categories, which has been challenging. At the time of this writing there were 80 companies making one type or another augmented reality device, and I doubt I found all the military ones. This book is not meant to be a survey of suppliers as they will come and go, and hopefully the book will remain relevant and useful beyond the churn in the industry.

Ron Padzensky, who runs a blog-site on augmented reality called, Augmera [1], re-classified the above and created a taxonomy which is strictly hardware oriented (Fig. 2.3).

And yet another segmentation or taxonomy is the device itself. Augmented reality can be experienced in or on dedicate augmented reality devices, or non-dedicated devices such as TVs, mobile phones, tablets, and PCs.

Within dedicated visual see-through augmented reality systems, there are seven classes:

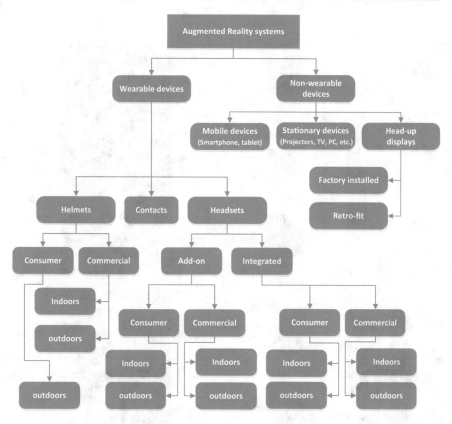

Fig. 2.2 Taxonomy of augmented reality

- Contact lens
- Helmet
- Head-up Display (HUD)
- Headset (Smart-glasses)
  - Integrated
  Indoors
  Outdoors
  - Add-on display and system for convential, sun, or safety glasses
  Indoors
  Outdoors
- Projectors (other than HUD)
- Specialized and other (e.g., health monitors, weapons, etc.)

The following is a list (in alphabetical order) of examples of the primary classes of visual see through dedicated augmented reality devices.

Ronald Azuma who is credited with defining the three main elements of augmented reality has yet another taxonomy [2]:

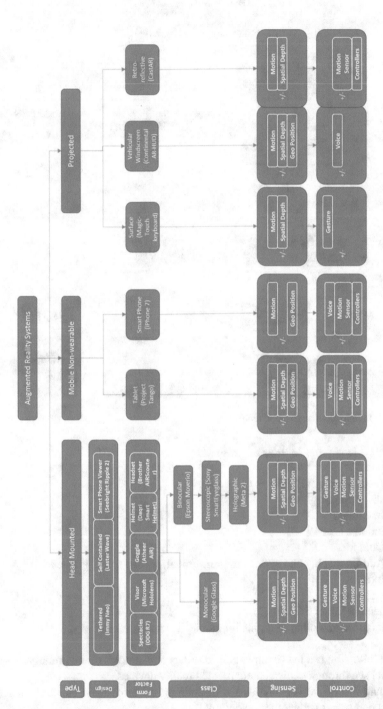

Fig. 2.3 Taxonomy of augmented hardware (Ron Padzensky)

1. Head-Mounted-Displays (HMD)
   (a) LCD-based, head-worn
   (b) Virtual retinal displays
2. Handheld displays
   (a) Flat panel LCD displays with an attached camera
3. Projection displays
   (a) Project the virtual information directly on the physical objects
   (b) Head-worn or fixed projector in the room objects with special surface reflecting the light
   (c) Projected images only visible along the line of projection

Presumably 3.c could include HUDs.

While Steve Mann in his book: *Intelligent Image Processing* (Wiley 2001) suggests the following:

Augmented Reality must be:

(a) Orthospatial (capable of mapping rays of virtual light collinearly with rays of real light);
(b) Orthotonal;
(c) Orthotemporal (interactive in real-time).

Says Mann, "An ideal reality mediator is such that it is capable of producing an illusion of transparency over some or all of the visual field of view, and thus meets all of the criteria above."

The following are some examples of types of products that make up the augmented reality market.

2.3   Contact Lens

Contact lenses for augmented reality are still in development and there are no commercial products available yet. The information on these intriguing devices can be found in the section, "Contact lens," Sect. 2.3.

2.4   Helmet

In the case of helmets, I classified a device as a helmet if it covered the user's ears, total head and most of the face (Fig. 2.4).

Some of the devices I put in the integrated smart-glasses category are quite large and look like a mini helmet so everyone may not agree with my classification (Fig. 2.5).

As in all categorization, distinctions can blur and overlap, which can at times cause confusion for someone new to the industry. Or in some situations it may just suit the developer, or the user to refer to the device in a certain way for easier communication. There are no hard rules in these classifications, just generalizations.

Fig. 2.4 This is a helmet
(Source: Daqri)

Fig. 2.5 This is not a
helmet, and is an integrated
smart-glasses AR HMD
(Source: Caputer)

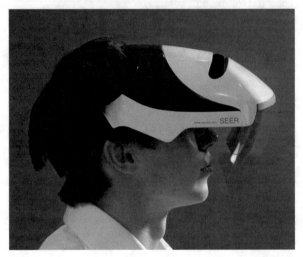

2.5   Head-Up Display

In the case of head-up displays, I only considered add-on or retrofit systems, not factory installed systems by vehicle manufacturers. The adoption of head-up displays in cars is rapid and difficult to track. The high-end cars from Audi, BMW, Cadillac, Lexus, Mercedes, and others have sensitized the consumers, as well as legislators who are proposing it be mandated.

A retro-fit head-up display is usually a low-cost device that either connects to an automobile's on-board diagnostics system (OBD2) connector and/or connects via bluetooth to a smartphone. Such devices sit on the dashboard, and project the vehicle speed, engine speed, water temperature, battery voltage, instantaneous fuel consumption, average fuel consumption, mileage measurement, shift reminders (if needed), and other warning conditions and project them to the inside surface of the windshield (Fig. 2.6).

Fig. 2.6 Kshioe's Universal 5.5″ Car A8 head-up display (Source: Amazon)

Fig. 2.7 Hudway Glass which offers navigation and a speed information from a smartphone (Source: Hudway)

Another example is one that uses the smartphone's application that displays vehicle speed and navigation information, available for the Android and iOS operating systems. In the following image, you can see the user (Fig. 2.7).

There is additional information on head-up displays for aircraft in the section on "Aircraft," section "Aircraft", and on automotive in the section, "Walking and Driving," section "Walking and driving".

It should be noted, HUDs are not limited to automobiles, and are being deployed in buses, trucks, and even ships.

2.6   Smart-Glasses

As mentioned earlier, I have subdivided the smart-glasses suppliers into integrated and add-on, and both of those categories are further subdivided regarding their ability or design to be used indoors, or outdoors. Obviously indoors is an implied subset of outdoors, however, there are some consumer smart-glasses that are integrated with sunglasses and would be inappropriate to wear indoors.

2.6.1   Integrated Smart-Glasses

The distinction between an add-on augmented reality device, and an integrated device may seem arbitrary. The distinction I made was if the device could be attached to, or worn with regular glasses, it was an add-on device. If it included and integrated lenses and other elements (such as a microphone, camera, or earphones) then it is considered as integrated smart glasses, augmented reality headset.

2.6.1.1 Indoors and Outdoors
I have further subdivided integrated smart-glasses into consumer and commercial, and those into indoors and outdoors. It's an important distinction. Consider a sports headset like Intel's Recon. However, for augmented reality glasses that have a time-of-flight depth/distance measuring technology, like Microsoft's Hololens, the sensors depend on non-visible light that does not agree with UV outdoors (and can also be affected indoors by sunlight coming through windows). In other cases, the display may not be bright enough to overcome the ambient light from outside.

2.6.1.2 Consumer
Smart-glasses can vary widely from the newer consumer type of spectacles offered by companies like GlassUp's UNO, Laforge Shima, and Ice's Theia. These devices have a small real time OS on board and communicate via BTLE (Bluetooth low energy) with any smartphone (or tablet) running Android or iOS. It displays to the user any kind of message that the smartphone has already elaborated, and uses the smartphone's GPS, gyro, accelerator, and other sensors (Fig. 2.8).

Consumer smart-glasses are mobile battery-powered, and look close to if not exactly like regular glasses. Some consumer versions of smart-glasses have a small box or package, typically the size of a smartphone, connected by a thin cable to the glasses. The box is worn on the belt or in a pocket.

Fig. 2.8 GlassUp's UNO consumer augmented reality glasses (GlassUp)

Included in the consumer category are smart-glasses designed for specific functions such as sports and exercise such as Intel's Recon, and Kopin Solos.

I do not include Google Glass or its imitators as consumer since they are conspicuous and call attention to themselves and the wearer, just the opposite of what is desired to be worn in public.

2.6.1.3 Commercial

Other smart-glasses are designed for commercial, scientific, and engineering uses and are more powerful, and usually tied to a computer via a tethered umbilical cord. Companies like Atheer Labs, Meta, Osterhout, and many others are in this class.

And some companies like GlassUp make both consumer and commercial smart-glasses.

Also, included in this category are special smart-glasses for people with eye disorders or partial blindness such as LusoVU Eyespeak (Fig. 2.9).

The Atheer Labs head-mounted display is an integrated smart-glasses example because it has ear temples on both sides and has built-in lenses.

2.6.1.4 Binocular Verses Monocular

Some integrated smart-glasses have only one display (and all add-on smart-glasses only have one display). Binocular provides much better, more natural viewing. Often, monocular devices can cause headaches, have screens that obstruct the view rather than overlay, etc. Binocular also provides greater field of view than most monocular glasses.

2.6.1.5 Prescription Smart Glasses

Some companies have taken one additional step in the development of their smart glasses, and added prescription ground lenses. One of the questions often asked of smart glasses manufacturers is, "Can I use it with my glasses?"

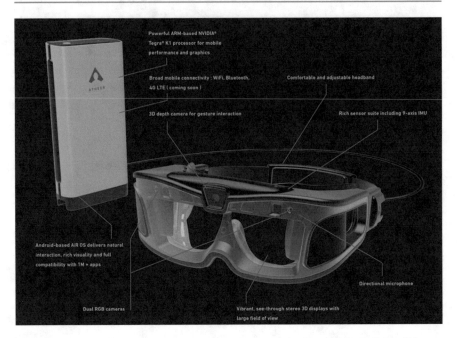

Fig. 2.9 This is an integrated augmented commercial reality head-mounted device (Source: Atheer Labs)

As is mentioned later (Laforge, Sect. 6.1.4), as of this writing, only a few companies are offering consumer-class augmented reality eyewear with a normal look.

Rochester Optical, a renowned optical company founded in 1883 by William H. Walker [3] (1846–1917) has provided prescription lenses that can be used with other firms augmented reality glasses. In November, 2015, Hong Kong Optical Lens Co., LTD established a partnership with Rochester Optical in offering Smart Solutions for five types of smart glasses and providing optical corrections users. Rochester Optical had designed its Smart Solutions optimized for people who felt discomfort while wearing smart glasses. The company developed two types of prescription glasses. Very thin and light frames that can be used under augmented reality headsets (and virtual reality head-mounted displays too), and custom frames that can accept add-in augmented reality displays such as Recon, Vuzix, Epson, Atheer, and others.

Jins Mem also offers type of smart glasses in a conventional frame with prescription lenses. However, they do not have a camera, and connect to a companion application in a smartphone via Bluetooth. They're equipped with a gyroscope, six-axis accelerometer, and electrooculography (EOG) sensors for tracking eye movement. The Meme smart glasses are designed for fitness tracking and can measure posture and identify when fatigue is setting in.

Fig. 2.10 This is an add-on augmented reality display device (Source: Garmin)

2.6.1.6 Blue Light Filters

Smartphones, tablets, and displays in augmented reality headsets are common sources of blue-violet light. Close proximity to users' eyes intensifies the impact, and too much blue light exposure can contribute to eye fatigue, and potentially cause early-onset macular degeneration [4].

To combat this problem, lenses have been designed that can block harmful blue-violet light emitted by digital devices. Rochester Optical has made this a feature of their lens offerings. Laforge is also adding blue light to their lenses, in addition to UV filtering.

2.6.2 Add-On Smart-Glasses

Add-on augmented reality display devices, like the Garmin Varia-Vision, can be attached to sunglasses or prescription glasses (Fig. 2.10).

Add-on displays, or retro-fit displays, are usually limited to monocular presentation. Interestingly, the suppliers seem to favor the right eye, possibly influenced by Google Glass. Steve Mann's original EyeTap however, was worn over the left eye.

The other augmented reality devices such as contact lenses are discussed in the "Smart contact Lens," section on Sect. 8.7.5.3.

2.7 Projection

The use of projected specially treated light that can be seen through some type of a viewer has been worked on since the early 2010s. Advertised as holo-something, with the implication that it is some form or type of a hologram, and inspired by the famous image in the original Star Wars movie (now Episode 4) with a hologram of Princess Leia projected by R2D2 (Fig. 2.11).

To project an image requires some type of a reflective device or medium to send the light (photos) to the viewer's eyes; free space is not such a medium. However,

Fig. 2.11 Princess Leia's hologram projected into open space (Courtesy: Lucasfilm Ltd.)

special glasses, or a viewer (such as a tablet) can be. The glasses/viewer can see the basic scene, and receive the virtual information, classic augmented reality. It's not holographic, its mixed or projected reality.

To create the illusion, a display system needs two pieces of information: the exact position of the projection surface in 3D space, and the position of the viewer's eyes in the same 3D space. Together, these two provide enough information to set up the correct perspective projection.

Realview Imaging, Yokneam, Israel, introduced a 3D volumetric imaging system in 2012 targeted at the medical market for visualization by clinicians called the Holoscope. Based on acoustical interference, it was effective, but small, and expensive.

Since then the company has developed an augmented reality headset for viewing the models (Fig. 2.12).

Realview creates multiple depth planes at multiple distances in real time, projected simultaneously. Using multiple depth plans, says the company, eliminates the vergence confusion. Like other firms (Microsoft, Hololamp, CastAR, etc.) the term holograph is used casually, and incorrectly, holograms don't have focal planes. However, in the case of Realview, which is using depth planes, it may be definitionally correct. A holographic image of a real 2D image is still a holographic image, just not one of a 3D object. As Dr. Oliver Kreylos of the University of California at Davis points out, composing a holographic image from multiple slices of a 3D object is an approximation of creating a holographic image of the full 3D object, but it is still a real holographic image.

According to the Wikipedia entry for computer-generated holography, one of the simpler algorithms to generate the required interference patterns, Fourier transform, is only able to create holograms of 2D images. Another method, point source holograms, can create holograms of arbitrary 3D objects, but has much higher computational complexity.

Fig. 2.12 Realview's
Deep perception live
holography system
(Realview)

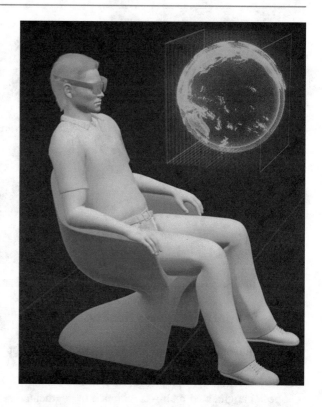

To create the illusion, a display system needs two pieces of information: the exact position
of the projection surface in 3D space, and the position of the viewer's eyes in the same 3D
space. Together, these two provide enough information to set up the correct perspective
projection.

A more affordable system, suitable for home use, is the one developed by
Hololamp. Founded in Paris France in early 2016, the company introduced their
augmented reality projector in early 2017. The Sony (Microvision laser-beam scanning) projector makes it possible for augmented reality to interact with real objects,
and no special glasses or smartphone are required to see its animated images
(Fig. 2.13).

HoloLamp is a structured light projection system that creates a 3D point-cloud of
the local area to generate the 3D objects in the field of view. The objects are then
used as markers for the superimposed virtual objects, and registered accordingly so
they behave physically correctly. The point of HoloLamp is to project images of
virtual 3D objects onto arbitrary surfaces. HoloLamp uses an additional set of cameras looking upwards to identify and track the viewer's face, using face tracking
algorithms. Based on that, the software can project 3D objects using one or more
projection matrices. The effect is monoscopic, and can only work for a single user.

Hololamp describes their approach as Spatial Augmented Reality.

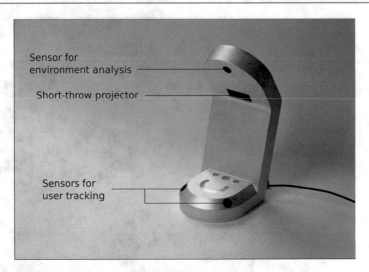

Fig. 2.13 Hololamp glasses free augmented reality projector (Hololamp)

2.7.1 Spatial Augmented Reality

Spatial augmented reality (SAR) is a term, and concept pioneered Oliver Bimber while at Bauhaus-University, Weimar, and Ramesh Raskar at Mitsubishi Electric Research Laboratory, Cambridge, MA, in 2004 [5].

Special augmented reality is a branch of augmented reality based on projectors that deliver a glasses-free and hands-free augmented reality experience. It exploits the way our eyes perceive 3D objects to allow you to perceive a 3D experience. Spatial augmented reality enables moving images on any surface by mapping the surface, tracking the user and then projecting an image that is warped so that from the user's point of view it is what they would expect to see as a 3D effect.

The Hololamp concept it is somewhat similar to the AR Sandbox, i.e., a set of cameras that scan a projection surface and a viewer's face, and a projector drawing of a perspective-correct image, from the viewer's point of view, onto the projection surface. It's also similar to what CastAR does.

The CastAR glasses project 3D images in front of the wearer's eyes and feel as if one is seeing a virtual layer on top of the real world, or feel like being immersed inside a game world. It uses shutter glasses with a forward facing (into the room) set of tiny projectors, and a reflective sheet-like material called retro-reflective. Theoretically one could use the reflective sheets to animate an entire room.

The U.S. National Science Foundation (NSF) funded AR sandbox—a multi-university project designed to develop 3D visualization applications to teach earth science concepts. It is a hands-on exhibit combining a real sandbox, and virtual topography and water created using a closed loop of a Microsoft Kinect 3D camera, powerful simulation and visualization software, and a data projector. The resulting augmented reality (AR) sandbox allows users to create topography models by

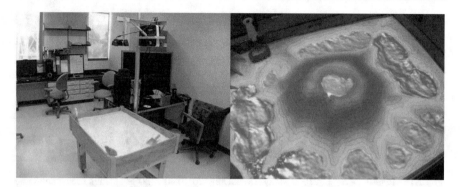

Fig. 2.14 *Left*: Sandbox unit when turned off. The Kinect 3D camera and the digital projector are suspended above the sandbox proper from the pole attached to the back. *Right*: Sandbox table when turned on, showing a mountain with a crater lake, surrounded by several lower lakes

shaping real sand, which is then augmented in real time by an elevation color map, topographic contour lines, and simulated water (Fig. 2.14) [6].

The goal of this project was to develop a real-time integrated augmented reality system to physically create topography models which are then scanned into a computer in real time, and used as background for a variety of graphics effects and simulations. The final product is supposed to be self-contained to the point where it can be used as a hands-on exhibit in science museums with little supervision.

2.7.2 CAVE

A classic CAVE Automatic Virtual Environment (better known by the recursive acronym CAVE) is an immersive virtual reality theater where 3D images are rear projected to between three and six of the walls of a room-sized cube. The first CAVE was conceived in 1991 and built by Professors Dan Sandin and Tom DeFanti at the University of Illinois at Chicago's Electronic Visualization Laboratory where grad student Carolina Cruz-Neira wrote the first software drivers for the CAVE. Since 2009, various CAVEs have been made from LCD and OLED panels with passive polarization, eliminating the need and space for projectors.

A CAVE can show a video projection of the outside world, so in once sense it is an obstructed view augmented reality system. Consider the giant CAVE at Stoney Brook University in New York (Fig. 2.15).

Combining augmented reality environments with immersive virtual environments can reduce interaction gaps and provide embodied interactions in distributed collaborative works. It can also provide many opportunities and degrees of freedom for collaboration in both real and virtual worlds.

Inside a CAVE there can be multiple people viewing the projections. They wear stereoscopic glasses (typically polarized and untethered and usually have reflectors on them for location sensing within the cave.

Fig. 2.15 Reality Deck" CAVE at Stony Brook Univ (2012) 40′ × 30′ × 11′ high room containing 308 LCD display—1.25 billion pixels

Fig. 2.16 University of California, San Diego's WAVE CAVE

CAVEs do not have to be six-sided rooms. The University of California, San Diego built the WAVE display, and true to its name, it is shaped like an ocean wave, with a curved wall array of 35, 55-inch LG commercial LCD monitors, that end in a 'crest' above the viewer's head and a 'trough' at his or her feet (Fig. 2.16).

WAVE is an acronym for Wide-Angle Virtual Environment, it was designed and built in-house by Qualcomm Institute's Director of Visualization Tom DeFanti, Professor of Visualization and Virtual Reality Falko Kuester and Senior Design Engineer Greg Dawe. The WAVE, a 5x7 array of HDTVs, is 20-feet long by nearly 12-feet high.

A CAVE can be as small as three walls, and as large as Stony Brook's.

2.8   Specialized and Other

Glasses, designated by the developer as smart-glasses, but with limited or no informational display capability are offered for fitness tracking and health monitoring, and in some cases navigation. Some of the glasses use audio as the information presentation (including navigation). Others, again designating themselves as offering augmented reality smart-glasses merely offer an embedded camera in a glasses frame.

Weapons with augmented reality mechanisms adapted to them are used by the military (e.g., shipboard defenses) and consumers (see Augmented Reality in Hunting, section "Augmented reality in hunting").

2.8.1   Watermarking Augmented Reality

In 2000, the Digimarc company in Portland OR, developed a water marking technology to thwart counterfeiting. As the web was spreading into all corners of commerce the company realized their technology could be used as a quasi-marker embedded in images and messages. Digimarc's process of embedding a digital watermark into an image involved dividing the image into blocks of pixels. Then the watermark is independently embedded in each of these blocks. That allowed the watermark to be detected from an image region as small as one block. Spread spectrum techniques are used to make the signal imperceptible and to combat the effect of image manipulation and filtering [7].

The reader reverses the operation of the embedder by extracting the synchronization signal from the frequency domain of the image. It uses the signal to resolve the scale, orientation, and origin of the watermark signal. Finally, it reads and decodes the watermark signal.

Digimarc developed a product they called the MediaBridge, which created a bridge between traditional commerce and electronic commerce (see Fig. 2.17, Sect. 2.8.1).

When a person used a digital camera or scanner to produce a digital image version of a printed MediaBridge image, the MediaBridge reader application detects and reads the embedded watermark. The embedded watermark represents an n-bit e.g., the Digimarc server. That index was used to fetch a corresponding URL from the database. Then the URL is used by the Internet browser to display the related Web page or start a Web-based application—it created a bridge between the printed material and the Internet.

Digimarc subsequently licensed the technology to several firms and it's in use in various places today.

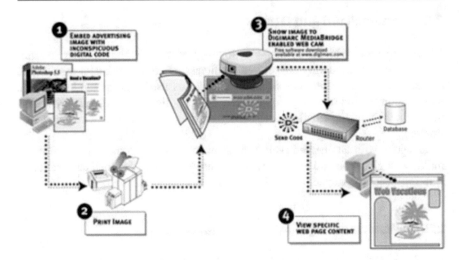

Fig. 2.17 Digimarc's watermarking technology was used to embed digital watermarks in printed images such as magazine advertisements, event tickets, CD covers, goods packaging, etc

References

1. http://augmera.com
2. Augmented Reality Part 1—Technologies & Applications. (2005, April). *Seminar, Smarte Objekte und smarte Umgebungen.* https://www.vs.inf.ethz.ch/edu/SS2005/DS/slides/03.1-augmented.pdf
3. http://www.historiccamera.com/cgi-bin/librarium2/pm.cgi?action=app_display&app=datasheet&app_id=231
4. Kitchel, E. *The effects of blue light on ocular health.* Louisville: American Printing House for theBlind.http://www.tsbvi.edu/instructional-resources/62-family-engagement/3654-effects-of-blue-light
5. Bimber, O., & Raskar, R. (2005). *Spatial Augmented Reality.* Natick, MA: A K Peters, Wellesley. http://web.media.mit.edu/~raskar/SAR.pdf.
6. Reed, S., Kreylos, O., Hsi, S., Kellogg, L., Schladow, G., Yikilmaz, M. B., Segale, H., Silverman, J., Yalowitz, S., & Sato, E. (2014). *Shaping watersheds exhibit: An interactive, augmented reality sandbox for advancing earth science education,* American Geophysical Union (AGU) fall meeting, Abstract no. ED34A-01.
7. Xerox Corporation. (1999, December 17). *DataGlyphs.* http://www.xerox.com/xsis/dataglph.htm

We'll All Be Experts Now

3

Abstract

Augmented reality uses a personal display, up close to the user, to show him or her information, text, drawings, 3D objects, generated locally or remotely, by a computer. The overlay information is registered to the scene by a forward-looking camera and can show the skeletal structure of a building, or the location of a store, or the pipes beneath the sidewalk. It can translate in real time street signs, menus, newspapers, and manuals. It will make us all experts, with massive data at out beckoning.

Augmented reality is blurring the boundaries between the digital and physical world and moving us into a new level of contextuality. Augmented reality delivers rich experiences derived from the use of sensors, computing, artificial intelligence, and big data.

3.1   Augmented Reality: We'll All Be Experts Now

Augmented reality uses a personal display, up close to the user, to show him or her information, text, drawings, 3D objects, generated locally or remotely, by a computer. The overlay information is registered to the scene by a forward-looking camera and can show the skeletal structure of a building, or the location of a store, or the pipes beneath the sidewalk. It can translate in real time street signs, menus, newspapers, and manuals. It will make us all experts, with massive data at out beckoning.

Augmented reality is blurring the boundaries between the digital and physical world and moving us into a new level of contextuality. Augmented reality delivers rich experiences derived from the use of sensors, computing, artificial intelligence, and big data.

Augmented reality will change our lives forever—for the better.

© Springer International Publishing AG 2017
J. Peddie, *Augmented Reality*, DOI 10.1007/978-3-319-54502-8_3

Fig. 3.1 A technician can use a tablet to "look at" a device and be given instructions on how to fix it or use it (Source: XMReality)

In the very near future, I believe we will all be wearing augmented reality glasses, just as we wear corrective and sun glasses today. The augmented reality glasses of the future will be lightweight, they won't be obnoxious or call attention to themselves, and they will be capable of providing us with a wealth of pertinent information, as well as being a logging device of our lives—think of it as your personal black box recorder. The augmented reality glasses of the future will be always connected providing you with information and sending information about you (with your approval and to your private storage locker). In one sense, augmented reality glasses will be the ultimate narcissist's dream. They will also be the honest witness in any insurance claims, or disputes with service personal, or family members.

However, the benefits of augmented reality are not limited to the future or just to glasses. A smartphone or tablet can today deliver augmented reality capabilities too. Basically, any device that has a forward-facing camera and back-facing screen, could be an augmented reality device. Theoretically a digital camera with a Wi-Fi or Bluetooth capability could be an augmented reality device. Your car could too if it has forward-facing cameras as are being proposed for autonomous driving. And if a car can, so can a boat, truck, bus, or a train.

Augmented reality is not necessarily a solitary experience. Using the camera and a Wi-Fi or mobile phone connection, a technician or first responder can show the situation to an expert at a remote location and get guidance. Or perhaps broadcast paths to safety in a disaster.

In their paper on the rebirth of augmented reality [1], Akif Khan, Shah Khusro, Azhar Rauf, Saeed Mahfooz described mobile augmented reality as sensitizing a new dimension of perception to see, hear and immerse in the real world via an interactive and enriched look and feel on physical world objects/places. This potential blend opens new vistas for overlaying information on physical infrastructure, places and object of interests (Fig. 3.1).

Fig. 3.2 BMW's
augmented reality
motorcycle helmet with
head-up display screen on
right (Source: BMW)

In addition to augmented reality glasses, also known as "smart-glasses," tablets, and phones, there are augmented reality helmets. Helmets for first responders, motorcycle riders, and for factory workers. Helmets with head-up displays (HUDs) are a logical and practical implementation of an augmented reality system, and the helmet offers more storage space for electronics and batteries (Fig. 3.2).

The head-up display in a motorcycle helmet could be a GPS-based navigation system for couriers as well as law enforcement, or even the pizza delivery person.

A helmet has room for a lot of electronics including a 3D sensing camera, an IR camera, an inertial measurement unit (IMU—often referred to as gyroscope), and of course a projected (on the visor) display (Fig. 3.3).

Augmented reality is a head-up display for the user, and can simultaneously be a telepresence device—the user of an augmented reality system can take family and friends on a tour with him or her. For instance, in the movie, *Her* [2], the protagonist Theodore (Joaquin Phoenix) becomes fascinated with a new operating system and carries a smart phone in his pocket with the camera facing outward so Samantha, the intelligent computer operating system, can share his experiences with him (Fig. 3.4).

As mentioned, augmented reality is not a new concept, Ivan Sutherland (1938 –) built the first working device in 1966, and Professor Steven Mann (1962 –) began real-world experiments with it in his childhood in the early 1970s (Fig. 3.5).

In the near future, the adornment of powerful augmented reality glasses will be as common as a watch or mobile phone, and by 2025 we'll wonder what life was

Fig. 3.3 The Daqri smart
helmet is also a certified
hard hat (Source: Daqri)

Fig. 3.4 Theodore carries
a camera in his shirt so
Samantha can see what
he's seeing (Source:
Warner Bros. Pictures)

like before augmented reality, much like we do today about the web, or our smartphones. In fact, it is entirely possible we will no longer need a smartphone. The
functionality of the smartphone could be built into our augmented reality glasses.
Alternatively, the smartphone will act as a server to our smart-glasses, connected
wirelessly and proving the network connection and local data storage, and reducing
the power consumption and weight of the glasses.

Augmented reality will become a part of everybody's life, you'll use it everywhere; we won't even consider it a technology anymore, it will be ubiquitous and
invisible and an intimate part of our lives. It will enrich and improve our lives.

Fig. 3.5 Steve Mann field tests his prototype augmented reality system circa 1980 (Source: Steve Mann)

New developments and technologies are leading to increased usage of augmented reality in several application areas. Due to these developments and the high growth potential, this an important area for study and understanding.

This book will discuss the history, applications, technologies, and opportunities that are bringing augmented reality to us all.

References

1. Khan, A., Khusro, S., Rauf, A., & Saeed, M. B. (2015, April). Rebirth of augmented reality – Enhancing reality via smartphones. *University Journal of Information & Communication Technologies 8*(1), 110. ISSN – 1999-4974.
2. https://en.wikipedia.org/wiki/Her_%28film%29

Overview of Augmented Reality System Organization

4

Abstract

In order to appreciate the developments and advances in augmented reality is it necessary to have a general understanding of what makes up an augmented reality system.

Prolonged use of conventional stereo displays can cause viewer discomfort and fatigue because of the vergence accommodation. Visual fatigue and discomfort occur as the viewer attempts to adjust vergence and accommodation appropriately. (Vergence is the simultaneous movement of both eyes in opposite directions to obtain or maintain single binocular vision.)

Although augmented reality has been with us since 1961, like many developments it has had multiple lives, and several fathers. The problem is augmented reality is largely thought of as a technology.

Augmented reality is a very subjective and personal thing; all users will not see the same view of information about the world unless they choose to. Users will be able to subscribe to the data streams they prefer. The two major uses for augmented reality are to provide general information and/or specific instructions. There won't be clear delineation between the two, but at the extremes the two will not overlap.

The major differentiation between informational and instructional augmented reality is the user's interaction with the information being presented and the place where the user is. Augmented reality is taking training, operational, and informational content to new levels of user experience. It is an incorporation of computer-generated assets superimposed onto the user's immediate surroundings through specialized hardware and software. Augmented reality has the unique ability to bridge the gap between training and operations, by integrating a highly-detailed 3D simulation and information of the most current equipment and facilities with which technicians, installation and repair personal, inspectors, engineers, and researchers will work.

© Springer International Publishing AG 2017
J. Peddie, *Augmented Reality*, DOI 10.1007/978-3-319-54502-8_4

4.1   Overview of Augmented Reality System Organization

In order to appreciate the developments and advances in augmented reality is it necessary to have a general understanding of what makes up an augmented reality system. The following block diagram shows the relative arrangement of the components of an augmented reality system.

Cameras—augmented reality devices will always have at least one camera in the visible spectrum, and may have two for depth sensing. There may also be an infrared (IR) camera in the device, used for heat mapping and/or depth sensing.

The acronyms used in the block diagram, consist of:

IMU—Inertial measurement unit, used as a gyroscope. It is a gyroscope, Accelerometer and often Magnetometer combined.

AP/FP—Application processor/function processor, fixed function engines, task-specific.

ISP—Image signal processor (for camera output).

DSP—Digital signal processor (for cameras, mic, range finders, and radio).

GPU—Graphics processing unit, also called the Image Generator (IG). For augmented reality the GPU needs to do alpha blending to make the objects appear to be in the room over real objects, and while the computational requirements are lower in terms of total scene polygons, the requirements for antialiasing and lighting are higher.

RTOS—Real-time operating system.

SLAM—Simultaneous localization and mapping (SLAM) is the computational problem of constructing or updating a map of an unknown environment. In some designs the SLAM is part of the ISP. SLAM allows an entity to track its location while simultaneously mapping its surroundings.

MEMs—Micro Electro Mechanical systems used for miniature gyroscope-like sensors.

The IMU and GPS help tell the user where he or she is, as well as provide location information for an external data base. The sonar and laser provide depth information, sonar for nearby, and laser for distance. The output is a display and audio. Not all augmented reality systems will have depth measurement capability, most mobile devices for example won't, and industrial helmets probably won't.

Processors used in mobile phones and tablets known as a system on a chip (SoC) contain a CPU, GPU, ISA, AP/FP, and usually a sensor multiplexor. Mobile phone semiconductor suppliers also make the radios (Gen5, Wi-Fi, Bluetooth), and of course a smartphone or tablet contains cameras, mic, speaker, and display; some even have 3D sensing sensors. Most SoCs have a built-in DSP allowing faster matrix operations.

The device's main operating system (i.e., iOS, Android, Linux, or some other) are selected by the device builder. The Real Time Operating Systems can be embedded in an AP/FP, or as a Kernel in the main OS.

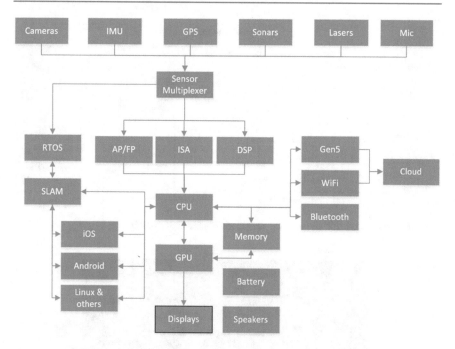

Fig. 4.1 Block diagram augmented reality system

4.1.1 What to See, What Not to See

The functions and capabilities that an augmented reality system must have to perform well, in addition to those in the above diagram (Fig. 4.1), are addressable occlusion and adjustable depth of field. Addressable occlusion is where the augmented image from the image generator has a synchronous and geometric correlation to a segmented part (or parts) of the image on display (screen) which blocks out light directly behind the augmented imagery. This is the only way to create photo realistic augmented reality, otherwise the image is ghosted (Semi-transparent). Secondly, the system needs to have an adjustable depth of field for the augmented reality image to correlate to the real world. If that isn't done there will be an accommodation-convergence conflict. There are several ways of accomplishing variable depth of field.

4.1.2 A Few Words About Convergence Conflict

Prolonged use of conventional stereo displays can cause viewer discomfort and fatigue because of the vergence accommodation. Visual fatigue and discomfort occur as the viewer attempts to adjust vergence and accommodation appropriately. (Vergence is the simultaneous movement of both eyes in opposite directions to obtain or maintain single binocular vision.) (Fig. 4.2): A graphical illustration of the issue can be seen in Fig. 4.3.

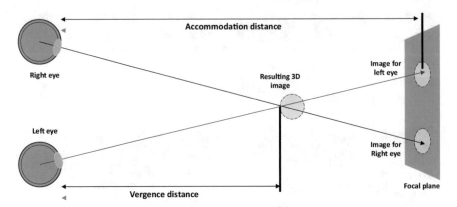

Fig. 4.2 Accommodation distance vs. Vergence distance in 3D viewing

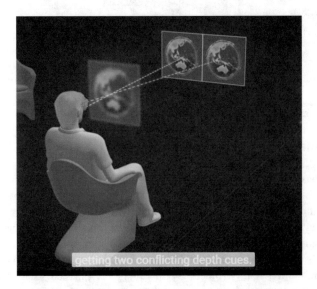

Fig. 4.3 Loss of depth image due to improper vergence will confuse the viewer (Realview)

In a conventional 3D-stereo projection one's brain can get confused between the overlapping projected view and the viewer's natural focus at his or her focal plane, creating two conflicting depth cues Your eye convergence is at the intersection of the view paths (the vergence distance), but the brain is tricked into seeing it in the distance (the accommodation distance), which creates the vergence accommodation conflict. It quickly becomes intolerable for close images, and is aggravated even more if the viewer tries touching the virtual 3D objects because the viewer's eye focus on his or her hand which makes the distant virtual image blur and become confusing. The result is the illusion of 3D is lost, and the viewer feels discomfort.

Various organizations have developed proprietary designs for accommodating convergence conflict. Augmented reality headset manufacturer IMMY uses two methods depending on the application, and with their optical method have created a way to dynamically vary the image plane. Magic Leap claim their breakthrough is due to a clever way of managing the convergence conflict.

Similar to virtual reality, a lot of factors have to come together to achieve immersion, as illustrated in the following diagram.

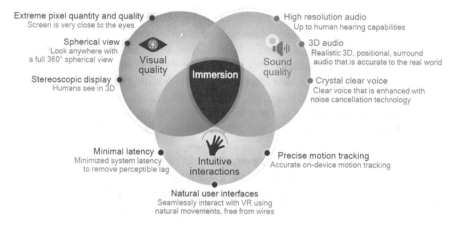

Visual, audio, positional, and UI all have to fast, accurate, and use little power in an AR HMD (Qualcomm)

Augmented reality introduces even additional requirements for immersion that need to be seamlessly integrated with virtual objects in the real world.

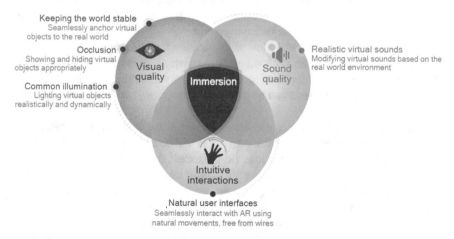

Immersion in AR requires knowing where you are and balancing the images generated with the environment. (Qualcomm)

Because of the needs of mobility (heat, wright, battery life), and the addition of cameras and geo-positioning sensors, combined with the geometric modeling to the real world, an augmented reality headset must do a great deal more work than a virtual reality system.

4.2   The Problem with Technology

Although augmented reality has been with us since the 1940s, like many developments it has had multiple lives, and several fathers. The problem is augmented reality is largely thought of as a technology. If you ask someone to explain what augmented reality is, inevitably they will do so by describing the components: a camera, a display, positional sensing sensors. It's like telling someone what time it is by describing how to build a clock. If you asked someone to describe TV they would say it shows moving pictures in your living room, and never mention the display technology, the source of the information, or that the information was live or from a stored media.

Technology-defined products are easier to market because they can be quantified. A PC has a processor that is so fast, a storage unit that is so big, and so much memory, etc. And because of the versatility and ubiquity of a PC, it would be difficult to describe what it is—it's a game machine, an engineering workstation, a photo editing device, a web browser, etc. Augmented reality suffers from that same versatility; it can be many things to many different people. And yes, augmented reality devices and systems do share some common technologies, but it is not the technology, or the components that define what augmented reality is, any more than the pistons in a car define what that is. Such use of components to define the substance of augmented reality fails to provide any insight into the use, benefit, potential, or difficulties of augmented reality. It also fails to provide a basis for any standardization, government, or safety oversight.

Augmented reality is a collection of applications, and those applications have different requirements from each other. Some require extremely high-resolution displays; others need very sensitive location sensors, while others need a super-fast, highly robust database. Some can be tethered, others must work for hours on just a battery.

One of the goals of this book is to develop a taxonomy of augmented reality. It is a daunting task, like defining what electricity is and how it is used. We will discuss the technologies, and the applications (to the extent they can be covered because there are so many of them). And hopefully we will leave you with the understanding that augmented reality is not a thing, not something you can go buy ten-pounds of. It's a solution to a problem, and problems we haven't even thought of yet.

To get to that realization, a brief understanding of how we got to where we are and some of the breakthroughs made along the way is called for, which is covered with a brief historical overview in the next chapter.

Historical Overview

5

Abstract

Although seeming new as it penetrates the consumer market, augmented reality can trace its roots back to the second world war, and conceptually even further to Pepper's ghost in 1862.

Overlaying one image with another was employed in various methods from entertainment to weapons, and as might be imagined, weapon development provided the most resources and emphasis. The first application of electronics to augmented reality was done by the English when they adapted an airborne RADAR navigation system in a WWII de Havilland Mosquito night fighter. But it didn't take long for the entertainment industry to employ the concept in TV right after the war. By the 1960s, small head-mounted displays were being experimented with and in the 1970s, with the ever-increasing miniaturization of electronics, augmented reality hit its stride, and things, as they always do, began to expand rapidly as more people got interested and involved.

5.1 Historical Overview: Ghosts to Real AR to DARPA

Augmented Reality is the enhanced or resultant image produced by overlaying another (could be computer-generated) image over a real-time view of one's surroundings.

- The first electronic HUD was in a de Havilland Mosquito night fighter, in **early 1940** by the Telecommunications Research Establishment in the UK.
- The first augmented reality helmet device was done by the Philco Corporation, Philadelphia, PA, USA, in **late 1950s** when they began developing a closed-circuit television surveillance system with a helmet-mounted display.

© Springer International Publishing AG 2017
J. Peddie, *Augmented Reality*, DOI 10.1007/978-3-319-54502-8_5

- Augmented reality in TV: The teleprompter, **1950**; Chroma-key virtual sets, early **1970s**; augmented reality based weather visualizations, **1981**; the scrimmage line in football, **1998**.
- First augmented reality smart glasses were developed by MicroOptical in **1997**, and the first commercial glasses product, Glasstron, was offered by Sony.
- First augmented reality system on a consumer mobile phone was shown in **2004** by Mathias Möhring, Christian Lessig, and Oliver Bimber at the Bauhaus University.

The following is a summary of developments in augmented reality, and although hopefully thorough, it is not meant to be an exhaustive chronical of the technology or the developers.

The first mention of an augmented reality-like device is believed to have been in L. Frank Baum's (1856–1919) (author of *The Wonderful Wizard of Oz*) 1901 novel, *The Master Key: An Electrical Fairy Tale*, [1] where he described a set of electronic glasses called a "character marker" that could reveal a person's hidden personality traits and give insight into a person's character (Fig. 5.1).

The first practical implementation of an Augmented Reality-like device was the teleprompter developed in 1950 by Hubert Schiafly [2] (1919–2011) which was based on the concept of Pepper's Ghost.

1862: Pepper's ghost is an illusion technique used in theatre, amusement parks, museums, television, and concerts. It is named after John Henry Pepper (1821–1900), a scientist who popularized the effect in a famed demonstration in 1862 (Fig. 5.2) [3].

Fig. 5.1 Lyman Frank Baum (May 15, 1856–May 6, 1919), better known by his pen name L. Frank Baum (Wikipedia)

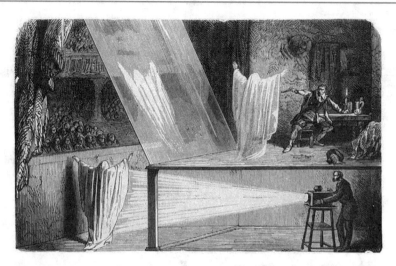

Fig. 5.2 Pepper's Ghost (1862) seeing things that aren't there (Wikimedia)

The basic trick involves a stage that is specially arranged into two rooms, one that people can see into such as the stage, and a second that is hidden to the side, or below the stage. A plate of glass is placed at the edge of the stage, at an angle that reflects the view of the second room towards the audience. When the second room is lit, its image (the ghost in the room) reflects off the glass toward the audience.

1901: An adaptation of Pepper's ghost was put forth in 1901 by Sir Howard Grubb (1844–1931) an optical designer from Dublin, who patented "A New Collimating-Telescope Gun Sight for Large and Small Ordnance (Fig. 5.3)."

Ambient lighting of the reticle was improved by placing it facing up and bouncing it off a relay mirror then off a concave collimating mirror. A modern-day version of the idea can be found at Augmented Reality in Hunting (section "Augmented reality in hunting").

The concept was extended to aircraft in WW I, and then enhanced with electronic displays in WW II aircraft creating the first head-up display systems.

1942: The history of augmented, or mitigated reality in the form of a head-up display (HUD), can be traced back to the early 1940s during World War II, in England. In October 1942, the Telecommunications Research Establishment (TRE), in charge of UK radar development successfully combined the image from the Airborne Interception Mk. II radar (AI Mk. II) radar tube with a projection from their standard GGS Mk. II gyro gunsight on a flat area of the windscreen of a de Havilland Mosquito night fighter [4].

The heads-up display (HUD) was adapted from WW II era gyro gunsight technology in the late 1950s [5] with the objective of supplying basic flight information

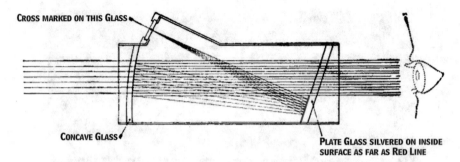

Fig. 5.3 A diagram of a version of Howard Grubb's collimating reflector sight designed to make a compact version suitable for firearms and small devices (Wikipedia)

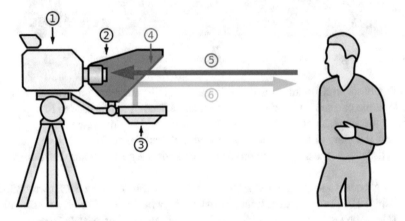

Fig. 5.4 A teleprompter system (Wikipedia) [7]

on the windscreens of military planes to minimize the need to glance down and change focus from the horizon [6].

1950: The teleprompter, developed by Hubert Schiafly in 1950, consisted of a transparent panel placed in front of a speaker like a podium, and a projector projected the speaker's text or script on it. The text was only visible to the speaker. That allowed the speaker to look straight ahead and not look down to consult written notes, he appears to have memorized the speech or to be speaking spontaneously, looking directly into the camera lens (Fig. 5.4).

The above image is of a teleprompter systems with: (1) Video camera; (2) Shroud; (3) Video monitor; (4) Clear glass or beam-splitter; (5) Image from subject; (6) Image from video monitor.

1953: The first synthetic-vision aircraft system was the Army-Navy Instrumentation Program (ANIP) [8]. Conceived in 1953 for the purpose of providing a new

Fig. 5.5 Artificial horizon image from ANIP system (Douglas Aircraft)

concept of flight data instrumentation which would make possible the optimum use of performance capability and true all-weather operation of aircraft (Fig. 5.5).

One of the objectives of ANIP was to unburden the pilot by providing carefully designed, artificially generated, more natural displays. The program was intended to be applicable to surface vessels, submarines and ground vehicles as well as aircraft.

1961: Philco is credited with having developed the first augmented reality-like head-mounted system, they called Headsight. It features a helmet with a cathode-ray tube and had magnetic head-position tracking (Fig. 5.6).

Philco employees Comeau and Bryan, built Headsight and demonstrated it in 1961. It used a magnetic tracking system and a single CRT mounted on a helmet, and gave a remote viewer a video image according to the wearer's head direction. It could be classified today as a telepresence device in that it didn't superimpose any data over the image the wearer saw.

The device was used with a remote controlled closed circuit video system for remotely viewing dangerous situations and to monitor conditions in another location, using the magnetic tracking to monitor the user's head movements. The device was reported on in the November 1961 issue of *Electronics* magazine [9].

1962: Hughes Aircraft also had a head-mounted device in the same time period, called the Electrocular (Fig. 5.7) [10].

It was designed to be a remote camera view device by projecting a video camera's output to a head-mounted one-inch diameter (7-inch long) CRT with a semi-transparent mirror that projects the image in front of the wearer's right eye.

Fig. 5.6 Philco' s
Headsight headset with
CRT display (Source:
Electronics magazine)

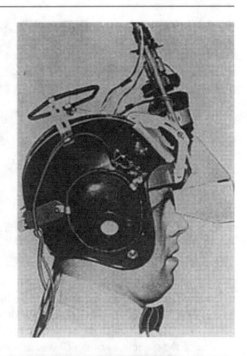

Fig. 5.7 Third Eye for
Space Explorers, Hughes
Aircraft's Electrocular
(Popular Electronics)

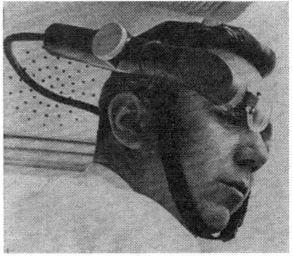

1963: Bell Helicopter Company in Fort Worth, Texas was experimenting with a
    servo-controlled camera and remote viewing device on a headset. The display
    provided the pilot with an augmented view of the ground, captured by an infrared
    camera under the helicopter. The camera was slaved to the headset so it would
    move as the pilot moved his head basically giving him remote vision and not too
    dissimilar from the Philco system (which probably was the inspiration for the
    Bell system).

The Bell Helicopter system was designed to help make landings at night, providing a real-world view enhanced in real-time. This system would be the first video see-through augmented reality system, but there wasn't any computer-generated imagery in it.

1965: Ivan Sutherland, famous for his SketchPad project at MIT in 1962 took a position as an associate professor at Harvard University. He envisioned augmented reality in his 1965 essay entitled *The Ultimate Display* [11].

The ultimate display would, of course, be a room within which the computer can control the existence of matter. A chair displayed in such a room would be good enough to sit in. Handcuffs displayed in such a room would be confining, and a bullet displayed in such a room would be fatal. With appropriate programming, such a display could literally be the Wonderland into which Alice walked.—Ivan Sutherland

While at Harvard he heard about the project at Bell Helicopter and went there to see it. Sutherland watched the Bell Helicopter people test the system by having one employee sit in the office wearing a prototype of the headset and watch two colleagues playing catch, up on the roof. When one of them suddenly threw the ball at the camera, the employee in the office ducked. "It was clear," said Sutherland, "that the observer thought he was at the camera and not comfortably safe inside the building.

Modestly Sutherland said, "My little contribution to virtual reality was to realize we didn't need a camera—we could substitute a computer. However, in those days no computer was powerful enough to do the job so we had to build special equipment."

1967: Tom Furness (April 19, 1943–) was working in the Air Force on pilot head-mounted displays for weapon aiming. Approximately 22 years later, he started the Human Interface Technology lab (HIT Lab) at the University of Washington (Fig. 5.8).

Produced under contract by Hughes Aircraft Company, the first USAF HMD used a one-inch electromagnetic deflection CRT producing a raster scanned image that was magnified and projected to produce a 30-degree field of view virtual image. It could be used to display on left or right eye.

In **1968**, Sutherland, with his student Bob Sproull (1945–), Quintin Foster, and Chuck Seitz, a grad student at MIT, built the headset with head-tracking and a special purpose computer to generate a single cube with some lettering on the sides (Fig. 5.9). They used the same display Bell Helicopter used, with two CRTs (one for each eye) and developed a head-mounted display suspended from the ceiling, which became named, "The Sword of Damocles."

The unit was partially see-through, so the users were not completely cut off from their surroundings. This translucence combined with the other features is why it is often cited as a precursor to augmented reality technology (Fig. 5.10).

Later that year, Sutherland moved to Utah, where he joined the Computer Science Department at the University of Utah founded by Dave Evans (1924–),

Fig. 5.8 Lt. Tom Furness
wearing first USAF Helmet
Mounted Display
(Armstrong Laboratory,
Wright-Patterson AFB,
OH)

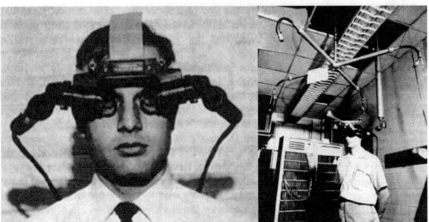

Fig. 5.9 The viewer saw computer-generated graphics—basically a floating wire-frame cube
(Courtesy: The Computer History Museum)

Sutherland had known Evans from his ARPA days at MIT. Together they founded
Evans & Sutherland Computer Corporation in 1968, the first computer graphics
company in the world, and a pioneer in CG.

Since **1965**, in an attempt to improve aircraft man-machine design, human-
factors engineers of the Aerospace Medical Research Laboratory (AMRL) at

Fig. 5.10 "The Sword of Damocles" (without gantry) head-mounted display (Courtesy: The Computer History Museum) [12]

Wright-Patterson AFB, Ohio, (a unit of Aerospace Medical Division) have been pioneering techniques to "visually couple" the operator to his weapon system.

In **1969** Myron Krueger (1942–) while earning a Ph.D. in Computer Science at the University of Wisconsin–Madison, developed a series of interactive computer artworks which he termed "artificial reality" in which he developed computer-generated environments that responded to the people in it. This technology enabled people to communicate with each other in a responsive computer generated environment despite being miles apart, the forerunner of telepresence. The projects named Glowflow, Metaplay, and Psychic Space were progressions in his research and in **1975** led to the development of Videoplace technology (funded by the National Endowment for the arts). It surrounded the users, and responded to their movements and actions, without the use of goggles or gloves. The work done in the lab contributed to his well received and often cited 1983 book, *Artificial Reality* [13].

Augmented reality is generally thought of as having an image displayed over some type of a view system like goggles, or a tablet.

During the **1970s** and 1980s, augmented reality was a research topic at some institutions, including the U.S. Air Force's Armstrong Laboratory, the NASA Ames Research Center, the Massachusetts Institute of Technology, and the University of North Carolina at Chapel Hill.

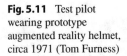

Fig. 5.11 Test pilot
wearing prototype
augmented reality helmet,
circa 1971 (Tom Furness)

1971: South Africa emerged as one of the pioneers and leaders in helmet-mounted
gun-sight technology. The SAAF was also the first air force to fly the helmet
gun-sight operationally.

That same year the visor projected display/tracking system developed for the
USAF under contract by Honeywell Inc., was finalized (Fig. 5.11).

The display image was generated by a one-inch CRT on the rear of the helmet
and relayed to the front of the helmet via a coherent fiber optical bundle. The image
was collimated and introduced onto a mirrored portion parabolic visor, reflected to
another mirror at the focal point of the parabola, reflected back into a second
dichroic coating on the parabola and then into the pilot's eye. The pilot would see a
virtual image subtended at a visual angle of 22° at optical infinity superimposed on
the outside world. The helmet was also tracked using an infrared triangulation on
photodetectors on the slide of the helmet creating the first see-through augmented
reality display that was not mechanical coupled.

1974: The US Navy were the first to field an operational helmet-mounted sight system in a fighter aircraft, the Visual Target Acquisition System, also known as
VTAS.

Also in **1974**: Steve Mann creates the concept of wearable augmented reality,
using wearable computers to overlay phenomenological signals onto visual reality.
Mann also creates the concept of, and implementation of, phenomenological augmented reality (Fig. 5.12), e.g. making otherwise invisible electromagnetic radio
waves visible, by way of his "S.W.I.M. (Sequential Wave Imprinting Machine)".

This was a real form of augmented reality, in the sense that the augmentation was
directly from the real physical world (reality itself) in which the alignment between
the real and virtual worlds was nearly perfect, with a near infinite bandwidth
(Fig. 5.13).

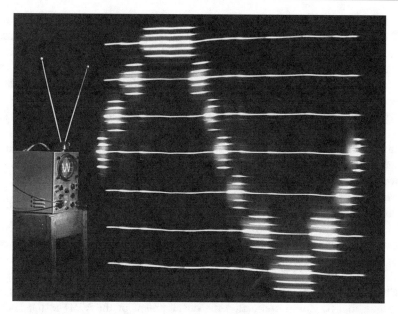

Fig. 5.12 Real Augmented Reality—visualization of information with no mediation (Mann)

Fig. 5.13 Steve Mann field tests his prototype EyeTap augmented reality system at MIT circa 1980 (Source: Wikipedia Steve Mann)

1980: Steve Mann's WearComp 1, cobbled together many devices to create visual experience. It included an antenna to communicate wirelessly and share video. Mann later re-named the next version, "Eyetap."

1981: The idea of overlaying computer and RADAR augmented reality data over a TV image was developed by Dan Reitan (1960–) for television weather broadcasts which brought augmented reality to TV. Reitan is credited with inventing the original augmented reality-based weather visualizations at KSDK St. Louis, Mo. The inventions went live on-air at KSDK, WGN and many other stations; not just overlay, but mixed real-time images from multiple radar imaging systems and satellites in real-time. Reitain went on to develop an application called ReinCloud, and obtained serval patents [14].

1985: Jaron Lanier (May 3, 1960–), who is credited with coining the term 'virtual reality' (in 1987) and fellow ex Atari researcher Thomas G. Zimmerman (1957–) founded VPL Research. It sold products such as the Data Glove (invented by Thomas Zimmerman [15]), which lets people use their hands to interact with a virtual environment, and the EyePhone, a head- mounted display.

1985: While working at the Armstrong Laboratory at Wright-Patterson Air Force Base, Thomas Furness conceived the idea of a virtual retinal display as a means of providing a higher luminance helmet-mounted display for pilots. About the same time in 1986, Kazuo Yoshinaka (1916–2001) while working at Nippon Electric Co also developed the idea. (In November 1991, Furness and his colleague Joel S. Kollin completed the development of the VRD at the Human Interface Technology Laboratory at the University of Washington and filed a patent in 1992.)

1986: As part of the US Air Force Super Cockpit project, Tom Furness developed a high-resolution heads-up overlay display for fighter pilots, supported by 3D sound (Furness, 1986).

1989: Reflection Technology introduced The Private Eye head-mounted display. It had a monochrome array of LEDs in a 1.25-inch display that was scanned vertically using a vibrating mirror. Images appeared to be like a 15-inch display at 18-inches distance (Fig. 5.14).

1990: The term "Augmented Reality" is attributed to Thomas P. Caudell, and David Mizell [16] former Boeing researchers [17]. Caudell and Mizell worked at Boeing on simplifying the process of conveying wiring instructions for aircraft assembly to construction workers, and they referred to their proposed solution of overlaying computer represented material on top of the real world as augmented reality. In 1992 it was published in a paper in the Proceedings of the Twenty-Fifth Hawaii International Conference on System Sciences. Krueger pre-dates that with his 1983 book, *Artificial Reality* [13], and his work at the University of Wisconsin in 1969.

1991: Ben Delaney launched CyberEdge Journal. From January 1991 until January 1997, CyberEdge Journal was the voice of the virtual reality industry [18].

1992: Louis Rosenberg (1969–) developed Virtual Fixtures, one of the first functioning augmented reality systems, for the Air Force Research Laboratories. This allowed the military to work in remote areas [19]. In 1993, Rosenberg founded the virtual reality company, Immersion Corporation. Then in 2000, Rosenberg then founded Outland Research, a company specializing in advanced methods of

Fig. 5.14 Steven Feiner's Private Eye (photo by Dan Farber)

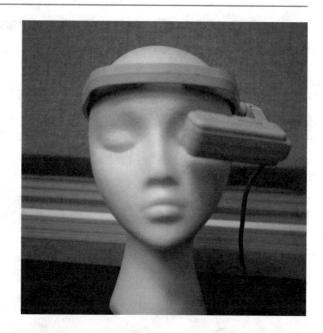

Fig. 5.15 Augmented reality intended to show toner cartridge and show location of and identify paper tray (Courtesy: Blair MacIntyre)

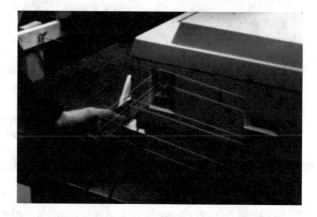

human-computer interaction and in 2001 Google purchased Outland Research, along with its patents.

1992: Although several working prototypes of augmented reality had been demonstrated, Steven Feiner (1952–), Blair MacIntyre, and Doree Seligmann are credited with presenting the first major paper on an augmented reality system prototype, KARMA (Knowledge-based Augmented Reality for Maintenance Assistance) [20, 21], at the Graphics Interface conference (Fig. 5.15).

1992: Neal Stephenson publishes Snow Crash introducing the concept of the Metaverse. Stephenson joined the Magic Leap company in 2015.

1993: Lizzy—Thad Starner (1969–) starts constantly wearing his computer based on Doug Platt's design [MIT]. Using an Intel 80,286 PC, and a Private Eye dis-

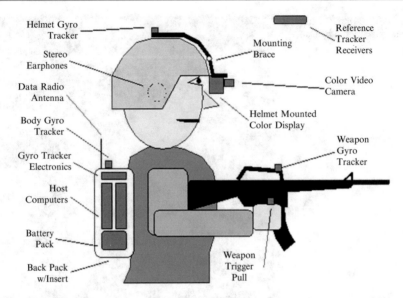

Fig. 5.16 Augmented Simulation (AUGSIM) system (Source: Peculiar Technologies) [24]

play by Reflection Technology (see above). [22] and calls the system, "Lizzy," after the Ford Model T.

1993: Loral WDL, with sponsorship from STRICOM, performed the first demonstration combining live augmented reality-equipped vehicles and manned simulators (Fig. 5.16). (Unpublished paper, J. Barrilleaux, "Experiences and Observations in Applying Augmented Reality to Live Training", 1999 [23].)

1994: Augmented reality was first used for entertainment purposes when Julie Martin created what is believed to be the first Augmented Reality Theater production, "Dancing in Cyberspace." Funded by the Australia Council for the Arts, featuring acrobats and dancers manipulating body–sized virtual objects in real time, projected into the same physical space and performance plane.

1994: SixthSense is a gesture-based wearable computer system developed at MIT Media Lab by Steve Mann in 1994 [25] and 1997 (head worn gestural interface), and 1998 (neckworn version), and further developed by Pranav Mistry (also at MIT Media Lab).

1996: Steven Feinberg, professor of computer science at Columbia University, created the first outdoor mobile augmented reality system using a see-through display.

1997: Ronald T. Azuma's, A Survey of Augmented Reality, examined the varied uses of augmented reality such as medical, manufacturing, research, mechanical operation and entertainment.[1]

---

[1] Azuma, Ronald T., http://www.cs.unc.edu/~azuma/ARpresence.pdf

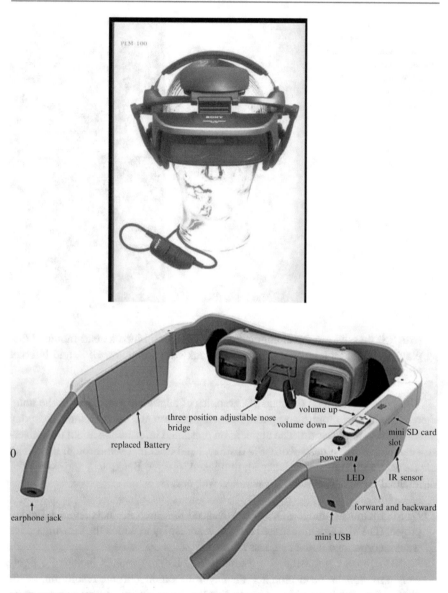

Fig. 5.17 Sony Glasstron augmented reality headset (Source: Wikipedia)

1996: Sony released the Glasstron, a head-mounted display which included two
LCD screens and two earphones for video and audio respectively. It also had a
mechanical shutter to allow the display to become see-through (Fig. 5.17).

1997: Mobile Backpack augmented reality, The Touring Machine, developed at
Columbia starting in 1996, was the first mobile augmented reality system

Fig. 5.18 Touring
Machine—First mobile
augmented reality system
Backpack augmented
reality with head-worn
display (Columbia
University)

(MARS) that did graphical augmented reality. It combined a head-mounted display, handheld tablet display, and a backpack with computer, GPS, and Internet
connection (Fig. 5.18) [26].

The system combined overlaid 3D graphics of augmented reality with the untethered freedom of mobile computing, proving support for users in their everyday
interactions with the world. The application presented information about the university campus. It had a head-worn, 3D display, head-tracking, see-through handheld,
2D display with stylus and trackpad, untracked, opaque Backpack, and computer,
differential GPS, digital radio for wireless web access.

1997: MicroOptical, under a Defense Advanced Research Projects Agency funded
project (DARPA), demonstrated the eyewear display in which the viewing optics
were incorporated in the eyeglass lens.
1998: IBM Japan demonstrated a wearable PC. Its components included a lightweight monocular head-mounted display with a monochrome resolution, headphones for sound and video, a controller / microphone for control and a control
unit. It ran Windows 98 and featured a 233 MHz Pentium MMX, 64 MB of
RAM, a 340 MB IBM.
Late 1990s: Augmented reality became a distinct field of research, and conferences
on augmented reality were started, including the International Workshop and
Symposium on Augmented Reality [27], the International Symposium on Mixed
Reality, and the Designing Augmented Reality Environments workshop.
Organizations were formed such as the Mixed Reality Systems Laboratory
(MRLab) in Nottingham and the Arvika consortium3 in Germany [28].

Fig. 5.19 Mark Billinghurst and Hirokazu Kato developed the pioneering and widely used augmented reality Tool kit (Courtesy: Thomas Furness and Hirokazu Kato)

1997: Ronald Azuma is credited with establishing the three main elements that define augmented reality [29]:

- it connects real and virtual worlds
- it's interactive in real time
- it allows movement in 3D

1998: augmented reality in sports broadcasting—Sportvision, The use of augmented reality was introduced in a wide variety of graphics overlays used in sports broadcasting. The most well-known one was the (yellow) scrimmage line in U.S. football.

1998: Concept of spatial augmented reality (SAR) introduced at the University of North Carolina, where virtual objects are rendered directly within or on the user's physical space without a headset [30].

1999: The ARToolkit developed by Mark Billinghurst and Hirokazu Kato by the Human Interface Technology Laboratory at the University of Washington. The technology was first demonstrated publicly at SIGGRAPH in 1999. It was released open source in 2001 by the HIT and commercialized by ARToolworks under a dual licensing model (Fig. 5.19).

ARToolKit was acquired by DAQRI and re-released open-source starting at version 5.2 on May 13, 2015.

1999: NASA turns to augmented reality with the X-38 program, which would allow researchers to better understand what technologies would be needed to build inexpensive and reliable spacecraft.

Fig. 5.20 Mann wearing
his wearing his EyeTap
Digital Eye Glass from
1999 (Photo by: Dan
Farber for Cnet) [31]

1999: Naval researchers begin Work on Battle-field Augmented Reality System
(BARS), the original model of early Wearable systems for soldiers.
1999: Steve Mann is one of the earliest pioneers in digital eyewear and what he calls
"mediated" reality. His breakthrough development was the enabling of mobile
augmented reality. He is a professor in the department of electrical and computer
engineering at the University of Toronto and an IEEE senior member, and also
serves as chief scientist for the augmented reality startup, Meta (Fig. 5.20).

An EyeTap is worn in front of the eye, recording what is available to the eye and
superimposing the view as digital imagery. It uses a beam-splitter to send the same
scene to both the eye and a camera, and is tethered to a computer in a small pack. In
2000, Steve Mann was recognized as "The Father of the Wearable Computer" (IEEE
ISSCC 2000), and the Founder of the Wearable Technologies field; specifically,
Nicholas Negroponte, Director of the MIT Media Lab, stated, "Steve Mann is the
perfect example of someone who persisted in his vision and ended up founding a
new discipline."

2000: Outdoor gaming *ARQuake,* developed by Wearable Computer Lab University
of South Australia used a head-mounted display, a mobile computer, head tracker,
and GPS system to provide inputs to control the game (see "Games," section
"Games").
2001: MRLab finished their pilot research, and the symposia were united in the
International Symposium on Mixed and Augmented Reality [32] (ISMaugmented
reality), which has become the major symposium for industry and research to
exchange problems and solutions.
2004: First augmented reality system on a consumer mobile phone was accomplished by Mathias Möhring, Christian Lessig, and Oliver Bimber at the Bauhaus
University (Fig. 5.21) [33].

Fig. 5.21 Video see-through example on a cell phone

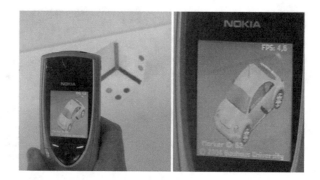

Fig. 5.22 Tomohiko Koyama (aka Saqoosha) developed FLARToolKit bringing augmented reality to web browsers

The researchers presented a first running video see-through augmented reality system on a consumer cell-phone. It supported the detection and differentiation of different markers, and correct integration of rendered 3D graphics into the live video stream via a weak perspective projection camera model and an OpenGL rendering pipeline.

2009: In January, LEGO, the Danish toy manufacturer launched its DIGITAL BOX, based on Metaio technology. Angela Merkel and the Governor of California pose with the product. The interest level in augmented reality jumps.

2009: NyARToolKit was ported to Flash by Tomohiko Koyama (aka Saqoosha) to create FLARToolKit and enabled augmented reality to be viewed in a web browser for the first time (Fig. 5.22) [34].

Fig. 5.23 Esquire featured
an augmented reality
experience within its
magazine in 2009 (Source:
Hearst Publishing)

LARToolKit is based on NyARToolkit, a Java ported version of ARToolKit. FLARToolKit recognizes the markers from input image. And calculates their orientation and position in a 3D world.

2009: Esquire—Augmented Reality Issue. The December 2009 issue of Esquire magazine featured six Augmented Reality experiences triggered by a black and white block "marker" printed on the cover and with several articles and ads. After downloading the custom software, holding up the marked pages started playback of the associated experience, with actors performing in virtual environments that changed with the orientation of the magazine page (Fig. 5.23).

Esquire Magazine can be credited with popularizing the idea of augmented reality, and shortly thereafter new companies started forming faster than ever (see Fig. 9.1: Companies entering the augmented reality market since 1988, Sect. 9.1.1).

2009: Qualcomm launches project Vuforia, an Augmented Reality Software Development Kit (SDK) for mobile devices that enables the creation of Augmented Reality applications. In 2015 Qualcomm Connected Experiences, a subsidiary of Qualcomm, sold its Vuforia augmented reality platform to Computer-Aided Design (CAD) and Product Lifecycle Management (PLM) software maker PTC (formerly Parametric Technology Corporation) for $65 million, to enable applications in the Internet of Things.

Fig. 5.24 Epson Moverio
BT-100 augmented reality
glasses (Source: Epson)

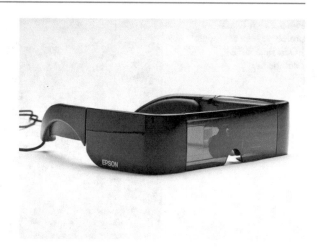

2010: Microsoft launches project Baraboo, to develop mixed reality smart-glasses. The HoloLens can trace its lineage to Kinect, an add-on for Microsoft's Xbox gaming console that was introduced in 2010.

2011: The HIT Lab NZ staff and students demonstrated the CityViewAR app to the public during the weekend of 10–11 December, 2011, at the Cashel Mall in downtown Christchurch. CityViewAR showed the city of Christchurch as it was before the 7.1-magnitude 4 September 2010 earthquake there.

2011: Magic Leap Raise $50 million in investment, the largest augmented reality investment in history. By 2014, when the company officially announced its funding, it had raised $1.4 billion.

2011: Epson showed a prototype of an augmented reality system, the Moverio BT-100 and promised more fashionable glasses for 2014 (Fig. 5.24).

Epson released three more versions and in 2016 brought out the Moverio Pro BT-2000 with a depth camera.

2011: Google Glass project was developed by Google X, the facility within Google devoted to technological advancements such as driverless cars, led by Jaque Aldrich (Fig. 5.25).

The product was publicly announced in April 2012, and in April 2013, the Explorer Edition was made available to Google I/O developers in the United States for $1500.

2013: Car manufacturers use augmented reality to replace vehicle service manuals. The Volkswagen MARTA application (Mobile Augmented Reality Assistance) for example, provides detailed information for service technicians, While the Audi augmented reality application uses the iPhone camera to provide details on 300 elements about the vehicle from windscreen wipers to the oil cap [35].

Fig. 5.25 A Glass
prototype seen at Google
I/O in June 2012
(Wikipedia)

2013: Toshiba introduces a 3D augmented reality hybrid theatre planning application for medical procedures.

2014: Wearable augmented reality headlines began appearing, mostly due to Google
Glass, and other companies like Epson, which developed Smart glasses. A startup
company, Innovega, announced it would offer its iOptik system, augmented reality contact lens. In 2017 the company changed its eyeware name to eMacula.

2016: Super Ventures, the first incubator and fund dedicated to augmented reality
was launched [36]. Investment in augmented reality companies and startups
reached $1.5 billion in 2016 with Magic Leap capturing $800 million of it that
year (in addition to earlier investments).

Microsoft entered the market with its $3000 HaloLens, which had been under
development as Project Baraboo, since 2010.

5.1.1   Trend Spotting

In my research for this book I realized that many people were explaining augmented
reality (and virtual reality); what it is, how it works, who invented what and when.
I think that is the measurement of newness. If you know how something works, even
just basically (how many people know in any detail how a car works) its considered
common place, maybe even commoditized, perhaps ordinary. But when something
is new, and therefore exciting, maybe promising, then we want to know what it is,
how does it work, what's the magic? We are interested in it. And we express our
interest by asking about it, reading about it, searching on the web about it.

No one explains today how a smartphone works, a PC or TV work. They, and all
other technologies that we live with and take for granted, are part of our environment, part of our metaverse.

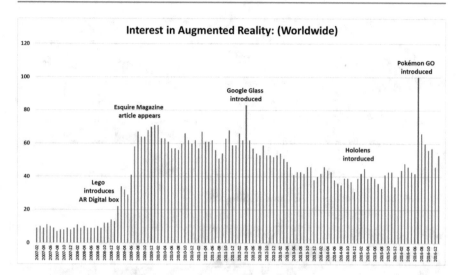

Fig. 5.26   Interest over time of Augmented Reality

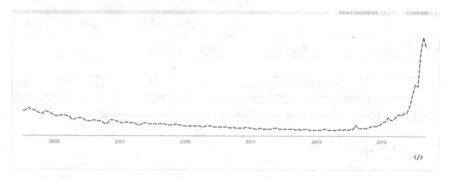

Fig. 5.27   Interest over time of Virtual Reality

Maturity of a market (or technology) is not just when there is a consolidation of suppliers, but when people stop explaining what it is, stop investigating it.

5.1.1.1 Interest Over Time Google Trends
Using Google's Trends monitoring system [37] one can enter a subject and see what the search activity of a topic, based on Google's search engine data, has been (Fig. 5.26).

The (vertical) values represent search interest relative to the highest point on the chart for the given region and time. A value of 100 is the peak popularity for the term. A value of 50 means that the term is half as popular. Likewise, a score of 0 means the term was less than 1% as popular as the peak(Fig. 5.27).

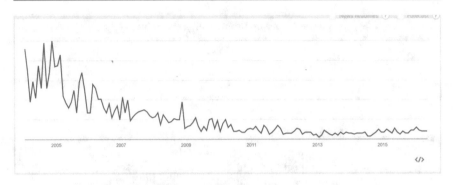

Fig. 5.28 Interest over time of Artificial Intelligence

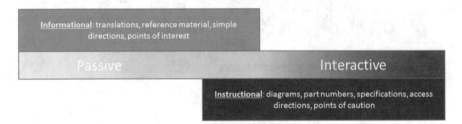

Fig. 5.29 The spectrum of use of augmented reality with some overlap

The next big spike will be the release of this book of course. However, in comparison to other popular technologies (see following charts) augmented reality has the longest high level of interest extending back to 2006 (Fig. 5.28).

One could look at this as an extension or augmentation to the hype curve (developed by Gartner in 1995) [38].

When the hyper, the above average interest in a topic or company falls off, the topic is no longer faddish, and may be on its way out, or at least quiescently evolved into a normal part of our lives.

5.1.2   Real Time Content in Context

Augmented reality is a very subjective and personal thing; all users will not see the same view of information about the world unless they choose to. Users will be able to subscribe to the data streams they prefer. The two major uses for augmented reality are to provide general information and/or specific instructions. There won't be a clear delineation between the two, but at the extremes the two will not overlap (Fig. 5.29).

As will be pointed out later there are dozens of suppliers offering dedicated augmented reality devices, as well as even more applications that run on general purpose mobile devices such as smartphones, tablets, and notebook PCs. That large population of devices and applications is testament to the diversity of augmented reality and the richness it will bring to millions of users.

5.1.2.1 Informational

A head-up display in which information is displayed on a windshield or at the top corner of a user's field of view to provide digital content and text is a passive augmented reality situation, and used for information only. Some researchers and commentators suggest that is because the information does not overlay digital content on top of real world content, but instead displays them more or less side-by-side, it is not considered augmented reality. The informational type of augmented reality is sometimes called the Terminator view (see Fig. 1: The augmented reality eye of The Terminator). However, informational augmented reality is most likely going to be the biggest use case, and the one used mostly by consumers. The illustrations in Figs. 6.24, 6.52 and 6.60 are prime examples.

5.1.2.2 Instructional

The major differentiation between informational and instructional augmented reality is the user's interaction with the information being presented and the place where the user is. Augmented reality is taking training, operational, and informational content to new levels of user experience. It is an incorporation of computer-generated assets superimposed onto the user's immediate surroundings through specialized hardware and software. Augmented reality has the unique ability to bridge the gap between training and operations, by integrating a highly-detailed 3D simulation and information of the most current equipment and facilities with which technicians, installation and repair personell, inspectors, engineers, and researchers will work.

However, for instructional information to be effective and useful, it has to look realistic. In addition to addressable occlusion and adjustable depth of field (see "What to see, what not to see," Sect. 4.1.1), the virtual objects in a scene have to have correct coloring and lighting to be realistic, and immersive. For example, in (Fig. 5.30) the TV on the wall, the sofa, and rug, do not look realistic in terms of their lighting, even though they are geometrically correct.

Correct lighting considers the position, intensity, and orientation of all light sources in the real-world scene and applies proper augmented reality environmental processing. To obtain realism and immersion, virtual objects must look real and be correctly placed. Dynamic lighting is used to correct for the environment which makes solid objects look solid, materials look physically correct, and move smoothly and interactively. Notice the difference in the feeling of the image in (Fig. 5.31) where correct lighting is used.

To get correct lighting in an augmented reality scene requires intelligent, fast interaction between many different sensors and rendering systems. Computer vision and global illumination algorithms are also needed to dynamically render and overlay realistic augmented reality objects.

Fig. 5.30 Incorrectly lighted virtual objects in an augmented reality view (Qualcomm)

Fig. 5.31 Correctly lighted virtual objects in an augmented reality scene (Qualcomm)

Vector Graphics vs. Raster

One of the question being discussed among augmented reality watchers, engineers, and manufacturers is whether augmented reality and virtual reality are going to cause a resurgence of vector graphics (VG)—since one can store so much visual information in a tiny amount of space compared to 3D or raster graphics. VG will be especially helpful for augmented reality. In virtual reality, it is problematic due to shading issues (think games and videos).

The answer is probably yes, because as a technology develops and evolves every imaginable concept is tested in a Darwinian-like manner, with the best solutions surviving and becoming dominant.

References

1. Baum, L. F. (1901). *The master key: An electrical fairy tale*. Indianapolis: Bowen-Merrill Company.
2. http://www.smithsonianmag.com/history-archaeology/A-Brief-History-of-the-- Teleprompter-175411341.html
3. *Timeline for the history of the University of Westminster*. University of Westminster. Archived from the original on 16 May 2006. Retrieved 28 August 2009.
4. Clarke, R. W. (1994). *British aircraft armament: RAF guns and gunsights from 1914 to the present day*. Yeovil: Patrick Stephens Ltd.
5. *Gunsight Tracking and Guidance and Control Displays*, SP-3300 Flight Research at Ames, 1940–1997. https://history.nasa.gov/SP-3300/ch6.htm
6. Jarrett, D. N. (2005). *Cockpit engineering*. Surrey: Ashgate/Taylor & Francis.
7. CC BY-SA 3.0. https://commons.wikimedia.org/w/index.php?curid=334814
8. *Army-Navy Instrumentation Program (ANIP)*, ES 29101, Douglas Aircraft, https://archive.org/ stream/armynavyinstrumentationprogramanip/army-navy%20instrumentation%20program%20(anip)_djvu.txt
9. Comeau, C. P., & Bryan, J. S. (1961, November 10). Headsight television system provides remote surveillance. *Electronics, 34*, 86–90.
10. *Third Eye for Space Explorers*, page 84 July 1962 Popular Electronics. Also Modern Mechanix August 1962: *Seeing Things' with Electrocular*, and *Second Sight*, Friday, April 13, 1962, Time Magazine
11. http://www8.informatik.umu.se/~jwworth/The%20Ultimate%20Display.pdf
12. http://www.computerhistory.org/revolution/input-output/14/356
13. Krueger, M. (1983). *Artificial reality*. Reading: Addison-Wesley.
14. http://www.businesswire.com/news/home/20141119005448/en/ReinCloud-Invents-Interactive-Immersive-Media-Key-Patent
15. https://en.wikipedia.org/wiki/Wired_glove
16. Caudell, T. P., & Mizell, D.W.. (1992, January 7–10). *Augmented reality: An application of head-up display technology to manual manufacturing processes, research. & technology*. Boeing Computer Services, Seattle, WA, USA, System Sciences, 1992. Proceedings of the Twenty-Fifth Hawaii International Conference on (Volume:ii).
17. Lee, K. (2012, March). Augmented reality in education and training, (PDF). *Techtrends: Linking Research & Practice to Improve Learning* 56 (2). Retrieved 2014 May 15.
18. http://bendelaney.com/write_arch.html
19. Rosenberg L. B (1992). *The use of virtual fixtures as perceptual overlays to enhance operator performance in remote environments* (Technical Report AL-TR-0089), USAF Armstrong Laboratory, Wright-Patterson AFB OH.
20. http://graphics.cs.columbia.edu/projects/karma/karma.html
21. http://www.cs.ucsb.edu/~almeroth/classes/tech-soc/2005-Winter/papers/ar.pdf
22. https://en.wikipedia.org/wiki/Thad_Starner
23. Barrilleaux, J. *Experiences and observations in applying augmented reality to live training*. Retrieved June 9, 2012, Jmbaai.com
24. http://jmbaai.com/vwsim99/vwsim99.html

25. Mann, S., *Wearable, tetherless computer–mediated reality,* February 1996. In Presentation at the American Association of Artificial Intelligence, 1996 Symposium; early draft appears as MIT Media Lab Technical Report 260, December 1994.
26. Feiner, S., MacIntyre, B, Höllerer, T, & Webster, A. *A touring machine: Prototyping 3D mobile augmented reality systems for exploring the urban environment,* Proceedings First IEEE International Symposium on Wearable Computers (ISWC '97), 1997, pp 74–81. Cambridge, MA. http://ieeexplore.ieee.org/xpl/freeabs_all.jsp?arnumber=629922 (PDF) http://graphics.cs.columbia.edu/publications/iswc97.pdf
27. IWaugmented reality'99: Proceedings 2nd International Workshop on Augmented Reality, San Francisco, CA, USA, October 20–21 1999. IEEE CS Press. ISBN 0-7695-0359-4.
28. ISaugmented reality'00: Proceedings International Symposium Augmented Reality, Munich, Germany, October 5–6 2000. IEEE CS Press. ISBN 0-7695-0846-4.
29. Azuma, R. (1997, August). A survey of augmented reality. *Presence: Teleoperators and Virtual Environments, 6*(4), 355–385.
30. Raskar, R., Welch, G., Fuchs, H. First international workshop on augmented reality, San Francisco, November 1, 1998.
31. http://www.cnet.com/pictures/google-glass-ancestors-45-years-of-digital-eyewear-photos/2/
32. ISWC'00: Proceedings 4th International Symposium on Wearable Computers, Atlanta, GA, USA, Oct 16–17 2000. IEEE CS Press. ISBN 0-7695-0795-6.
33. Video See-Through augmented reality on Consumer Cell-Phones, ISMaugmented reality '04 Proceedings of the 3rd IEEE/ACM International Symposium on Mixed and Augmented Reality, Pages 252–253, https://www.computer.org/csdl/proceedings/ismar/2004/2191/00/21910252.pdf
34. https://saqoo.sh/a/labs/FLARToolKit/Introduction-to-FLARToolKit.pdf
35. https://itunes.apple.com/in/app/audi-ekurzinfo/id436341817?mt=8
36. https://gamesalfresco.com/
37. https://www.google.com/trends/
38. https://en.wikipedia.org/wiki/Hype_cycle

Key Applications

6

Abstract

The possibilities of augmented reality run the gamut from basic informational purposes to enterprise needs, fulfilling training and onsite job assistance. With modern computer-aided design (CAD) programs, it is possible to generate elaborate 3D representations of data that can lead us to spectacular insights of very complex relationships and to extend the value of the original design out to service and maintenance, facilities management, operations, etc.

Augmented reality will completely alter the education sector from training to sports to remedial education.

One of the first applications for augmented reality was how to repair a copying machine, and automotive repair. Augmented reality is also used as a tool for design review and to evaluate present models while design is still in the development stage. Virtual models that replace real ones are being used to inform customers and public about new products.

The medical field is so broad that there are dozens of applications, enough for a book of its own. From enabling health care workers in a hospital or doctor's office to be mobile and still be able to access health records and/or enter data into forms, to providing telesense capabilities so a remotely located field medic can be guided by a physician from a hospital across the world.

The military has played an important role in the creation and development of wearable augmented reality, starting back in 1963 with Bell helicopter which inspired Ivan Sutherland

Augmented Reality is not a single thing, say like a PC or a smartphone. Rather it is collection of hardware and software capabilities with an almost endless list of applications. This is the good news in terms of the market opportunity and growth, and the bad news if you want to chronicle and analyze the technology and market.

© Springer International Publishing AG 2017
J. Peddie, *Augmented Reality*, DOI 10.1007/978-3-319-54502-8_6

It cannot be said too often that the needs and uses of commercial and enterprise augmented reality users are dramatically different from consumers. Whereas consumers are mostly concerned with appearance and price, commercial and enterprise users are more concerned with functionality and return on investment.

6.1   Key Applications

The possibilities of augmented reality run the gamut from basic informational purposes (such as telling a user which constellation they're looking at) to enterprise needs, fulfilling training and onsite job assistance. What does the future hold for this sector of wearables? What are its top use cases? And what does this panel of experts predict augmented reality to be years from now?

Augmented reality systems have the most demanding requirements of any kind of three-dimensional synthetic graphic systems. Augmented reality systems must register computer graphics (such as annotations, diagrams and models) directly with objects in the real-world. Most of the augmented reality applications require the graphics to be precisely aligned and geometrically fitted with the environment. For example, if the augmented reality system shows an outline, or wire frame diagram of a building, the computer-generated diagram may have to be distorted to compensate for the angle of the viewing and display device. Therefore, an accurate tracking system and a detailed model of the environment are required. Constructing those models can be an extremely challenging task as even a small error in the model can lead to significant errors in the display of the overlay, undermining the effectiveness of an augmented reality system. Also, models of urban structures contain a very large number of different objects (buildings, doors and windows just to name a few). Laser scanning of buildings and constructing a model of it have proven to be very helpful in building databases of urban objects, as well as objects in machines, buildings and homes, automobiles, and other devices.

In this section, we will look at some of the more popular applications, but by no means all of the possible augmented reality applications; that list would be almost endless as new ideas are cropping up every day. The purpose of this section is to give the reader an overview and expand thinking about all of the myriad possibilities augmented reality offers.

I have tried to segment the applications into three main segments in terms of potential buyers of augmented reality systems:

- Scientific, Engineering, and Government
- Commercial and Enterprise
- Consumer

However, some applications, such as real estate, cut across segments (such as commercial and consumer), and medicine cuts across all three segments.

6.1.1 Scientific, Industrial and Government

Augmented reality will eventually revolutionize industries and enterprises, and Increased productivity, efficiency, and safety in several industries:

- Healthcare—more efficient patient care, diagnosis and treatment assistance, surgical training and visualization will be aided and improved.
- Industrial & manufacturing—guided training and remote support, plus improved safety, and real-time factory diagnostics.
- Education—immersive, self-guided, interactive visual learning, in any subject, from history and physics to vocational.
- Military—instructional training, and in-the-field assistance.
- Engineering—3D visualization and CAD—colleague collaboration and communication.
- Emergency response—police, fire, security response, as well as potential improvements in safety, response time, and saving lives.

It's not just productivity in terms of getting more work done, but it's also higher quality work. The thing that engineers and technicians and repairman and doctors will do when being aided in real-time with augmented reality glasses, will be done better. When a technician knows that he or she must turn three bolts on a cover to secure an electrical panel, for example, he or she will know that the torque on that screw should be 35 foot pounds, and won't over-torque it or under-torque it. The quality of the work that is produced will be faster and better.

The technologies for augmented reality are steadily improving and becoming more cost effective. Industries such as aerospace, automotive, marine, and commercial vehicles are learning to use augmented reality for design, manufacturing and production, operations, and service and repair, as well as training. Augmented reality is proving to be a tool that can be used throughout a product's life cycle.

6.1.1.1 Architecture, Engineering, and Construction

With modern computer-aided design (CAD) programs, it is possible to generate elaborate 3D representations of data that can lead us to spectacular insights of very complex relationships.

Industrial designers, mechanical engineers, architects, interior decorators, etc. who use CAD or similar 3D design programs can employ augmented reality systems to great advantage. Field and on-the-job inspection use augmented reality to compare results to design.

In the early 1990s augmented reality was being used to allow a user to see the otherwise hidden structural systems of a building as a graphical representation of a building's structural systems on the user's view of a room within the building [1]. This overlaid virtual world showed the outlines of the concrete joists, beams, and columns surrounding the room, as well as the reinforcing steel inside them (Fig. 6.1).

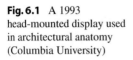

Fig. 6.1 A 1993
head-mounted display used
in architectural anatomy
(Columbia University)

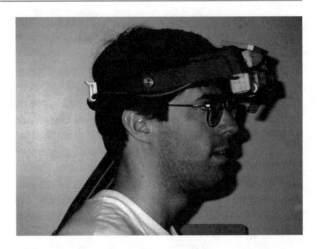

The augmented reality system used a Reflection Technology Private Eye display and Logitech ultrasonic tracker. Its graphics were rendered at 720 × 280 resolution and, in the application described above included 3D vectors without hidden-line removal. Since then CAD suppliers such as Autodesk, Bentley Systems, PTC, Siemens, and others have provided support for augmented reality to be used with their programs.

Speaking on the topic of augmented reality in construction, Stéphane Côté of Bentley Systems says, "One day, we may see all construction workers equipped with high end smart phones integrated into their clothes, with wireless display on their digital contact lenses, following detailed visual and verbal instructions from a construction app that is carefully coordinating the work of all the workers on the site."

Contrary to what one might think, the process of interpreting a 3D structure on a 3D piece of paper is neither simple, nor immediate. And, what one perceives, another may interpret differently. 3D in construction is powerful, effective, and valuable.

While Côté speaks of the issue of putting the power of 3D in the hands of construction workers, augmented reality in the hands of urban planners, designers and structural engineers is similarly powerful. We can see this kind of simulation and modelling capability in products like computational design software that allow for rapid model development, perhaps hundreds of iterations, before deciding upon the optimal structures.

Augmented reality enables large, complex 3D CAD data to be transferred to a tablet device and then used for mobile visualization and comparison to real world conditions. This enables real time, actionable manufacturing insight for in-process inspection, assembly, guidance, and positioning.

One company, MWF-Technology, based in Frankfurt, Germany (and acquired by FARO Technologies in 2016) specialized in mobile augmented reality solutions, particularly technology allowing for mobile visualization and real-world comparison of 3D CAD data.

Additional discussion on these companies' involvement in augmented reality can be found in the section on "Manufacturing," Sect. 6.1.1.5.

Design

There are multiple methods of using augmented reality in design, with both see-through (optical) and video mixed reality devices.

Microsoft HoloLens is a see-through optical headset (even though they market it as mixed reality), and Cannon's MREAL system is a mixed reality system using a camera.

Cannon, a company well known for their cameras, developed its augmented/mixed reality head set in 2012 and introduced it into the market in 2013. The device is aimed at the design and engineering markets, but the company says it can also be used by first responders (Fig. 6.2).

HM-A1 (MERAL) and the software platform MP-100 generates video of one's surroundings using a pair of cameras positioned in front of the wearer's eyes, which is combined with computer-generated graphics. The result is displayed on a pair of small monitors with 1920 × 1200 (WUXGA) resolution to create three-dimensional images. Amongst the potential target audiences for the product are automotive designers, manufacturers, university researchers and museum exhibit curators.

Fig. 6.2 Cannon's HM-A1 MERAL headset with HD cameras (Cannon)

Canon's also planning to open up its SDK to developers, so applications will likely only increase.

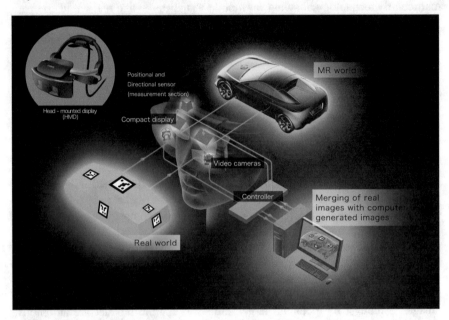

The Canon MREAL System for Mixed Reality (Cannon)

The Canon MREAL System for Mixed Reality—which consists of a head-mounted display (HMD) HM-A1 and the MR Platform Software MP-100, sells for $125,000, and works with design applications including Siemens CAD/CAM/CAE, PLM Software's NX software, and the 3D visualization software RTT DeltaGen.

6.1.1.2 Aviation and Aerospace

Aviation has led the way in the development and application of head-mounted display technology going back to the Bell Helicopter work that motivated Ivan Sutherland in 1965. In the early 1990s, the potential of head-mounted displays for mounted and dismounted Warfighters was fully recognized. That led to several development programs that focused on the differing requirements for head-mounted displays intended for ground applications. However, the fundamental characteristics of the ground-based head-mounted displays are the result of decades of lessons learned from aviation-based head-mounted displays development programs.

The most sophisticated airborne head-mounted display deployed was the design for the F35. Iowa-based avionics company Rockwell Collins, in collaboration with Israel's Elbit Systems Ltd, which developed one of the most expensive and advanced pilot helmets, the F-35 Gen III Helmet Mounted Display System (HMDS). This head-mounted display is priced at $400,000, and is designed for pilots flying the Lockheed Martin F-35 Lightning II or other multi-role combat aircraft. The helmet was delivered in July 2014 (Fig. 6.3).

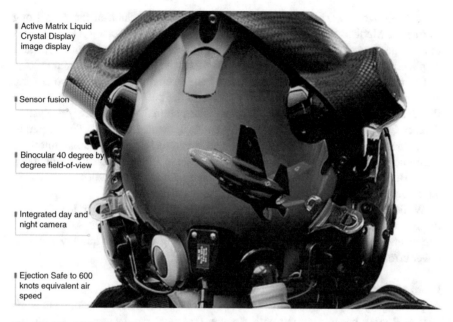

| Active Matrix Liquid
Crystal Display
image display

| Sensor fusion

| Binocular 40 degree by
degree field-of-view

| Integrated day and
night camera

| Ejection Safe to 600
knots equivalent air
speed

Fig. 6.3   The F35 helmet (Source: Rockwell Collins)

The HMDS provides the pilot video with imagery in day or night conditions combined with precision symbology to give the pilot enhanced situation awareness and tactical capability. The F-35 JSF was the first tactical fighter jet aircraft to fly without a dedicated head-up display, and used the HMDS to provide that functionality. The display in the helmet is two 0.7-inch diagonal SXGA resolution (1280 × 1024) AMLCDs. The HMDS provides a field-of-view (FoV) of 40-degree (H) and 30-degree (V).

Augmented Reality in the Aerospace Industry

Christine Perey is a widely-recognized consultant, researcher and industry analyst focusing on enabling technologies for and use of Augmented Reality since 2006. She is the founder and, from 2013 to 2016, the first Executive Director of the AR for Enterprise Alliance (AREA), the only global member-based organization focusing on accelerating adoption of Augmented Reality in enterprise, the founder and chair of the Augmented Reality Community, a global grassroots organization seeking to accelerate development of open and interoperable Augmented Reality content and experiences, and the founding Director of PEREY Research & Consulting, a boutique consulting firm.

Ms. Perey has offered the following observation on the use of augmented reality's uses in the aerospace industry. One of many augmented reality areas she follows.

Christine Perey

There are many use cases for Augmented Reality in the aerospace industry and the leaders in this industry have a long history with the technology.

In 1969, while working in the Human Engineering Division of the Armstrong Aerospace Medical Research Laboratory (USAF), Wright-Patterson AFB, Thomas Furness presented a paper entitled "Helmet-Mounted Displays and their Aerospace Applications" to attendees of the National Aerospace Electronics Conference.

Over 20 years later the paper was one of eight references cited by two Boeing engineers, Thomas Caudell and David Mizell. In their 1992 paper published in the Proceedings of the Twenty-Fifth Hawaii International Conference on System Sciences, Caudell and Mizell coined the term "Augmented Reality." The degree to which the team drew from the work of Furness, who had started the Human Interface Technology Lab (HIT) at University of Washington in 1989, is unclear but the focus of the Boeing team was on reducing errors when building wire harnesses for use in aircraft and other manual manufacturing tasks in aerospace.

While the technology was not sufficiently mature to leave the lab or to deliver on its potential at the time, they suggested that with an augmented reality-assisted system an engineer would in the future be able to perform tasks more quickly and with fewer errors.

Proof of Concepts

Approximately 15 years later, in 2008, Paul Davies, a research & development engineer at Boeing began working with Boeing Technical Fellow, Anthony Majoros. Together, Davies and Majoros picked up where the Caudell and Mizell paper left off. They used commercially-available technologies such as Total Immersion's D'Fusion platform to show how technicians building satellites could perform complex tasks with Augmented Reality running on tablets.

Airbus has also been experimenting with Augmented Reality for over a decade. In a paper published in the ISMaugmented reality 2006 proceedings, Dominik Willers explains how Augmented Reality was being studied for assembly and service tasks but judged too immature for introduction into production environments [2]. The paper, authored in collaboration with the Technical University of Munich, focused on the need for advances in tracking.

Since those proof of concept projects, augmented reality technology has advanced to the point that it is being explored for an increasing number of use cases in the aerospace industry. In parallel with the expansion of use cases, the pace of applied research into augmented reality-enabling technology components has not abated.

Augmented Reality in Aerospace in 2017

While today augmented reality may not be found in many aerospace production environments, the promise of the technology to increase efficiency is widely acknowledged.

The European Space Agency sees a variety of use cases on Earth and in space. Inspection and quality assurance, for example, could benefit from the use of augmented reality-assisted systems.

Although most barriers to adoption can be considered as technological in nature, there are also significant obstacles stemming from human factors and business considerations.

Augmented Reality in Astronaut Training

Augmented reality, where 3D and 2D images are overlaid on a user's natural field of view like a head-up display, is being developed for use in manned space applications. NASA, through its augmented reality-eProc program, and the European Space Agency, through MARSOP, have demonstrated the potential of augmented reality to improve hands-on training and just-in-time training (JITT).

This research demonstrates the feasibility and tests the performance of hands-free, remote or proximity, and instantaneous collaboration or mentoring between individuals in the augmented reality environment to augment audio communication for training, task completion, and other space applications. Real-time augmented reality collaboration provides flexible spontaneous communication capabilities not found in previous systems. Collaboration is facilitated by drawing on, or annotating, preexisting augmented reality graphics using tablets or gesture detection which can also be viewed by other individuals in real time. Hands-free operation is accomplished by utilizing radar-based gesture recognition transceivers which are environment-robust and embeddable in rigid materials. They precisely measure motion in 3D, allowing for gestures adapted to limited ranges of motion. Embedded gesture sensors and augmented reality headsets enable potential expansion of use to extravehicular activity (EVA) or other space suit applications. The potential for augmented reality control in EVA applications opens future development in augmented reality communication with autonomous systems.

Christine Perey is the executive director of the Augmented Reality for Enterprise Alliance (AREA), and the founder and principle analyst of PEREY Research & Consulting. She provides highly strategic research, business- and market-building related services with an emphasis on building robust strategies leading to the successful introduction and widespread adoption of mobile Augmented Reality products and services.

PEREY Research & Consulting is a leader in the mobile Augmented Reality industry, advising vendors, technology and application providers, research institutes and network operators on the design, launch and operation of mobile Augmented Reality- and Internet of Things- based technologies, products and services. The firm is also a charter member of the AREA.

6.1.1.3 Education

Augmented reality will completely alter the education sector from training to sports to remedial education.

Augmented reality applications can complement a standard curriculum. By imposing a graphic, video or text, and audio into a student's text book in real time. Textbooks, flashcards and other educational reading material are all vehicles for additional and supplemental information, and a way to keep textbooks current and up to date. Early examples used pages with markers that, when scanned by an augmented reality device, produced supplementary information to the student rendered in a multimedia format [3].

In higher education, there are applications that can be used to help students understand physics, math, geometry, electrical, chemical, or mechanical engineering concepts. These are active learning processes where students learn to learn with technology. In chemistry for example, augmented reality can help students visualize the spatial structure of a molecule and interact with a virtual model of it that appears in the virtual reality viewing device, which could be a smartphone or tablet. Augmented reality has also been used in physiology to visualize different systems of the human body in 3D.

Primary school children can learn through experiences, and visuals designed to help them learn. Children will be able to better understand the solar system when using augmented reality devices and being able to see it in 3D. For teaching anatomy, teachers could visualize bones and organs using augmented reality to display them on the body of a person [4]. Languages can be taught using translation applications and supplemental information [5].

Augmented reality applications are emerging in the classroom every semester. The mix of real life and virtual reality displayed by the apps using the mobile device's camera allows information to be manipulated and seen as never before.

Welding

One of the first augmented reality training systems to teach welding was developed by Soldamatic in 2013 in Huelva, Spain. Students work in a real welding environment, with all the real elements used in workshops (welding torches, welding helmet, work pieces, etc.) and augmented reality technology is used to make all these elements interact, and to draw computer generated graphics welding effects, offering realistic welding training experiences (Fig. 6.4).

Soldamatic is a digital tool to teach welding techniques in the safety of a virtual world.

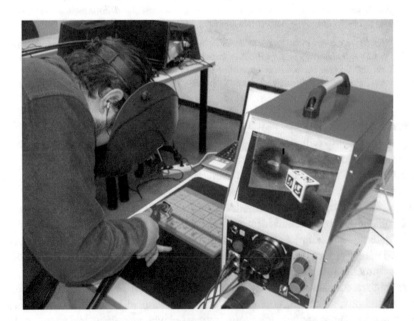

Fig. 6.4 Soldamatic augmented welding training

Medical Training

Augmented reality has been applied across disciplines in higher education, including; environmental sciences, ecosystems, language, chemistry, geography, history, and medicine. Some of the uses of augmented reality in medical applications were done in ultrasound imaging in 1992 [6]. In medical training and simulation, the learning potential of augmented reality is significantly amplified by the capability of the system to present 3D medical models in real-time at remote locations.

Clinical care is also interested in augmented reality because it provides doctors with an internal view of the patient, without the need for invasive procedures. Since students and medical professionals need more situational experiences in clinical care, especially for the sake of patient safety, there is a clear need for additional use of augmented reality in healthcare education. The wide interest in studying augmented reality over recent years has highlighted the following beliefs [7]:

- Augmented reality provides rich contextual learning for medical students to aid in achieving core competencies, such as decision making, effective teamwork and creative adaptation of global resources towards addressing local priorities.
- Augmented reality provides opportunities for more authentic learning and appeals to multiple learning styles, providing students a more personalized and explorative learning experience.
- The patients' safety is safeguarded if mistakes are made during skills training with augmented reality.

Some practitioners still think augmented reality is in the early stages of application within healthcare education but acknowledge it has enormous potential for promoting learning in healthcare (Fig. 6.5).

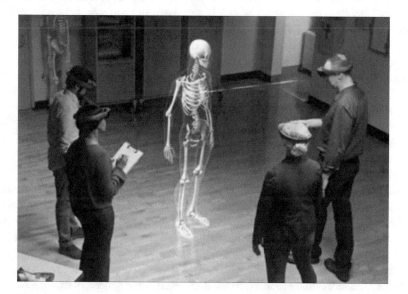

Fig. 6.5 Students at Case Western Reserve University learn about human anatomy using Microsoft HoloLens (Source: Case Western Reserve University)

Augmented reality, while not a new technology, is becoming well-known and gaining momentum in medical education, helped in no small part by products such as Google Glass and Microsoft's HoloLens. Not only can augmented reality aid in student education, but it can also impact patient care through its ability to enhance medical training. Medical libraries can partake in this new endeavor by being aware of applications in augmented reality that can benefit students and educators.

Medical training can be interactive or passive. Interactive training involves augmented reality. Passive (viewing) does not. (see, "Video Recording Not Augmented Reality," section "Video recording not augmented reality".)

6.1.1.4 Inspection and Maintenance

One of the first applications for augmented reality was how to repair a copying machine. (See. Fig. 5.15, Sect. 5.1), and automotive repair. Augmented reality employing real time computer graphics, overlaid on and registered with the actual equipment being maintained, can significantly increase the productivity of maintenance personnel, both during training and in the field [8].

Augmented reality can support maintenance tasks by acting as an "x-ray" like vision, or providing information from sensors directly to the user.

Technical Documentation with Augmented Reality

Technical documentation is being visualized and made mobile by augmented reality. Whether in training, operations, troubleshooting or maintenance (and in particular when it comes to complicated machinery or equipment), when employees need instructions they need them to be clear and accessible right away. Undoubtedly, when technicians have to stop and look for printed or digital documents, they lose valuable time searching for the right information. Augmented reality opens up a totally new dimension: with only a few clicks, the 3D instructions are projected directly "onto" the machinery. The data is also the most up to date, unlike old printed manuals and loose field alerts (Fig. 6.6).

Kothes! Technische Kommunikation GmbH, a consulting and service provider of technical documentation and CE marking based in Kempen Germany, has integrated augmented reality into the realms of technical documentation. The SIG company's Combibloc carton packaging machine required the existing manual to be virtually expanded to provide an added tangible benefit for the user. The specific task was to view the content of the technical documentation directly on the machine using color coded, clearly arranged and linked interactive content. Furthermore, the user can access more details or receive step-by-step augmented reality instructions for machine operation if necessary.

Kothes! created a prototype for an intuitively mobile and easy to navigate user manual for operation, repair and maintenance. The user points his or her tablet at the machine to scan the unique barcode so that the tablet can identify the machine. The virtual guide that appears is context sensitive and colorfully structured to scale for optimal use.

The closer the user is to the machine, the viewing screen displays more relevant details of the individual modules; in addition, each angle generates the next level of the component (Fig. 6.7).

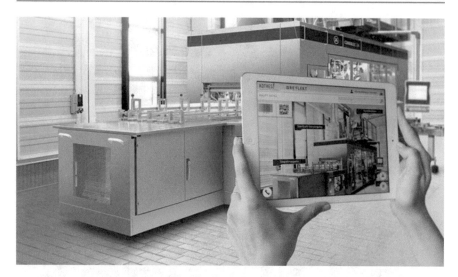

Fig. 6.6 Augmented Reality handbook visualized onto the machine (with permission of Kothes/ SIG)

Fig. 6.7 Step-by-step instructions for replacing a vapor filter (Source: Kothes/SIG)

The clarity is increased enormously as well as the definition for each module of information that is displayed in full screen. In the case of the Re'flekt and Kothes! jointly developed application, the user can select the option of choice to receive detailed information and guidance in a visual form—directly inside the working environment. München Germany based Re'Flkt develops augmented reality applications for automotive, industry and real estate.

Fig. 6.8 Augmented reality guide to find parts and check items in a car (Source: AR-media)

Maintenance and Repair

Car engines and equipment can be a totally unknown universe for many. Even if one is an experienced amateur (or professional) mechanic, he or she might not know where in the engine the most relevant parts are exactly located. Today users can install augmented reality apps on their smartphones and tablets that will turn the user into a mechanic. Applications like I-Mechanic from Inglobe Technologies augmented reality-media, based on computer vision 3D tracking software, enables the user to contextually access the instructions required to maintain their car (Fig. 6.8).

One of the major breakthroughs for these types of applications was the development of markerless image processing, using the actual objects for identification and registration. That in turn required the application of simultaneous localization and mapping (SLAM) vison processing technology.

Automotive, Trucks, and Heavy Equipment

Head-up displays in automobiles, buses, and motorcycle helmets will be commonplace, and make us uncomfortable when not available. However, pedantically speaking, augmented reality is expected to include tracking between the superimposed information, data, and images and some portion of the real world, and early automotive head-up displays didn't do that, providing only speed and fuel level information. A modern head-up display in an automobile that includes directional information and assistance that does change its data due to its location, and could even give pertinent information about near-by points of interest such as a coffee shop or gas station.

Head-up display enabled vehicles have had somewhat mixed reactions. While many drivers appreciated the ability to keep their eyes on the road (and the futuristic thrill it gives to driving), others worried about the device blocking their view of what's ahead. However, it has proven itself and is available on many midsize and above cars today. head-up displays will help keep drivers safe in the future as more features are enabled and it becomes available in an increasing number of vehicles.

Head-up displays in automobiles are a consumer product, and discussed further in "Navigation and Control," Sect. 6.1.3.6.

6.1.1.5 Manufacturing

In the second half of 2015, the manufacturing industry changed. Apple bought Metaio, which had the second largest market share of augmented reality after Vuforia. Then Google invested in Magic Leap, Microsoft announced HoloLens, and the Needham MA-based computer-aided design and product development software company, Parametric Technology Corporation (PTC), bought Vuforia from Qualcomm. These moves by the technology superpowers ignited conversations around augmented reality and, inevitably, what it could be used for outside of the consumer space.

> *"Like the introduction of the steam engine in the 1800s, augmented reality is going to change everything in manufacturing and construction." Dexter Lilley EVP and COO of Index augmented reality Solutions*

Augmented reality is already, and will play a larger role in day-to-day operations and training in the manufacturing sector. Companies have reported training times cut in half, and retention extended due to augmented reality. Day-to-day activities such as inspection, logistics, building, operations and maintenance all have use cases that will enable workers and technicians to do more, reduce the times some steps take and totally eliminate other steps (Fig. 6.9).

Clearly, augmented reality will be ubiquitous in industrial environments. There will be an on-going evolutionary trend of usage which will rapidly become revolutionary as companies begin to understand the tremendous impact that augmented reality technology can have on their top and bottom lines.

Reduced Errors in Manufacturing

Boeing instated one of the first industrial applications using augmented reality in 1989 to reduce errors when building wire harnesses for use in aircraft. As mentioned earlier, the term 'Augmented Reality' is attributed to Thomas P. Caudell, and David Mizella of Boeing [9].

At the Arise'15 conference, at the University of Sheffield in the UK, Paul Davies of Boeing gave a presentation [10] about a wing assembly study Boeing did in collaboration with Iowa State University [11]. Davis showed the results when complex tasks are performed using conventional 2D work instructions versus Augmented Reality. The differences in performance were dramatic.

Fig. 6.9 Construction workers building a factory without blueprints or drawings by using augmented reality (Source: Index augmented reality Solutions)

Three teams were tasked with assembling parts of a wing, which had over 50 steps and used 30 different parts. Each group performed the task using one of three different methods of instruction:

A. A desktop PC with its monitor displaying the instruction in a PDF file.
B. A tablet displaying the instruction from a PDF file.
C. A tablet displaying Augmented Reality software showing the work instructions as guided steps with graphical overlays. A four-camera infrared tracking system provided high-precision motion tracking for accurate alignment of the augmented reality models with the real world.

Davies and the Iowa State people had each team assemble the wing twice. The observers measured trainees with little or no experience to perform an operation the first time (known as, "first time quality").

The A-team had to go from the PC to the assembly area (called a "cell"), and then back for the next instruction. The B-team, and C-team took their tablet with them, and could walk around the assembly as needed.

The team's movements and activities were recorded using webcams positioned around the work cell.

The observers counted and categorized the errors each team made, and discovered team-B and C made significantly fewer errors than team-A with the stationary desktop PC.

Team-A made an average of eight errors the first time, and reduced that to four the second time, showing the effects of experience and familiarity with the issues. Team-B made only one error on average and did not improve on the second time. Team-C, using guided augmented reality instructions made less than one error the first time, and none the second time.

Fig. 6.10 Visualizing and planning where new pumps and equipment will go in an aircraft carrier (Source: Huntington Ingalls)

The study showed, and quantified, how complex tasks performed for the first time can benefit from augmented reality work instructions. If the task is done with fewer errors and faster, the impact on productivity is highly significant.

6.1.1.6 Marine Vehicles (Submarines to Pleasure Craft to Aircraft Carriers)

Augmented reality is used as a tool for design review by some of the leading shipyards around the world. Using augmented reality, participants of various disciplines and stakeholders have an opportunity to test and evaluate present models while design is still in the development stage. Virtual models that replace real ones are being used to inform customers and the public about new products, e.g., ships and offshore installations.

In 2011, Newport News Shipbuilding began a research and development project to learn how to apply Augmented Reality to shipbuilding. They called the project "Drawingless Deckplate." After a year, it was apparent that the potential cost savings in shipbuilding were big enough to start forming a dedicated team. By 2017, the augmented reality team had over 30 projects either completed, in process, or in backlog.

The company that builds the U.S. Navy's aircraft carriers is using augmented reality technology to bring shipbuilding into the twenty-first century (Fig. 6.10).

Huntington Ingalls uses augmented-reality tablets to allow shipbuilders to "see through" a ship's hardware and overlay designs and other information onto a real space as technicians move around. It is part of a larger plan to make shipbuilding paperless. Huntington Ingalls built the third ship in the CVN class, CVN 80—the Enterprise, as the first ship built without drawings.

Fig. 6.11 Oxsight's Smart Specs for people with limited vision (Source: Oxsight)

6.1.1.7 Medicine

The medical field is so broad there are dozens of applications, enough for a book of its own. Listed here are a couple of the more popular or interesting. From enabling health care workers in a hospital or doctor's office to be mobile and still be able to access health records and/or enter data into forms, to providing telesense capabilities so a remotely located field medic can be guided by a physician from a hospital across the world.

Help the Visually Impaired with Augmented Reality Smart Glasses

Augmented reality smart-glasses developed by researchers at Oxford University can help people with visual impairments improve their vision by providing depth-based feedback, allowing users to see better (Fig. 6.11).

Smart Specs are designed to enhance the images of everyday objects such as a friend's face, or items on a table. Where they are really important is in detecting large obstacles in the dark, such as walls, tables, doorways, sign posts (Fig. 6.12).

Oxsight's Smart Specs employ a 3D camera and a smartphone program to enhance the visibility of nearby objects. The software hides the background and highlights edges and features to make many objects easier to see. Many of the features work in darkness and at any time, the video can be paused or zoomed to provide greater detail.

The augmented reality spectacles are designed to help people with serious visual impairments see. Smart Specs was developed by Neuroscience Researcher Dr. Stephen Hicks (1960–) and his research team at Oxford, the glasses use cameras to augment vision. Hicks says, "When you go blind, you generally have some sight remaining, and using a combination of cameras and a see-through display, we're able to enhance nearby objects to make them easier to see for obstacle avoidance and facial recognition."

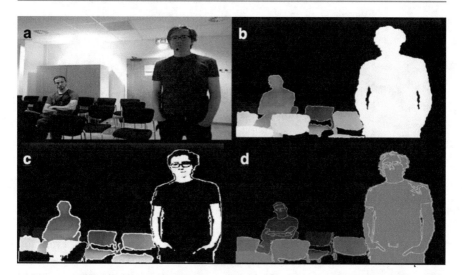

Fig. 6.12 Smart Specs can show a natural color image, or a simplified high contrast display depending on the needs of the user (Source: Oxsight)

Hicks says the glasses are different from other products—depth perception a unique facet of the smart-glasses technology. Collaborated with a British blind charity and the UK government, early prototypes have shown promise—Google helping fund the research after it won an award. After testing the glasses outside a laboratory setting, the final challenge before production will be to make them smaller.

In another example, Intel demonstrated its RealSense technology being used to help visually impaired people understand their surroundings. Rajiv Mongia, Intel's director of the RealSense sInteraction Design Group. His team created a prototype that combines RealSense 3D camera technology with vibrating sensors integrated alerted visually impaired people to "sense" when a person was nearby. Intel has announced that the source code and design tools will be made available to allow developers to continue this work [12].

Help Immobile People Communicate Using Their Eyes

The EyeSpeak augmented reality headset from LusoVu is a communication system that uses one's eyes, and is especially designed for people with extreme mobility and communication limitations caused by different types of illness or injury. The EyeSpeak consists of a pair of glasses in which the lenses have displayed a screen with a virtual keyboard. It has a micro camera that detects the position and the movement of the eyes and, in this way, identifies the key to which the user is looking at (Fig. 6.13).

Ivo Vieira, CEO of LusoVu was looking for a way to help his father, who had been diagnosed with Amyotrophic Lateral Sclerosis, and began to lose mobility in one arm. Viera commented that LusoVu had already worked in augmented reality glasses for astronauts, "I realized that I could design a computer screen in their

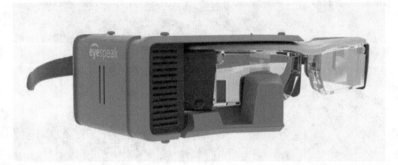

Fig. 6.13 EyeSpeak as adapted its eye racking sensor to augmented reality glasses (Source: LusoVu)

lenses and put a micro camera to do the tracking of eye movements. From this moment, the mission of LusoVu in designing the EyeSpeak was drawn."

The EyeSpeak consists of a pair of glasses in which the lenses display a screen with a virtual keyboard. It has a micro camera that detects the position and the movement of the eyes and, in this way, identifies the key the user is looking at.

The user selects the keys with the movement of the eyes, being able to write words and phrases. Then, using the built-in speaker system, the user translates what was written into sound by selecting the key "speak" after typing a word or phrase.

The system is somewhat similar to the eye-tracking and blinking system Stephen Hawkins uses to communicate.

Help Blind People See with Their Ears and Fingers

Google has developed an application that translates what a camera (such as one in a smartphone) "sees" into descriptions for blind people. Voice for Android is a free downloadable application Google introduced in 2016.

The vOICe for Android application adds a sonic augmented reality overlay to the live camera view in real-time, thereby giving even totally blind people live and detailed information about their visual environment that they would otherwise not perceive. It may also serve as an interactive mobile learning app for teaching visual concepts to blind children. The vOICe for Android is a universal translator for mapping images to sounds. The application can run on a smartphone, tablet, or suitably equipped pair of smart-glasses.

Once the application is started, it continuously takes snapshots. Each snapshot is translated into sounds via a polyphonic left-to-right scan through the snapshot while associating height with pitch and brightness with loudness. For example, a bright rising line on a dark background sounds as a rising pitch sweep, and a small bright spot sounds as a short beep. The visual encoded have a visual resolution of up to 176×64 pixels (which is greater than an implant with 10,000 electrodes).

Talking compass speaks the current heading. By default, it only speaks heading changes, but options for continuous heading feedback and for disabling the talking compass are available. Together with the camera-based soundscapes the talking compass may help to walk in a straight line, and of course the compass continues to work in the dark where the camera fails to give useful feedback.

Talking locator announces nearby street names and intersections as determined from GPS or local cell towers. It can upon request tell you the current speed and altitude, and the user can change verbosity.

Talking face detector announces the number of human faces detected by the camera. It can detect and announce up to dozens of faces in a single view. On the other hand, if only one face is detected then it will additionally say whether the face is located near the top, bottom, left, right, or center of the view, as well as announce when the face is within close-up range. It can also be set up to notify about skin color. The face detector is not a face recognition system, so there are no privacy concerns. Moreover, the talking face detector can be turned off.

Haptic feedback is offered that allows the user to feel the live camera view using the touch screen. The perceptual effect is quite crude and limited by the simplicity of the phone's vibrator.

Help Patients with Chronic Intractable Phantom Limb Pain

Dr. Max Ortiz Catalan at Chalmers University of Technology has developed a method of treating phantom limb pain using machine learning and augmented reality.

Many people who have lost an arm or leg often experience a phenomenon known as phantom limb pain It is, to the person, as if the missing limb was still there and can become a serious chronic condition reducing the person's quality of life. It is unknown what causes phantom limb pain and other phantom sensations (Fig. 6.14).

Dr. Ortiz Catalan's treatment consists of using muscle signals that would have gone to the amputated limb to control augmented and virtual environments. Electric signals in the muscles are picked up by electrodes on the skin. Artificial intelligence algorithms translate the signals into movements of a virtual arm in real-time. The patients see themselves on a screen with the virtual arm in the place of the missing arm, and they can control it as they would control their biological arm. Ortiz Catalan calls the new method phantom motor execution [13].

Surgical Navigation for Image-Guided Spine, Cranial and Trauma Surgery

Using a combination of 3D X-ray imaging and optical imaging is providing surgeons with an augmented-reality view of the inside and outside of a patient during surgical procedures.

Spine surgery was traditionally an 'open surgery' procedure, accessing the affected area via a large incision so that surgeons could physically see and touch the patient's spine in order to position implants such as pedicle screws. In recent years, however, there has been a definite shift to the use of minimally-invasive techniques, performed by manipulating surgical tools through small incisions in the patient's

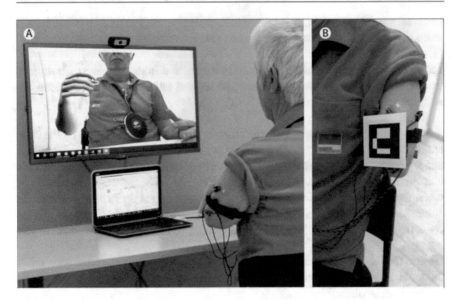

Fig. 6.14 A webcam provides live video of the patient displayed on a computer screen. A virtual limb is added to the video feed in the location indicated by a fiducial marker. (B) Surface electrodes over the stump record synergistic muscle activation during motor volition of the phantom limb (phantom motor execution). Myoelectric pattern recognition is used to decode motor volition and voluntarily control the virtual limb (Source: Lancet)

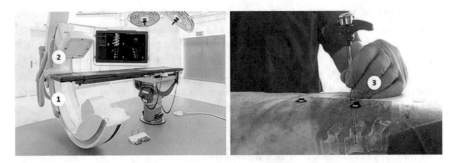

Fig. 6.15 Low-dose X-ray system (*1*) optical cameras on flat panel X-ray detector (*2*) image the surface of the patient. It then combines the external view captured by the cameras and the internal 3D view of the patient acquired by the X-ray system to construct a 3D augmented-reality view of the patient's external and internal anatomy (*3*) providing a real-time 3D view of the patient's spine in relation to the incision sites (Source: Philips)

skin in order to minimize blood loss and soft tissue damage, and consequently reduce postoperative pain.

Due to inherently reduced visibility of the spine during these procedures, surgeons have to rely on real-time imaging and navigation solutions to guide their surgical tools and implants. The same is true for minimally-invasive cranial surgery and surgery on complex trauma fractures (Fig. 6.15).

Philips developed an augmented-reality surgical navigation system to be used with its low-dose X-ray system. The system uses high-resolution optical cameras mounted on the flat panel X-ray detector to image the surface of the patient. It then combines the external view captured by the cameras and the internal 3D view of the patient acquired by the X-ray system to construct a 3D augmented-reality view of the patient's external and internal anatomy. The real-time 3D view of the patient's spine in relation to the incision sites in the skin improves procedure planning, surgical tool navigation and implant accuracy, as well as reducing procedure times.

Augmented Reality Telepresence
In 2013, a surgical team at the University of Alabama at Birmingham performed one of the first surgeries using a virtual augmented reality technology from the Virtual Interactive Presence and Augmented Reality (VIPAR) company. The remote doctor views a screen on a computer that is being fed by the camera in the local doctor's headset. The remote doctor has a black pad about 18-inches square, and a camera above it that sends a video feed of his hand which is projected into the display of the remote doctor's headset. The result is the local doctor sees the patient, and super-imposed on the patient is the remote doctor's finger, pointing to where the local doctor should do something (such as make an incision).

Diet Management
Research conducted at University of Tokyo in 2012, developed a specialized goggle to trick one into thinking food tastes better. Professor Michitaka Hirose who led the project said the computer-enhanced goggles had the ability to alter people's senses by visually changing the apparent size of the food the person was eating. When a cookie appeared twice as large, subjects ate almost 10% less of it. When cookies looked half their actual size, subjects ate 15% more.

The experiment involved an examinee eating a cookie while wearing a camera-equipped special goggle which made the cookies look larger. The goal was to help users' diet at Hirose's laboratory. Hirose conducted an experiment, asking examinees to eat as many cookies as they wanted with and without the glasses. The results showed they ate 9.3% less on average with the goggle showing cookies 1.5 times bigger than they were and ate 15% more with cookies looking two-thirds of their real size (Fig. 6.16).

Another of their projects, nicknamed a "meta cookie," tricked subjects into thinking they were eating something sweet. The headgear not only had a visual component to make the food look more flavorful, it had a scent bottle that gave off the aroma of whatever food they were trying to trick the subject into thinking they were eating. For example, even though they were given plain biscuits, scientists were able to make the subjects think they were eating strawberry or chocolate cookies with an 80% success rate.

Reality is in your mind, said Professor Michitaka Hirose.

Neither the university or Professor Hirose have any plans to sell either device.

Fig. 6.16 Augmented
Satiety is a method for
modifying perception of
satiety and controlling
nutritional intake by
changing the apparent size
of food with augmented
reality (Source: Cyber
Interface Lab, University
Tokyo)

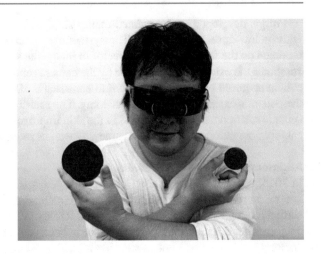

Seeing Veins

Evena Medical, in Roseville, CA introduced an ultrasound and near-infrared head
mounted smart-glasses for vein viewing for clinicians. The first version of the
Eyes-On glasses used Epson's Moverio technology for displaying an image laid
over the wearer's field of view.

The glasses project both infrared light and ultrasound onto the skin, the first for
viewing peripheral veins, while the latter for deeper targets such as the femoral vein
and artery. The returning images are captured by their respective sensors and turned
into an image that's viewed right over the patient's skin in real time (Fig. 6.17).

The IR emitters are on the corner of the headset. Two digital cameras are mounted
in the center and provide a zoom capability to see even the smallest veins. The system also offers telemedicine transmittal to a nurse's station or other remote locations. An additional benefit is the nurse doesn't require an extra hand to use the
Eyes-On glasses and can quickly move between patients without pushing a cart
around (Fig. 6.18).

Illuminating a patient's arm with IR and wearing IR filtered glasses to see peripheral veins for blood tests and intravenous injections has been in use for years. This
takes it to the next stage by using augmented reality technology and incorporating
more sensors.

Video Recording Not Augmented Reality

Also in 2013 surgeons in the U.S. preformed surgeries while wearing Google Glass
headsets. The headsets were used to record and transmit (stream) what the surgeons
were doing. However, that's all they were used for. No information was fed to the
surgeons, and in fact they made a point of saying that they were not distracted from
their surgical work by the glasses. Such video streaming can be useful for
students.

Fig. 6.17 Veins exposed with infrared can be seen in augmented reality glasses for accurate syringe placement (Source: Eveba Medical)

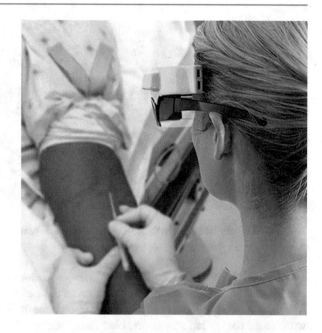

Fig. 6.18 Using a contact Ultrasonic sensor, the clinician can see femoral veins and arteries (Source: Evena Medical)

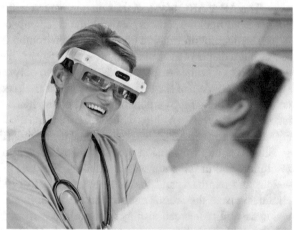

6.1.1.8 Military

The military could be considered the father of wearable augmented reality, starting back in 1963 with Bell helicopter which inspired Ivan Sutherland (see p. 84).

Traditional information systems that are not worn (dismounted in military-speak) require soldiers to look down at maps or mobile devices to access tactical information. In so doing, their head is 'down' and their attention is drawn away from what is happening directly in front of them. Augmented reality systems that a soldier can wear enables the soldier to acquire time-critical tactical information with their 'head-up' and 'eyes-out' on the environment (Fig. 6.19).

Fig. 6.19 Military-based ruggedized wearable augmented reality system for soldiers (Source: Applied Research Associates)

Applied Research Associates (ARA) developed an outdoor augmented reality system that delivers head-up situational awareness to the dismounted warfighter. Rather than looking down at a 2D map or smartphone device, the soldier sees virtual icons (e.g., navigation waypoints, blue forces, aircraft) overlaid on his real-world view. The ARA ARC4 system uses an augmented reality fusion engine that incorporates head tracking sensors, network management software, and a user interface to overlay iconic information on the user's environment. It integrates with daytime see-through displays as well as night-vision goggles. The system shown in the figure leverages a Lumus display for demonstration purposes (Fig. 6.20).

Elbit, developers of the F35 augmented reality helmet (see p. 115) took that technology and applied it to a tank helmet. The tank has a camera mounted on top, as inconspicuously as possible, while inside the tank commander can look around 360-degrees for what is called, "situational awareness (Fig. 6.21)."

Elbit says that Iron Vision provides images in real time with zero latency, high resolution, and in full color with a seamless 360° line of sight. The visors are lightweight and compact, and the software uses a distortion-correction algorithm to eliminate visual distortions and motion sickness. In addition, the system has night vision capability and can display relevant information directly in front of the commander. It also has head-tracker technology that locks on potential threats and targets, and follows them with just a glance from the commander (Fig. 6.22).

The system literally gives the tank commander x-ray vision enabling him or her to effectively see through the tank.

6.1.1.9 Power and Energy

Augmented reality can provide technicians in the field with immediate access to expert knowledge. They can access the latest documentation for all of the power plant, sub-station, or underground equipment on their tablet or augmented reality headset. Technicians can overlay a 3D model on an actual piece of equipment. They

Fig. 6.20 ARA's ARC4
helmet mounted
augmented reality system.
This is not a helmet, and
could be considered a
special case of a smart-
glasses head-up display
(Source: ARA)

may also view the internal components of a piece of equipment and explore its inner
workings. System repairs and upgrades are faster than ever before.

Augmented reality also improves operational safety. Not only does augmented
reality facilitate better employee training, but it also allows for better visualization
of underground assets and complex components, reducing accidents.

In early 2015, The Electric Power Research Institute (EPRI), a nonprofit organization focused on and funded by the electric utility industry, conducted a large-scale
experiment with some of the biggest utilities around the world to see how augmented reality could fit into the industry's workforce. EPRI's DistribuTECH brief-
ing laid out how data from geospatial information system (GIS) and asset
management systems could give field workers an augmented view of equipment
that needs to be checked or repaired.

The project is called "Field Force Data Visualization" (FFDV) and relies on three
technologies:

Augmented reality—overlay GIS data, measurements, menus, and documentation
    on an interactive view of the utility distribution or transmission environment.
GIS context awareness—knowing the location of the worker relative to utility
    assets, customizing the user's experience and defining what the user can and can-
    not do.
Common Information Model (CIM) messaging—using CIM to communicate with
    multiple back office systems to accomplish the allowed workflows.

Fig. 6.21 Elbit's Iron Vision helmet uses sensors and software and a user-friendly interface (originally developed for aircraft) to transmit video images from inside and outside the tank to the commander and driver's visors (Source: Elbit)

Fig. 6.22 Elbit's see-through armor (STA) technology (Source: Elbit)

EPRI's research in augmented reality started with the question: "if you can project a first down marker on reality at a football game, why can't you project GIS information on reality in a work environment?"

6.1.1.10   Public Sector

With careful planning, the public sector can deploy augmented reality to improve operations and deliver services to citizens when it matters most. Augmented reality can enhance a variety of government tasks, including building inspections, fleet maintenance, planning and risk assessment, security, first responders, search and rescue, and training.

Many state agencies use mobile devices for planning and risk assessment, where it's useful to incorporate photographs of the interior dimensions of a facility. Other areas include fleet maintenance, where technicians with wearable glasses could read barcodes and order machine parts, and inspection of buildings.

Augmented reality can improve security screening at travel hubs, border crossings and public events:

The citizen and the public service staff benefits from a tech-evolved public sector in the workplace. The advantages of an augmented reality aware, tech-evolved, workplace, as cited by employees, signify a culture where information and communication can be better streamlined. More than half the public workers believe that establishing a tech evolved workplace will give them better access to the information they need to do their jobs and help them to complete tasks faster, while improving collaboration. It's exciting to think that new technology could help alleviate the pressure on public sector organizations trying to increase efficiencies and boost citizen-facing services.

First Responders

First-responder training methods for police, paramedics, firefighters, and search and rescue teams have remained practically unchanged for decades despite the emergence of new technologies. This is due in part to the concern that a new technology may malfunction or require a steep learning curve that impedes its effective use. Augmented reality devices and applications for first responders will increase the effectiveness of paramedics, firefighters, and other first-responder training. However, to be effective, such tools must integrate seamlessly, enhance existing training methods and co-exist with rather than replace them.

Augmented reality headsets for first responders must provide a real-time link of position and point-of-view display between the responders and the situation manager, and stream information for later analysis and to make rescuing the responders possible if necessary. This information increases the coordinators' situational awareness by allowing them to monitor the activity of the responders precisely from an overhead view or from the perspective of any member of the response team (Fig. 6.23).

First responders need as detailed and accurate information of the environment as possible and a hands-free, heads-up display. This enables the responders to

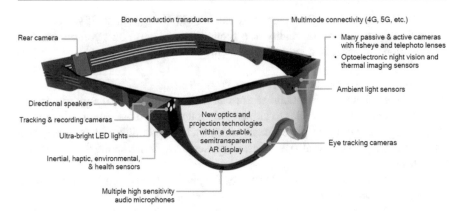

Fig. 6.23 Design concept for the next generation of first responder augmented reality glasses (Qualcomm)

visualize the path they have to take (and later follow to exit) and provide for display of virtual beacons that indicate important positions or objects in the environment.

Engineers at École polytechnique fédérale de Lausanne (EPFL) Switzerland have created VIZIR, an augmented reality smart visor for firefighters that will allow them to see thermal images through their breathing mask visor while keeping their hands free.

In addition, technology such as Google's project Tango can be used to create real-time maps to assist early responders in navigating unknown environments. The company is making its SDK available to developers.

Civic Augmented Reality

Governments and public service organizations like transportation organizations (bus, trolley, subway, etc.) are adopting augmented reality and offering localized applications for smartphones and tablets to aid citizens and visitors find places of interest, bus routes and schedules, translations, and emergency assistance.

Utah.gov launched a transit tracking application that lets residents track public transit data in real time and receive SMS notifications when a bus or train is nearby. A map helps them find public transportation stops and routes.

Civic Resource Group (CRG) in Los Angeles, CA, developed applications for their Civicaugmented reality product line that enables governments and public sector agencies to deliver information and services directly to citizens and communities in a highly contextual way for mobile devices (Fig. 6.24).

In Santa Monica, CA, CRG installed an online travel and information system for visitors and citizens that connected a variety of City and third-party provided data sources in a cloud-based data platform. That then provided real-time information to public users via smartphone, web, interactive kiosks and digital way-finding signage. Citizens were encouraged to seek ride matches and form carpools and van-pools, to bike, take transit and walk, and to track their trips. The goal was to streamline the transportation demand management and administrative process for the City.

Fig. 6.24 CRG's Civic
augmented reality
application, using
markerless image
recognition, applies
augmented reality for local
public information
(Source: Civic Resource
Group)

Airport Security

Travelers entering an airport will be scanned by cameras positioned throughout the facility. Their data will record passenger's behavioral, gestural, and kinematic characteristics, and feed this information into a highly-sophisticated data management system (Fig. 6.25).

The data management system will analyze the feed through video analytics, facial identification software, and threat recognition algorithms, and work in concert to generate a threat profile for the traveler. By the time a passenger reaches a screening person, such as the Transportation Screening Agency (TSA) agent's in the U.S., that stand just beyond the check-in area, the passenger's number and threat profile are overlaid into the agent's field of vision via a pair of augmented reality glasses.

U.S. Postal Service

In 2009, the US Postal Service (USPS) launched an augmented reality application named the 'Virtual Box Simulator' that ensured customers wouldn't have to worry about whether or not their shipping items would fit into standard USPS boxes.

The Virtual Box Simulator is a simple application of 3D augmented reality provided as a web service by the USPS) (Fig. 6.26).

To choose the right size of Flat Rate Box, the user holds up a printed "marker" page to their Webcam to position a virtual translucent box. Then they hold up the materials they want to ship and compare it to the available box sizes.

Fig. 6.25 Airport security and threat assessment will be sent to security guard's augmented reality glasses (Source: Deloitte)

Fig. 6.26 US Post Office's Priority Mail virtual box simulator uses augmented reality application with user's PC's web camera to pick the right (standard) size box for a package

Having a Little Fun

During the 2014 holiday season in the U.S., the USPS launched a mobile marketing campaign that transformed its 156,271 blue mail collection boxes across the country into a holiday mobile experience using augmented reality.

Fig. 6.27 U.S. postal boxes were turned into holiday cards (USPS)

"Whether you're walking down a busy city street or a main street in a small town, you can find one of our iconic blue boxes all across the country," said Nagisa Manabe, chief marketing and sales officer for the Postal Service. "Instead of just dropping off mail, smartphone users can use our USPS augmented reality application to transform these boxes into a unique and interactive experience during the holidays (Fig. 6.27)."

The innovative use of augmented reality featured fun activations like flashing holiday lights or dancing animated penguins, followed by prompts to order free shipping boxes or stamps.

The Postal Service has been promoting augmented reality as a way for marketers to add a digital component to direct mail campaigns to generate a greater return on investment.

In 2015 the USPS expanded the augmented reality to allow you to be photographed with Peanuts characters. Using the USPS application, users had the ability to take a photo of themselves next to characters like Charlie Brown and Snoopy at real world locations (Fig. 6.28).

Adding the popular Peanuts franchise to its augmented reality promotions indicated the USPS had no intention retreating even as email and application-powered delivery services continue to encroach on its turf.

6.1.1.11 Real Estate

Augmented reality in the real-estate sector is used to project information about properties on the market to provide images of the interiors of the houses. The overlaid data is visible to the users when they point their augmented reality device, typically a mobile device toward the houses. In some cases, buyers can not only see the overlaid data, but they can also see how the interior of the house will look after completion.

Fig. 6.28 Have you picture taken with your favorite Peanuts character and postal; box (USPS)

Buyers can visit potential new homes without having to enter the house. They can walk or drive by houses in construction and browse them. Seeing the positions of other houses in the locality and the location of their preferred house helps them in making the right purchase decision.

Probable buyers can check out how a prospective home will look when decorated in different ways, making the house more appealing to the buyers. There are augmented reality apps which can change the color of the walls thereby showing how the house will look when painted with their favorite shades. There are apps which can give a detailed view of the homes with their interior design planning even without placing any real object in the house. These apps can place furniture virtually inside the homes.

Augmented reality allows the shopper to avoid the real-estate sales person, and eliminates the restrictions of open house times.

Augmented Reality's Benefits to Realtors
With the use of augmented reality, realtors can benefit as much as the buyers. They will be able to set up a faster communication with their consumers. This technology will also help them to generate new clients. Realtors can provide the right message

at the right time with a geo-fencing feature that is available in most of the augmented reality apps.

There are also apps which can help realtors learn when a prospective buyer is viewing a property and know its location in real-time. They can find out when the users see a print advertisement. Based on this information, they can send push notifications to interact with the potential customers. With interactive logos, images, and listings it will be highly beneficial for the realtors to draw the attention of the prospective buyers towards the properties. Marketing costs will be reduced significantly with the use of augmented reality. By communicating instantly with prospective buyers, the chances of generating more revenue increases for the real estate agents.

Augmented Reality's Benefits to Potential Buyers
In addition to the above, with augmented reality buyers can take a virtual tour of a home using their mobile device. They can scan a flyer, banner or any other printed material which has augmented reality integrated in it, to see the property come to life. Searching for properties will become much easier.

Augmented reality will help buyers find out the location of the properties, know the exact distance from their current location to that of the property. They will be able to view the photos of the property with an augmented reality application. The technology will help you with detailed information about a property such as the price, total area of the house, number of rooms, etc. Some apps also provide the option to contact the listing owners directly. All this information will assist the buyer when making the final decision of buying a property.

6.1.1.12 Telepresence
Telepresence refers to a set of technologies which allow a person to feel as if they were present, to give the appearance of being present, or to have an effect, via telerobotics, at a place other than their true location.

Telepresence could be considered a subset of augmented reality in that it doesn't (by definition) include the superimposition of synthetic information on the viewer's vision. It can be thought of as "augmented reality lite," or augmented vision. Several companies (e.g., AMA XpertEye, Interapt, CrowdOptic, and others) use augmented reality headsets and helmets as a telepresence device to put a report expert in the locality of a situation (i.e., an ambulance, a repair operation, a conference room, etc.).

6.1.1.13 Summary
Augmented Reality is not a single thing, say like a PC or a smartphone. Rather it is collection of vertical applications. Therefore, the list is almost infinite, which is good news in terms of the market opportunity and growth, and bad news if you want to chronical and analyze it. One of the best places to keep up to date on the industrial and scientific developments in augmented reality is Augmented Reality for Enterprise Alliance—AREA. http://thearea.org/.

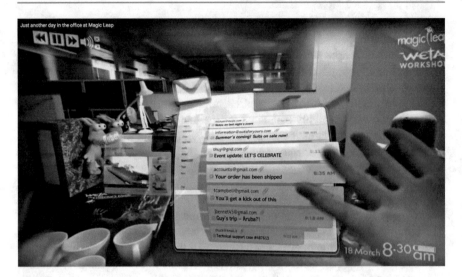

Fig. 6.29 An augmented reality virtual desktop, superimposed over an actual desktop, conveyed through Magic Leap's lightfield technology headset (Source: Magic Leap)

6.1.2   Commercial and Enterprise

The needs and uses of commercial and enterprise augmented reality users are dramatically different from consumers. That can't be said too often. Whereas consumers are mostly concerned with appearance and price, commercial and enterprise users are more concerned with functionality and return on investment (ROI). However, commercial users will also have consumer facing applications and have to rely on the consumers to have appropriate viewing devices, which initially were smartphones and tablets.

In the "back rooms"—the warehouse, engineering, maintenance, and fleet management (to name a few), the companies (the commercial and enterprise companies) will have complete systems consisting of database servers, communications systems, glasses, and/or helmets.

In this section, a few of the many augmented reality applications used or suggested for use by commercial and enterprise organization are offered.

6.1.2.1 Email with Personality
One vision of how augmented reality will change is offered by Magic Leap. They envision an email client superimposed on whatever you are looking at (Fig. 6.29).

Such a system could be highly interactive and become a video-conferencing system. Imagine instead of exchanging four or five emails to get a meeting scheduled your email system called the person you wanted to meet with and the two or three or more of you discussed it in real time.

Fig. 6.30 A typical QR
code (Wikipedia)

6.1.2.2 Advertising and Marketing

Visual, or augmented marketing is the practice of using images and objects to enhance brand communications and utility via image recognition, augmented reality and visual discovery. Various augmented reality marketing apps help to deepen and inspire brand conversations with consumers with immersive digital information on everyday objects.

The first wave of augmented marketing items were advertisements in magazines and used QR codes. QR code (Quick Response Code) is the trademark for a type of 2D matrix barcode designed for the automotive industry in Japan (Fig. 6.30).

QR codes are probably the most common form of marker-based augmented reality, other forms exist as well, and are discussed elsewhere. (See "Natural Feature Tracking Using Markers," Sect. 8.9.2.)

Some commercial augmented reality applications are described as, "consumer facing." That means they are applications designed by a commercial organization to be used by consumers. Greeting cards are one such example. The first versions had simple characters or objects encoded in them (using a marker typically embedded (coded) in the image in the card, although some early versions used a QR code marker.

Hallmark, the giant greeting card company in Kansas City, Mo, introduced the first augmented reality greeting card in January 2010 for Valentine's Day [14]. The person receiving the card could view a 3D animated feature by holding the card up to a web camera on a PC, after a downloaded application had been installed. Later in June the company introduced an iPhone/iPad application for viewing their greeting cards.

The first magazine to use augmented reality was *Esquire* in 2009 (see Fig. 5.23, Sect. 5.1). Since then several magazines have employed the technology in advertisements and editorials.

Augmented reality has been used in various advertising campaigns. For example, in the mid 2010–2020s, the Coca-Cola company introduced its Magic application that used an augmented reality technology application created by Arloopa. It allowed the user, through specially selected augmented reality markers (QR-code markers), to have three experience options:

- discover the surprise on Coca-Cola Christmas bottles,
- explore the branded bus stations in the city,
- find Santa's message behind Coca-Cola signs in the malls and youth-active places (Fig. 6.31).

Coca-Cola Magic
       Markers

Thee simple steps to see the magic:

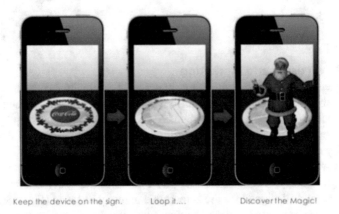

Keep the device on the sign.   Loop it....   Discover the Magic!

Fig. 6.31 Coca Cola's holiday augmented reality advertising (Source: Arloopa)

From interactive product packaging and marketing collateral to print ads, and billboards, augmented reality is opening up a new range of marketing opportunities. AR allows to easily engage with information using mobile devices they already own and when and how they please. If accessing product information easy, convenient, and maybe even fun, customers will automatically have a more positive inclination towards the brand.

Retailers
Retailers, often referred to as "brick and mortar," establishments, have been under pressure to survive due to competition from the web. Stores that sold commodity products with little to no differentiation, offering only the convenience of immediate availability (assuming you were willing to go get it, during store hours). In the US retail sales represent about a $4–5 billion industry, but on-line eCommererce sales are worth over $300 billion [15]. Augmented reality offers a way to blend the two. augmented reality offers numerous, implications in retail and design capacities within a business.

Companies use 3D models in the design of their products. By using those models in augmented reality prospective customers can evaluate them before any production is ordered, and, depending on the supplier, ask for customizations. This helps companies demonstrate prototypes more effectively, and more to the production phase much faster than ever before.

Retailers use augmented reality packaging, displays, and signage to engage customers as they shop in-store. Many toy companies have implemented kiosks in-store where customers can scan a product's packaging and see a 3D version of the finished product.

For other shops, however, the web has become their catalog and advertising vehicle. And with augmented reality it even becomes their customer service source. Neal Leavitt, who runs an international marketing communications company, offers a view on how that will work.

How Augmented Reality Is Changing the Way Consumers Shop

Neal Leavitt established Leavitt Communications in 1991 bringing more than 25 years of marketing communications and journalism expertise to clients. He received his Bachelor of Arts degree in communications from UC-Berkeley and a Master of Arts degree in journalism & public affairs from American University in Washington, DC. As a journalist Neal served as a city editor, copy editor and reporter for major metropolitan newspapers in California, covering everything from business to technology to travel. He is a regular contributor to a number of technology and marketing publications such as Computing Now, published by IEEE Computer Society, and iMediaConnection.com. He has worked in a variety of vertical markets in both the public and private sector including: biotech, education, engineering, entertainment, environment, financial, healthcare/medical, industrial, municipalities, public agencies (state and federal), real estate, sports, and technology.

Neal Leavitt

For years, furniture buying was often a leap of faith. You could measure the available space for a sofa, chair, dining room table, perhaps take some pictures, then walk into a store, select what you think would work, and hope for the best.

Homeware retailer Ikea conducted research in 2014 that seemingly corroborated the challenges customers face in selecting furniture:

- More than 70% said they didn't know big their homes were;
- 14% of customers purchased wrong-sized furniture for their rooms;
- 33% said they were confused about how to properly measure for furniture.

Those days are long gone.

Enter augmented reality. The technology lays a computer-generated image over an image picked up on the camera of a smartphone or tablet – in effect, it adds a layer of digital data or images to the real world.

Now furniture retailers and customers benefit from Google's Tango that was initially available on a Lenovo smartphone, the Phab 2 Pro. Using motion-tracking cameras, sensors and software, Tango enables a mobile device to create 3D maps of indoor spaces and also reorient the map based on where the phone is in those spaces. The Phab 2 phones have depth perception thanks to a sensor that utilizes infrared light to ascertain depth by how light is shaped by various objects in a room. So, with Tango, sofas, chairs, etc. can be integrated into the simulation along with the actual motion of your body (Fig. 6.32).

"Once a Phab 2 phone creates a map of a room and stores it, you'll be able to select a digitized image of a piece of furniture, insert it on to the 3D map, and then

Fig. 6.32 Visualizing how something (e.g., furniture) might look in a given environment (Google)

move it around so you can see how it looks in different places and from different angles," notes the Smithsonian.

And Forbes added that a "Tango enabled device knows where doors, windows, shelves and the like are so that in the future, when you visit a large store, you can find what you need right down to the exact shelf."

Retailers are seeing gold in the technology. Lowe has a Tango application called Lowe's Vision. Shoppers can point a Phab 2 at their laundry room and see how different washers and dryers will fare in that space.

And Wayfair Inc., a home furnishings company, offers WayfairView, a first-party smartphone augmented reality application available in Google Play. The company says the application allows shoppers to visualize furniture and décor in their homes at full-scale before making a purchase. Via the Phab 2, a customer can choose a Wayfair product and virtually fit in a room to see if passes muster in that space. Wayfair says shoppers can move and rotate products "to visualize various layouts and perspective and when ready to make a purchase, shoppers are seamlessly connected to Wayfair's shopping application in Google Play."

And while augmented reality probably won't preclude getting in the car and driving to the furniture store or outlet, some furniture executives think that's just fine.

Scott Perry, VP of digital for Jerome's, a well-known regional furniture chain, said he doesn't see augmented reality replacing the store experience.

"We want them to see it, feel it, love it before they buy it, because that makes for a happier customer," said Perry. However, shoppers, noted Perry, who virtually see items in their home are 35% more likely than other website visitors to call the company or get directions to a store location, and 65% more likely to buy.

Fig. 6.33 Yelp's Monocle app identifying stores based on what the camera is looking at the user's location (Yelp)

Many experts believe augmented reality will help bolster brick-and-mortar retailers.

"I do think it's a game-changer for the retail industry," said Artemis Berry, VP of retail for Shop.org and the National Retail Federation. "What we know right now, though, is that it's in the very early stages."

Neal Leavitt, who runs an international marketing communications company. Mr. Leavitt also serves as a contributing editor for a number of leading interactive marketing and high technology publications including Computer (published by IEEE), and iMediaConnection. com. His articles have appeared in a wide variety of print and online publications nationwide and overseas.

Product Reviews

Letsee, a South Korean company, has developed an application that uses augmented reality on a smartphone to scan a product for instant product reviews. The company claims that Web 2.0 has made consumers into prosumers by enabling direct interaction between users and contents. This is an early application, but a good idea. It's a platform to scale to create value so that there are many unbiased reviews for many products. For example, Letsee has developed an app for beer drinkers that lets them point their smartphone at bottles of beer to access information about the beer and see other users' hashtag ratings.

Another example is Yelp's resource finder, that alerts people to nearby services. Introduced in 2009, the Yelp Monocle adds a 3-D layer to what your phone's camera is seeing. This technology pulls graphics from your TV/Computer/Phone displays and into your environment with augmented reality (Fig. 6.33).

The Monocle feature can be access from the Yelp app and it uses the camera, GPS and compass in an Android phone to look at businesses in their surroundings and see reviews. The advantage here is obvious, Yelp already has a wealth of reviews on every topic, it's more or less trusted. Monocle makes it more valuable to the person wandering in an unfamiliar location.

Post Augmented Reality

Product placement in a TV show or movie, where a company pays to have their product conspicuously shown in a scene, or scenes, is a practice that dates back to the 1960s. Prior to 2011 in the UK where one pays a TV license fee (to support ad free shows) product placement on TV was prohibited and strict guidelines were imposed to stop companies from advertising their goods. Today it's possible to insert products into almost any TV shows or movies by digitally imposing adverts into regular, or older TV shows—applying augmented reality historically.

Ironically, it was a UK company, Mirriad, founded in 2008, that developed the idea and technology. Using sophisticated feature detection and tracking, the company tracks objects and backgrounds through the videos. One technique is to track features, which are special points that are able to be accurately located and identified in each frame (Fig. 6.34).

To understand where to integrate brands into video automatically, Mirriad splits the scene into regions identifiable over the whole video sequence. To place objects into an open space in a 3D scene with a moving camera, 3D tracking is essential. This calculates the camera position and orientation in every frame. To place images such as logos on flat surfaces such as walls or signs in windows, planar tracking is used, and it can do it even if the surface is moving. it's even possible to change brands depending on the audience (Fig. 6.35).

This technology has created a form in advertising where a brand integration is less expensive, scalable, and can be run in multiple pieces of content. The resulting ads are seamless, authentic, and work across all types of screens. In 2013 they won an Academy Award for their imaging technology. However, it could be ridiculous or offensive if modern products were placed in the background of iconic TV shows. It would be absurd to see a smartphone or computer set in an older time when such things didn't exist.

6.1.3   Consumer

Augmented reality is here today, but it is still in its infancy from a consumer's point of view. Like smartphones, the augmented reality evolution will take years but has the potential to be huge. Consumers will engage with augmented reality for:

- Marketing & advertising—personalized ads based on context, as well as consumer data—what they like, what they look at, etc.
- Retail—try before you buy: clothes, furniture, car, real estate shopping, etc. Also, navigation to products and personalized coupons.

Fig. 6.34 Markers are picked in the scene to develop a 3D model (Mirriad)

Fig. 6.35 Same scene, two different ads in the windows (Mirriad)

Cognitive technologies are key for augmented reality adoption. Cognitive augmented reality will greatly expand our human abilities. By understanding the environment and providing personalized assistance, augmented reality will:

- Assist the visually impaired—help the visually impaired map their environment and get around.
- Make travel easier—describe the landmarks around you and translate street signs.
- Become a pro—make a gourmet meal, fix your car, or perfect your jump shot.

Augmented reality is the future, but for universal consumer use, there are still some obstacles.

Augmented reality, like virtual reality, is and has been, used for industrial, military, and scientific applications in controlled environments, and by professionals who understand and tolerate the technology's limitations (while simultaneously helping to improve it). The problem with our society is that when an interesting technology like augmented reality, virtual reality, or neural gaming gets a little coverage, the press, and Wall Street jump to conclusions and extrapolate it to be the

Fig. 6.36 "Tom Lea—
2000 Yard Stare" by US
Army

next revolution, the new DVD, MP3, or UHD. Then, when that doesn't happen
within their short-range vision, they declare it a failure and go looking for the next
shiny thing—the well-known well-documented Hype Curve.

Augmented reality, virtual reality, and neural gaming may suffer such fates too,
just like 3DTV, and the S3D PC gaming promise failed. The other new thing people
are talking about is mixed reality. HoloLens and other mixed reality technologies
like CastAR and Magic Leap are different from augmented reality—and are different from virtual reality. The Immersive Technology Alliance likes to bundle all the
reality-removing or augmenting technologies into a basket they call immersive reality. I think that is a better overall name than mixed reality, or virtual reality or augmented reality, or neural gaming. But logic doesn't always prevail in big companies
with big marketing budgets.

However, I'm a big proponent of augmented reality and can't wait for it to happen. Nevertheless, I also see the obstacles and even have some suggestions.

First there is the 2000-yard stare, the Google glass vacant look as the wearer
focuses on the screen or out into space—it's obvious to the people around the
wearer, especially the person he or she is supposed to be talking to (Fig. 6.36).

My vision of an effective pair of augmented reality glasses is one which isn't
obnoxious, calling attention to itself, and that takes the wearer's attention away
from people, or potential.

Fig. 6.37 Google Glass
(Wikipedia)

Fig. 6.38 Tethered glasses
(Source: Aunt Lydia's)

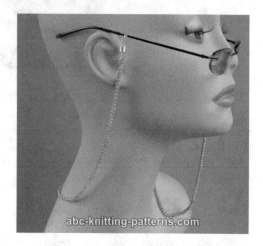

Looking at Google Glass specifically, one of the first success stories of consumer AR and its most renowned failure, the device was a low-resolution, one-eye, off-angle display with a 15-degree diagonal field of view. Humans have two eyes and 15-degrees is a very small field. Looking off-angle with one eye does not seem practical for consumer use (Fig. 6.37).

I think we will all wear augmented reality glasses just as we now wear corrective glasses and sunglasses, but the display will have to be smart and move its focal plane to where we are looking. Up close if we're reading or talking to someone, further out if we're walking or trying to find a street sign.

Second is power, less is better; I don't want to pull a Ground Power Unit around, or have to wear a battery belt.

The new generation of mobile devices such as SoCs from Qualcomm, MediaTek, and others are power misers, and are already being used. This will be used for the next generation of augmented reality glasses (AKA as smart glasses, since we have smart phones, I guess our glasses have to be smart too) (Fig. 6.38).

Fig. 6.39 Augmented
reality glasses make you
Tom Cruise in the Minority
Report (Source:
shutterstock.com)

Tethered glasses (AKA "Granny" glasses) are sensible, logical, and practical.
You never lose them; you can take them off when not needed and quickly recover
them when they are needed. Now envision the center rear of the chain holding an
AA battery, and the chain is a super lightweight flexible, and decorative power
cable. And maybe it's also an inductive antenna that is getting fed by force-sensors
in your shoe.

Third is content and big data, a variation on my second axiom, *the more you can
see, the more you can do* (**Fig. 6.39**).

For augmented reality to really augment our lives we need to have data streaming
at us, as well as locally stored. Our augmented reality glasses need to know where
we are, and where we're heading and anticipate what we might want or need to see
ahead. That's a potentially big data load and puts a big demand on the network.
Microcells will help manage that, and our glasses will advise our big-data suppliers
on our preferences. We may also do a mini flight plan and tell our glasses "I'm
going to the grocery store", or "I'm going to the bar, airport", etc. Then only relevant information in our path will be delivered, and also be potentially available to
our family, friends, and colleagues.

I've always wanted a camera somehow connected to my eyes. augmented reality
glasses could do that for me. If for example I blinked three times rapidly it would
take ten quick photos of wherever I was looking, if I blinked five times, it takes a
3-min video. Alternatively, maybe it records all the time and I blink to say save the
last 2 or 3 min. And "save" means to the cloud in case what I am capturing is life
threatening and I don't make it—my personal black box.

Of course, if the glasses were connected to all sources of information I'd never
get into such a situation. Augmented reality can't happen fast enough for me.

Fig. 6.40 Merging the online digital experience with the in-store experience (Source: Layar)

6.1.3.1 Markerless Identification of Things

Over the years, people have learned how to used quick response (QR) codes found on products and in commercials, to get more information. Blippar says they have taken that concept to the next level, providing the users with more interactive content. The company even created its own verbs—"blipping." And "Blippable.".

Ambarish Mitra, and Omar Tayeb, founded Blippar 2011, in the U.K. It is a supplier of an image-recognition and visual discovery application, using augmented reality and machine learning.

In 2015, the company introduced visual search capabilities in its application using machine learning and computer vision, which allows users to unlock information about an object by pointing their mobile device's camera at the object. The company demonstrated it could work on apples, dogs and cars.

In 2014, Blippar acquired Layar, a Dutch augmented reality company founded by Raimo van der Klein in 2009. Layar developed geo-located image recognition technology, that can run in a mobile device. It can recognize known (trained and classified) objects, and trigger/link a URL with a video, or a store, or a site with general information, which the company refers to as a "layer." (As in an image layer that is superimposed on the image the camera is showing).

For example, looking at an album cover through the Blippar app could generate content about that band including videos of the band, a source to buy tickets to an upcoming concert, details on what people are saying about them on Twitter, and photos of the band itself (Fig. 6.40).

Layar has thousands of content layers and more coming as developers increasingly use it as the platform for augmented reality. Many fit right into an urban lifestyle, while others are particular to a locale. However, every layer has to be individually developed. Google on the other hand, wants to bring the entire Web to

(Android) smartphone users through augmented reality and a function called "visual search." Visual search enables people to take a picture of whatever they would like to know more about, such as a car, a dress, a painting, or a building, and information found via Google search appears on the user's screen (or in his or her smart glasses).

In 2014 Blippar acquired Layar, forming at the time the world's largest augmented reality user base. Blippar then demonstrated its new 'visual browser' application at the South by Southwest (SXSW) conference in Austin, Texas, in March 2015.

By just pointing the application at everyday objects, it identifies and categorises nearly everything in the frame. The application "sees" the object you point at and then identifies it. For example, if you pointed your smart phone, or smart glasses at your keyboard, it would label it a keyboard, and put it in a little window at the bottom of the application. The company has built its own knowledge graph, Blipparsphere, and combined with our visual search engine, you can get info about that keyboard.

If you were looking for something, say maybe a keyboard, this would save you a tremendous amount of time locating local providers of the thing.

Blippar's Mitra believes augmented reality can overcome the economic barriers of language. Using the Visual Web, people will be able to buy and sell things online, wordlessly, by image recognition. Mitra is particularly passionate about removing illiteracy as a barrier to development in third-world countries.

"People have disrupted the automotive industry, the retail industry, people disrupted banking. This is like disrupting 5000 years of social structures and bringing knowledge parity in the world," Mitra said.

Christine Perey of Perey Research & Consulting, and AREA, says that augmented reality holds the promise of turning the world into one huge "interactive catalog,"

6.1.3.2 Virtual Fashion Items

Augmented reality has found its way into fashion items for consumers. From clothes to glasses, to makeup, and hair, developers are coming up with clever ways to have a camera look at and scan a person and then create a 3D model, and then apply something to that model such as a hair style, cosmetics, clothes, and other accessories.

It's not as easy as it sounds, and it has been tried, and failed for decades. The difference is higher resolution, smaller and inexpensive cameras (thanks to the smartphone explosion), faster and less expensive processors (thanks to Moore's law), sophisticated 3D modeling software (thanks to a lot of hard work by legends of programmers), and real-time tracking or pose. Not least there is much more customer awareness of AR.

Clothing

Tesco in the UK introduced large screens equipped with camera and image recognition software to create "magical" mirrors that let consumers interact with the mirrors through augmented reality. When a consumer engages these mirrors, they have the option to browse a wide variety of clothing and try these clothes on, in a digital sense. Augmented reality is used to superimpose these articles of clothing over a consumer's reflection thereby giving them an idea of how they will look with that particular piece.

The other innovation Tesco has introduced is a digital mannequin. The mannequin has a physical representation in the world, but is animated through a variety of augmented reality holograms. The figure can interact with its surroundings and has some personality through recorded audio to engage consumers and get their attention as they browse Tesco stores.

FaceCake's introduced an augmented reality, virtual dressing room to online retail sites they called Swivel in February 2011, and is used in Bloomingdale's department stores. The technology lets you stand in front of a connected camera and "try on" different pieces of clothing by having their digital images superimposed on your body (as described above). It even lets you try out different accessories like purses and belts. If you raise your arms, the outfits adjust accordingly, and you can even turn to see the sides and back.

Neiman Marcus is also experimenting with new technology and mirrors. The company worked with Palo Alto, California company MemoMi Labs to create a full-length dressing room mirror with a 70-inch LCD, an HD camera and a computer to power it. Right now the use is not true AR, it's video. The mirror records a short video of someone trying on the dress and turning for the camera. Customers can then see the videos side by side rather than re-trying on clothes and they can share them with friends. MemoMi has also developed a feature that allows customers to see clothing in different colors, but Neiman's is waiting to employ that feature.

Glasses

One of the first augmented reality projects I was involved with in the early 2000s was putting virtual glasses on a person sitting in front of a camera, looking at a screen. Seemed simple. It wasn't. Turns out no two people have the same distance between eyes, thickness of head, height and arch of nose, or height of eyes above the nose. That's why when you buy glasses, they have to be fitted and adjusted. Needless to say, the project didn't succeed, the technology and knowledge just wasn't there yet.

3D-scanning company Fuel3D developed a smart mirror for facial-recognition, which finds and catalogues all the unique nuances in a person's face. Then, working with eyewear developer Sfered, the company created a 3D-scanning mirror for retail optical locations that makes finding a pair of spectacles that fit perfectly as simple as glancing in a smart mirror.

Fuel3D built a highly accurate facial scanning system that enabled the collection of all metrics required for fitting custom-fit eyewear in a single scan. The mirror scanner captures true facial 3D data in 0.1 seconds, allowing data capture of all the relevant data needed to create custom eyewear — including pupillary distance, nose bridge width, facial width, and distance to ear. The system also allows opticians and optometrists to virtually fit frames to customers for an enhanced customer experience.

Makeup

FaceCake (mentioned above) introduced a mirror that lets the viewer try on makeup before buying it. Manufactured by the USA TV builder Element Electronics, the NextGen vanity mirror uses cameras and built-in lights to create an augmented reality experience of the viewer's face.

The smart mirror uses cameras to capture faces, while augmented reality software allows users to try on makeup in real time, including cosmetics already owned, to avoid odd combinations or products not yet in one's vanity case—a try before you buy option. The mirror will also make personalized product recommendations the developers say, as well as, of course, sharing looks to social media.

Besides just the virtual makeup samples, the mirror also uses sensors to detect the lighting in the room — since previewing makeup in natural light and artificial light can result in slightly different looks. Dual LEDs also help create ideal lighting for previewing the look, much like some vanity mirror.

ModiFace is a firm that is offering an augmented reality for 55 of the top makeup brands like Sephora, P&G and Unilever. Unlike FaceCake, the ModiFace uses a portable device such as a tablet or smartphone, and the company's custom application. The user can go into a store's makeup counter and choose different styles of lipstick, eye shadow or whatever else, and ModiFace applies them to the user's skin in real-time on her screen. Move around, wink and smile, and the user can see their new style without the work or cost.

ModiFace can also simulate hair changes, anti-aging treatments and more (see following section).

Stores have reported increased sales because customers are more confident they'll be satisfied with what they're buying. Brands are paying $200,000–$500,000 a year to integrate ModiFace's augmented reality tech into their own apps.

Hair Styles

In computer graphics, hair is the most difficult and computationally intense part of any animal. Each hair has its own physics, light refection and absorption, length, and interactivity with other hairs, and it's almost never static, moved by wind, body motion and gravity.

The augmented reality app allows users to try new hairstyles and hair effects on their own photo and compare and share a photo collage consisting of multiple looks. The mobile-optimized app works on any mobile device enabling users to try the latest hairstyles and effects directly by taking a photo on their phone.

The Conair app provides a great way for consumers to experiment with new hairstyles and hair effects. The best part is, by saving a photo collage, users can share multiple looks instantly, get their friends and family to vote and comment on the best look, and they have something to take to the hairstylist to describe what they'd like. Aside from being very useful, this provides a great way for social engagement for Conair.

Fig. 6.41 Seeing things that aren't there—woman wearing augmented reality glasses at Smau, international exhibition of information communications technology in Milan (Image credit: Tinxt)

6.1.3.3 Art

Art galleries, museum exhibits, indoors and outdoors have been experimenting with and using augmented reality since the early 2010s to augment their exhibitions for combining what is on the gallery wall with images from the cloud as the visitor views it through their mobile device.

Museums have also offered supplemental "backstories" to pictures along with some history of the personalities involved (Fig. 6.41).

One clever application for augmented reality in a museum was the museum or Stolen Art (MOSA) in Hertogenbosch in southern Netherlands. It is an art initiative to let people enjoy art that the world has been deprived of because they were stolen (Fig. 6.42).

There is also virtual reality museum of stolen art started in 2014 by Ziv Schneider at NYU ITP.

In 2015, a group of students set up NO AD, an augmented reality project to make New York subway stations littered with movie posters, product adverts, become works of art through augmented reality (Fig. 6.43).

Designed and curated for the commuter crowd by RJ Rushmore of Vandalog, it consisted of 39 GIF artworks by 13 artists and collectives. Because the NOAD mobile application was an Art project and a proof of concept for what the world may be like once head-up displays become more ubiquitous, they shut it down after 1 year. Other pop-up augmented reality displays have appeared in museums since 2010.

Fig. 6.42 The Museum of Stolen Art is a gallery exhibition of works currently reported stolen or missing (Image credit MOSA)

Fig. 6.43 NO AD's superimposed art via augmented reality in a New York subway (Source: NO AD)

6.1.3.4 Entertainment

With augmented reality, entertainment will advance to new, immersive exciting and surprising levels. Augmented reality has been used effectively in PR and marketing for motion picture, television, and other promotional campaigns. Typically, these have included printed graphic or real life object recognition where the software identifies a unique symbol via web cam or cell phone camera. Other examples of augmented reality entertainment range from promotional film kiosks to interactive aquarium exhibits that are designed to educate children.

Some of the possible applications of augmented reality in entertainment are reviewed in this section.

Games

Game playing will reach across the world and throughout it. Early augmented reality games were simple games and usually associated with product advertising. Primarily used on mobile devices like notebook PCs, tablets and smartphones, augmented reality games in dedicated augmented reality devices such as glasses or helmets will soon be available.

Experiments for using augmented reality for gaming began in the late 1990s at MIT and the University of South Australia.

Like many new technologies, augmented reality was quickly employed in games. For a while it looked as if, outside of the military, augmented reality might be destined for just game applications. That didn't happen, because in site of the "cool technology," it was cumbersome to produce and operate. That changed in the late 2000s, but in between the tools had to be developed, like ARQuake.

ARQuake

In 2000, Bruce Thomas from the Wearable Computer Lab, part of the Advanced Computing Research Centre, located at the Mawson Lakes Campus of the University of South Australia demonstrated the very first outdoor mobile augmented reality video game. The game was the first to allow players to walk around without the use of a joystick or handheld controller (Fig. 6.44).

The first game was called ARQuake and all that was needed was a computer backpack and gyroscopes. This allowed users to simply flip down a head-mounted display and see a completely different view of the game based on their current physical location.

Smartphone

In the early 2000s, the first augmented reality applications were offered on smartphones, where people all over the world could enjoy the latest technology. The first application was for Symbian users and allowed them to use their mobile phone cameras to see different augmentations on the screen indicating points of interest. Later, gamers were offered this on the iPhone and Android phones.

Ironically, the first analog computer game was Tennis for Two, done at Brookhaven National Laboratory in 1958 [16]. And the first augmented reality game for a smartphone was a tennis game.

In 2005, Anders Henrysson, at the NVIS Linköping University ported the ARToolKit to the Symbian platform and created a collaborative game called, *augmented reality Tennis* [17]. In the game players would see a virtual tennis court superimposed over a piece of paper with the tracking squares on it (Fig. 6.45).

Augmented reality Tennis used a highly-optimized version of the ARToolKit computer vision library that was developed for the Symbian OS platform and

Fig. 6.44 ARQuake backpack circa 2000 (Used with permission of Dr. Wayne Piekarski and Prof. Bruce H. Thomas of the University of South Australia)

Fig. 6.45 Augmented reality Tennis circa 2005 (Courtesy Anders Henrysson)

combined with the OpenGL ES graphics library. The game was run on Nokia 6600 and 6630 phones.

Another augmented reality game that was developed at the same time was *the Invisible Train* in 2004–2005 by Wagner, Pintaric, and Schmalstieg at the Graz University (Fig. 6.46) [18].

Fig. 6.46 The Invisible
train (Courtesy Wagner,
Pintaric, and Schmalstieg)

The goal of this multiplayer game (PDAs connected via Wi-Fi) was to steer a
virtual train over a real wooden railroad track. The player was able to interact using
the touch screen to adjust the train speed and toggle track switches.

Console

The first console game to feature such technology was *The Eye of Judgment,* a turn-
based card battle video game for the PlayStation 3, released in October 2007
(Fig. 6.47).

Developed by SCE Japan Studio, the game used the console's PSEye camera to
gather real-world images and read the coded (marker) information on small physical
trading cards. This information allowed the game to bring the characters on the trading cards to life on the screen. The game was featured in the *Guinness World
Records Gamer"s Edition* 2010 [19].

Players conquer a play field by employing various creatures and spells, taking
turns playing cards of their choice strategically on the mat, and performing actions
through gestures that are captured through the PlayStation Eye camera.

Pokémon GO

Of all the augmented reality games for smartphones that were developed in the late
2000s and through to 2016, no other game did more to introduce the concept of
augmented reality to consumers than Nintendo's Pokémon GO. Pokémon GO was
a free-to-play, location-based augmented reality game developed and published by
Niantic for iOS and Android devices. It was initially released in selected countries
in July 2016, with downloads quickly exceeding 75 million. It has become a global
phenomenon, but Pokémon GO has been a popular franchise for many years.

Launched in Japan in 1996, it quickly spread around the world to encompass
merchandise such as trading cards, delighting children but annoying teachers and
even the police (Fig. 6.48).

Fig. 6.47 The Eye of
Judgment was the first
augmented reality console
game (Wikipedia)

Fig. 6.48 Encountering a
Doduo in Pokémon GO
(Wikipedia)

When Pokémon characters are found, one must throw the Poké Ball (by tapping
on the ball and flicking it up towards the Pokémon) at the character to capture it.

The game also raised concerns about privacy. Although it was the application
that took the world by storm, Pokémon GO also had privacy activists such as the

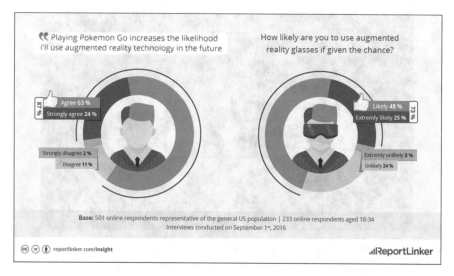

Fig. 6.49 Pokémon has influenced consumers positively toward augmented reality

Electronic Privacy Information Center criticizing its data collection practices with regard to consumer protection, and demanding the FTC investigate the application. However, Joseph Ansorge, a technology expert and author of *Identify & Sort,* commented at the time that, "Protecting one's privacy is no longer a realistic endeavor. Recent technological innovations have essentially removed the last shred of any anonymous public sphere. Instead of attempting to prevent this development, it is more practical to ensure that consumers have the right to control their personal data."

According to Wharton marketing professor David Bell, Pokémon GO and augmented reality can point the way to more local advertising and immersive marketing. "I see the direction for augmented reality going into advertising," says Bell. "The next evolution of the internet will be to immerse yourself into an environment... Augmented reality puts you in tune with the local environment and context is amplified (Fig. 6.49) [20]."

Pokémon GO has been credited with making augmented reality understandable and more accessible to millions of people who never interacted with an augmented reality game or device before.

Geo AR Games

The Auckland Council is the local government council for the Auckland Region in New Zealand. The governing body consists of a mayor and 20 councilors, elected from 13 wards. There are also 149 members of 21 local boards who make decisions on matters local to their communities.

In 2016, the Auckland Council formed a partnership with New Zealand's Geo AR Games, mixed reality experience designers founded in Sept 2015 to get kids off the couch and outside to play, ahead of the winter school holidays.

Fig. 6.50 Real Strike 3D augmented reality FPS application screen shot

Geo AR Games, said, "We can't reverse technology or progress, nor should we try. What we can do is create healthy relationships with technology by using the screen to get kids outdoors and moving around."

The Auckland Council signed an agreement to run a trial of Geo AR's "Magical Park" digital playground app in eight parks around Auckland for two months from 4 July to 4 September.

The digital playground experience is aimed at children aged 6–11, allowing them to explore digital content in the real world by viewing it through their smartphone or tablet.

Shooters

The concept of injecting images or actions into a view of the real world has been used for several years as smartphones and tablets became popular. One example which became controversial is an application called Real Strike. It mixes the camera's view of the local environment, and the real-time computed 3D gun animation into an integrated view, allowing the user to turn the forest, street, office or whatever environment they are in into a military simulation field. And, they can make a movie of what they do while they play (i.e., shoot) (Fig. 6.50).

The concept of shooting things, or people, with your smartphone has alarmed some people especially in the U.S. with its high murder rate and quantity of guns. In 2013, in Gray, Louisiana, in the U.S., a 15-year-old was arrested after posting a video on YouTube using the Real Strike app to shoot other kids at school, He said it was a result of him being frustrated and tired of being bullied. The video was removed from You Tube, the app is still available.

Porn

No form of visual entertainment has been developed that hasn't been used for the delivery of porn, and augmented reality is no exception [21]. Porn for adults with adults, and sadly child porn has also been developed and distributed. Second Life has been criticized for providing a platform and tolerance for porn of all types, including bestiality, and exploitation of children. For adults with adults, Pink Technology [22] has developed videos that allow the viewer to be in the scene, but not actively participating with the actors. Others like VRsexlab have been created, and more will be added no doubt [23]. In his book, *Augmented Reality Law, Privacy, and Ethics* [24], Brian Wassom examines the social, legal, and ethical issues surrounding augmented reality technology, and in chapter 13, examines the issues around addiction and pornography.

It can't, and shouldn't be ignored, and will always be with us.

6.1.3.5 Educational

Augmented reality applications are used to complement standard curriculum, from primary school to university. Graphics, text video and audio can be superimposed into textbooks, flashcards and other educational reading material through embedded markers. Furthermore, the augmented information can be regularly updated so school books won't go out of date and become obsolete.

Augmented reality enables layers of digital information to be displayed on top of the physical world that can be viewed through smart-glasses, tablets, and smart phones. augmented reality is a great interface for this because it can quickly bounce around many types of media such as detailed diagrams, engaging graphics, and interactive maps.

Students can learn mechanical engineering concepts, math or geometry through an application named, Construct3D, a Studierstube system (http://studierstube.icg.tugraz.at/main.php). It is an active learning process in which students learn to learn with technology. augmented reality can aid students in understanding chemistry by allowing them to visualize the spatial structure of a molecule and interact with a virtual model of it. Augmented reality can also enable students of physiology to visualize different systems of the human body in three dimensions.

The feedback loop between teachers and students is also improved by using augmented reality glasses. And the teacher has the opportunity to call on more reference sources in answering student's questions.

In 2013, in order to improve classroom interaction, researchers at the Carlos III University in Madrid developed a prototype of smart glasses based on augmented reality. When wearing the augmented reality glasses, the teacher could see above the student's heads, icons indicating their state of mind at any given time, i.e. showing when they have a question or whether they have or have not understood the point s/he is making (Fig. 6.51).

The prototype that the Madrid researchers have developed is controlled by gestures, captured with a Microsoft Kinect. The system, called Augmented Lecture Feedback System (ALFs), requires professors to wear augmented reality glasses in order to see symbols above students' heads and to facilitate communication between students and professors [25].

Fig. 6.51 Icons above students indicate their state of mind indicating when they have a question or whether they have or have not understood the point the teacher is making (Source: Atelier)

This reminds me of Frank Baum's novel, *The Master Key: An Electrical Fairy Tale*, where he described a set of electronic glasses called a "character marker," that could reveal a person's hidden personality traits. (see Sect. 5.1).

Chris Beyerle, a South Carolina math and engineering teacher, put together a list of 32 augmented reality applications for the classroom, which can be seen here: https://edshelf.com/shelf/cbeyerle-augmented-reality-for-education/.

Museums and Galleries
Students will also be able to employ smartphones, or augmented reality smartglasses of their own, or those provided for them at museums (Fig. 6.52).

Augmented reality can be a part of a school trip to a museum or a historical monument, where all the crucial data like facts and figures about relevant landmarks can be instantly displayed on the screen.

6.1.3.6 Navigation and Control
Augmented reality has been used for assistance in flying aircraft going back to 1937 in German aircraft.

Aircraft
Real world overlays flight information on what the pilot can see on the windshield.

Augmented reality in aircraft usually consists of three basic components: a projector, the screen or windshield (also called a combiner), and a computer generation system. A head-up display in general, and especially in an aircraft, presents data without requiring users to look away from their usual viewpoints. There are two types of computer generated display, actual or real world, and synthetic (Fig. 6.53).

Fig. 6.52 Students can learn more about exhibits with augmented reality (Source: British Museum)

Fig. 6.53 A real world copilot's head-up display in a C-130J aircraft (Wikipedia)

Fig. 6.54 The Landform synthetic vision display for helicopter pilots, circa 1997 (Wikipedia)

Head-up displays for pilots date back to the pre-World War II reflector sight, a parallax-free optical sight device developed for military fighter aircraft [26]. A gyro gunsight was added to a reticle that moved based on the speed and turn rate of the aircraft, and calibrated so the amount of lead needed to hit a target while maneuvering could be projected.

However, pilots must fly in all types of weather, and sometimes can't see, and have to rely on just the aircraft's basic six instruments. That is known as Instrument Flight Rules (IFR). To augment that synthetic vision was developed.

Synthetic vision was developed by NASA and the U.S. Air Force in the late 1970s and 1980s in support of advanced cockpit research, and in the 1990s as part of the Aviation Safety Program. Also known as Highway In The Sky (HITS), or Path-In-The-Sky, augmented reality was used to depict the projected path of the aircraft in perspective view.

Using augmented reality for navigation was first implemented in NASA's X-38 in 1998. It used what was called at the time a Hybrid Synthetic Vision system that overlaid map data on video to provide enhanced navigation for the spacecraft. The map data came from LandForm software, developed by Rapid Imaging in 1995. The X38 was one of the first in-manned system but the use of synthetic vision was used by manned helicopters in the late 1990s (Fig. 6.54).

Augmented reality became common in military, then in 1970 commercial aircraft, and later in drone aircraft and is now as common as a radio in an airplane. Later still it was adopted by private aircraft. In 1998, the Falcon 2000 was the first business jet to be certified (in Category III for a head-up display by the JAA and FAA) [27].

In 2014, Elbit Systems (developers of military augmented reality helmets and HMDs) introduced its ClearVisionan Enhanced vision system and SkyLens

Wearable head-up display and a fusion of sensor images and synthetic vision in its enhanced vision systems (EVSs) for commercial pilots.

In 2009, an independent Flight Safety Foundation study concluded that Head-Up Guidance System Technology would likely have positively influenced the outcome of hundreds of accidents [28]. The study found that 38% of all accidents were likely or highly likely to have been prevented if the pilot had a head-up display.

In 2012, one of the first private aircraft head-up display systems was shown at the Experimental Aviation Association's (EAA) annual gathering at the Oshkosh event. Italian based PAT Avionics demonstrated its G-HULP system at the Oshkosh in the USA (Fig. 6.55).

Like the military versions, the G-HULP head-up display uses laser projection technology, superimposing information on a transparent 7×3.5-inch (178×89 mm) display. The company has since gone out of business.

By 2015 more retro-fitable visor-mounted head-up displays were introduced (Fig. 6.56).

The MGF head-up display from MyGoFlight, contains three primary components: a projector unit, a combiner and an interface to an iPad or other computing source. The imagery appears to be floating out in front of the pilot, focused at infinity to minimize the time it takes to look at information and the outside world (Fig. 6.57).

Fig. 6.55 Retro-fitable head-up display for private aircraft (Source: PAT Avionics)

Fig. 6.56   Head-up display for private aircraft (Source: MyGoFlight)

Fig. 6.57   A DigiLens enabled HGS 3500 head-up display from Rockwell Collins for private aircraft (Source: Digilens)

Augmented reality for private aircraft can be a retro-fitted display as illustrated in the previous two images, or a pair of smart-glasses.

In 2011, NASA's Langley Research Center in Virginia, began development of an augmented reality headset for commercial pilots [29]. The research center's

Fig. 6.58 NASA's
prototype augmented
reality headset for
commercial pilots (Source:
NASA)

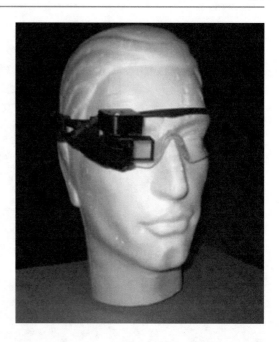

development of the augmented reality display system evolved out of NASA's
Synthetic Vision technology (Fig. 6.58).

The NASA system includes a head-worn display, a head tracker, computer hardware and software, and a voice recognition system. The system displays computer-
generated images of the airport, taxi route and traffic information on the head-up
display, replacing traditional paper airport maps that pilots typically carry. NASA
announced at the time it was seeking companies interested in licensing the rights to
manufacture, commercialize and market the system.

The first commercially available augmented reality smart-glasses for pilots was
introduced by Aero Glass at the annual EAA Oshkosh show in August 2014, in
Wisconsin (Fig. 6.59).

The glasses, made by Epson, gave the pilot a heading and direction, plus information about other aircraft in the area, and weather information (Fig. 6.60).

In 2015 Aero Glass introduced a new system based on Osterhout Design Group's
R-7 smart-glasses.

Consumers also began using augmented reality smart-glasses for flying drones.
In 2015, smart-glasses manufacturers began promoting the use of the glasses for
flying drones. Epson, one of the leading suppliers of smart-glasses at the time,
reported that sales to the enterprise over the past four years were outpaced by sales
to hobbyist drone pilots. The translucent smart-glasses allow pilots to see their
drones plus additional data, such as a live video feed from a drone's on-board camera, simultaneously.

Fig. 6.59   Areo Glass first
generation smart-glasses
for pilots (Source: Aero
Glass)

Fig. 6.60   What the pilot sees wearing augmented reality smart-glasses (Source: Aero Glass)

Walking and Driving

The most important functions in driving are being able to see and know where you
are going, A head-up display can project information on the windshield, to inform
the driver of the car's speed, where to turn, the location of lane markings, how close
the car in front of you is, and near-by points of interest such as gas stations, or parking lots.

The first automotive head-up display was introduced in 1988, by the Hughes and
EDS divisions of GM. It was offered as an option on the 1988 Oldsmobile Cutlass

Fig. 6.61   The Corvette, which got the industry's first color head-up display in 1996 (Source: Car and Driver)

Supreme Indy Pace Car replica. GM was also first with a color head-up display, in the 1996 Corvette (Fig. 6.61).

Those early automotive head-up displays only offered speed and fuel gauge displays. Navigation came with the introduction of GPS receivers in automobiles and inexpensive map data bases from Google and others. In-car navigation systems were first deployed in 2003, and the information made available to head-up displays. However, stand-alone GPS systems from Garmin and Tom Tom were also used as early as 2010 with independent head-up display suppliers.

The first automotive aftermarket head-up display was the WeGo offered in 2010 by Taiwan-based Springteg. It provided a virtual image in a head-up display system using the windshield (Fig. 6.62).

The head-up display can also be connected to the car's on-board cameras and adaptive cruise control so it could very well be one of the best safety systems of your car. Newer head-up display systems make use of infrared cameras to see through fog and detect the lines on the road, or the car ahead of you that may not be visible. It will also be able to show you how to maneuver around another car to avoid an accident or other road hazards. The cameras will also be used to spot and outline road signs for cautions or distances.

Swiss-based WayRay introduced a retrofittable system called Navion. The device projects holographic arrows on the windshield that coordinate with the road in front of you using a proprietary technology the company calls Infinity Focus. Only the vehicle's driver is able to see the projection. This enhances safety levels by keeping focus on the road, rather than looking down at an in-dash screen, or a smartphone (Fig. 6.63).

Fig. 6.62 Navigation data is projected via a head-up display directly in front of the driver onto the windshield (Source: Springteg)

Fig. 6.63 Navion uses gesture control and voice command for communications with the driver (Source: WayRay)

The system integrates with a smartphone. The company has apps that can be downloaded, projected onto the windshield,

The technology displays an image on a desired distance from driver's eyes—on the road ahead. It's comfortable for driver's eye's and makes driving safer, because the need for glancing away on your smartphone is eliminated.

Basically, it looks like a videogame where you follow the arrow in front of your car.

You can find several "smartphone HUDs" that simply have a holder for a smartphone and combiner (semi-mirror) for the display, which can be the windshield if properly positioned.

Road Signs

Automotive HUDs will also be used in the front facing cameras in cars with clever image processing software to see and then display highway signs such as speed limits, railroad crossing warnings, highway exits, and other road signs a driver might miss for one reason or another.

To ensure the car doesn't feed misinformation to the driver, such systems will cross-reference the information from the camera with navigation and current vehicle data to prevent a spurious warning that the limit is 70 mph (113 km/h) while driving on a two-lane suburban street.

Summary

Navigation on the ground by pedestrians and in cars using augmented reality became commercially viable in 2010. Consumer augmented reality navigation was introduced in the early 2010s. Wikitude Navigation was a proof of concept project with the first pedestrian and car navigation system that integrated an augmented reality display and eliminating the need for a map. First released in 2010, and originally titled "Drive," it presented users with turn-by-turn GPS based guidance, and the convenience and safety of not having to take their eyes off where they're going.

6.1.3.7 Translation

In 2011, Chinese social media giant Tencent introduced QQ Hui Yan, an augmented reality, optical character recognition (OCR) translation application. It used a smartphone's camera to read and translate words.

Prior to its acquisition in spring of 2014, one of the best language translation programs available was from Word lens, developed in 2009 by Otavio Good, John DeWeese, Maia Good, Bryan Lin, and Eric Park and released in 2010. Designed to run locally on a smartphone or tablet, Google wanted it as part of its Glass project which it brought out in 2014 and ended in 2015. Nonetheless, translation programs are now a standard feature in consumer augmented reality devices and are used daily all over the world.

Real-Time Text Translation

Google has made it easier to travel around the world without worrying about the language. It has upgraded its Google Translate application with augmented reality features in it and added many languages (Fig. 6.64).

The company is providing text translation in real time. Here is where augmented reality comes into play. Over 100 languages have been added to the application. All you need to do is open the Google Translate application and using your mobile device's camera you have to hold it over the text and you will see the translated

Fig. 6.64 Real-time sign translation using Google Translate (Source: Google)

word in English. The translation is not one-way. You can translate to and from English with the other languages, except Hindi and Thai.

6.1.3.8 Sports and Training

One of the best known and earliest examples of augmented reality was the synthetic yellow scrimmage-line shown in US football in 1998. However, the idea of generating an on-field marker to help TV viewers identify 1st down distances was conceived and patented by David W. Crain [30], in 1978. Crain showed it to ABC Sports and CBS, but they didn't think the broadcast industry could handle it. However, Sportvision used it and the rest of the industry and the world quickly followed.

Sportsvision expanded the concept of augmented reality in sports broadcasting to include showing the batter's box in baseball, and the trajectory of a thrown US football.

Fox Sports was another early innovator in augmented reality used in sports. The broadcaster introduced the FoxTrax puck tracking system in 1996. This technology made it possible for TV viewers to follow the puck by generating a red tail (Fig. 6.65).

The objective was to put a blue glow around the puck making it easier for people to see and follow during a game. Moreover, when the puck was shot at a speed of over 70 mph, a red tail would appear showing the puck's path.

A standard hockey puck was cut in half and infrared sensors were placed inside of it which sent signals to sensors placed around the arena. The data was transmitted to a FoxTrax truck outside with computers in it to generate the image, and superimpose and synchronize it with the broadcast signal from the cameras in the arena.

However, hockey fans severally disliked the glowing puck, eventually causing the National Hockey League (NHL) to abandon the technology after one game of the 1998 Stanley Cup Finals. Fox Sports spent a tremendous amount of time and

Fig. 6.65 The red tail seen on a hockey shot (Courtesy FOX sports)

money developing this system, yet due to the backlash from hockey's serious fans, had to abandon this innovation. The FoxTrax puck tracking system is a perfect example of how some ICT innovations, no matter how well-intentioned and thought out, can fail.

But Fox was not deterred and carried on with augmented reality techniques, applying them to tennis, football, baseball and golf (Fig. 6.66).

In 2001, Paul Hawkins developed the Hawk-Eye system in the UK. Originally designed for cricket, it became popular in tennis matches for settling disputes, and by 2014 almost every nation had adopted it. In June 2006, a group of investors led by the Wisden Group bought the company, and in 2011 Sony bought the company.

Augmented Reality Extended to Consumers in 2010 in the Form of Smart Glasses

The first augmented reality glasses for sports came from Recon Instruments. Founded in Vancouver, BC in 2009 the company introduced their Recon-Zeal Transcend augmented reality goggles, targeted at skiers and snowboarders in 2010. Using a micro LCD display, the goggles displayed speed, latitude/longitude, altitude, vertical distance traveled, total distance traveled, chrono/stopwatch mode, a run-counter, temperature and time.

In 2015 the company introduced their new lighter augmented reality sports sunglasses with side-mounted head-up display system which included a camera. Designed for running and cycling with an SDK it could be used for other

Fig. 6.66 Seeing where the ball will go, or should go, has greatly enhanced viewing of sports events (Courtesy of FOX Sports)

Fig. 6.67 Recon's Jet augmented reality glasses for sports (Source: Recon-Intel)

applications as well. Several generations of snow products were launched in between (Fig. 6.67).

Motorola invested in the company in 2013, and in 2016 Intel bought the company.

Augmented reality headsets designed for sports may incorporate additional biological sensors. For example, researchers at The University of Texas at Dallas have demonstrated a biosensor that can reliably detect and quantify glucose in human sweat [31].

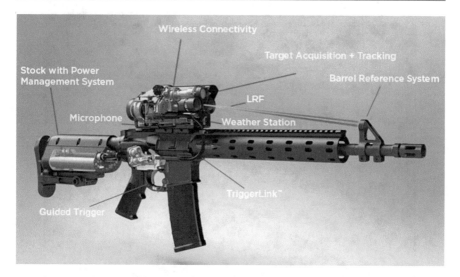

Fig. 6.68   The augmented reality weapon (TrackingPoint)

Augmented Reality in Hunting

Dating back to 1901 when Sir Howard Grubb patented his collimating-telescope gun-sight (see Sect. 5.1), people have wanted to have super shooting skills. With the rapid advancement of technology combined with smaller, lighter, less power-hungry electronics, and at low cost, it's now possible to have the same tracking and fire-control capabilities found in advanced fighter jets (Fig. 6.68).

Shooters of any skill level can now shoot better than the best shooters who ever lived. The TrackingPoint Precision-Guided Firearm provides precision at extreme distances and high target velocities (Fig. 6.69).

The augmented reality scope's digital display shows the field of view, range-to-target, target velocity, shot angle, compass heading, battery status, Wi-Fi status, wind velocity, and direction, kill zone size, ammunition type, temperature, barometric pressure, and time of day.

6.1.4   Summary

The number of augmented reality applications is almost endless and new ideas are being developed every year. For every company highlighted in the section, many more could just as easily have been mentioned and even more are being developed as this is being written. As the technology is further deployed even more ideas will be generated. Augmented reality brings such richness to our lives we will be asking it to do more and more for us for a very long time.

Google lit up the consumer's imagination about wearable augmented reality with Glass in 2012, Pokémon GO engaged them in 2016. Now augmented reality is recognized and anticipated. For the immediate future, the AR industry will continue to

Fig. 6.69 The weapon's HUD displays target, and vital pieces of data including range-to-target, target velocity, shot angle, compass heading, and battery status (TrackingPoint)

be supported and promoted by industrial, scientific and helmet applications (first responders, inspectors, dangerous repair situations, military, etc.). There are two classes of augmented reality: wearable and non-wearable. Non-wearable would include the head-up display in your car, or watching augmented reality on TV (e.g., scrimmage lines). This discussion is about wearable augmented reality.

Vuforia, one of the industry's most advanced and widely adopted augmented reality platforms has been used by more than 20,000 apps that have been downloaded more than 200 million times worldwide. And yet for all that effort, there are very few examples of mobile games or advertisements that became a runaway success because of the way they used augmented reality technology.

All the non-consumer wearable augmented reality systems and applications are specific, and have a specific ROI associated with them. The glasses or helmets are purpose built, not general-purpose, and each hardware supplier (in 2016 I identified 75 of them) is trying to satisfy a specific niche or two (or three if they are really not focused or overly ambitious).

Believe it or not (and sickness aside) virtual reality is actually much easier to do than augmented reality. In virtual reality the user is looking at a screen in a closed and controllable environment, and all of the screen is being used. In augmented reality, only a portion of the users FoV is used for computer generated content, and getting that area right-sized, with the right amount of transparency, in focus under varying conditions of glaze, presence, and consistency of content is immensely challenging, and so far, has many unsolved problems. The non-consumer users can tolerate a lot of fails in the overall system as long as the one key feature they need

Fig. 6.70 For consumers
to adopt augmented reality
the glasses will have to be
attractive and compelling
(Art by Patrick Farley,
from David Brin novel,
Existence)

Fig. 6.71 Laforge's
Augmented reality eyewear
with a normal look
(Laforge)

is done properly. For consumers, however, the machinery of the augmented reality experience should not be evident to the user (Fig. 6.70).

One of the most ambitious companies was LA-based Optical, which introduced Shima prescription augmented reality eyewear. Laforge Optical promised attractive consumer style augmented reality glasses, describing itself as a California dream, made in Italy. Ironically, the company was not named after the character Geordi La Forge from Star Trek who was blind and used augmented classes to see (Fig. 6.71).

One other company that proposed to offer consumer style augmented reality glasses is Meta, with the Meta Pro but then dropped it. Several other companies Like Ricon (Intel), and Sony have offered glasses with sidecar projectors like

Google Glass. These may be acceptable for special applications such as skiing, cycling and running.

Of the 80 companies, as of the writing of this book, Laforge is the only one promising truly consumer style augmented reality glasses. Whether or not Laforge can actually deliver such glasses is really beside the point; the point is none of the other 80 suppliers are even taking on the challenge.

Having said that I could then segment the hardware suppliers into consumer and commercial. BMW has offered an augmented reality helmet for motorcycle riders. The other motorcycle helmet company to announce, but shut down, was Skully. And, like Recon, BMW is addressing a special market.

A national survey company, Colloquy ran a survey that found American consumers thought wearable devices were too expensive (mind you, that includes watches and health monitor systems too, not just augmented reality) [32]. Over half of those surveyed said they didn't know enough about wearables and didn't understand them. On the other hand, 35% of consumers said wearable technology is nerdy, but "cool nerdy."

There is a gap in where the general media is pushing (believing) how wearables are going to enter our lives. However, they are not going start with the consumer, despite many companies' desire (or the media) for this to be the case. All of these devices need to find a practical application and usage, which is going to start in industry, enterprise, military, education, medical and entertainment. The notion of wearing a wearable beyond an immediate need or function is not real now. Some people think it could take 10 or 15 years for there to be enough functionality to make them more ubiquitous, and suggest people may use them (or don them) as needed, and not wear them all of the time.

I don't share that view, and I think as soon as we get low cost, good looking glasses, with useful apps, augmented reality wearables will allow users to put their smartphone in their pocket and forget about it. The phone will become a server, and comm center for our glasses. Moore's law and the imaginative, creativity of developers and suppliers will always surprise us. We are not just an information driven society, we are an ideas driven society, and it's almost impossible to predict what new ideas will appear. The people who do that do write science-fiction.

References

1. Feiner, S.K., Webster, A.C., Krueger III, T.E., MacIntyre, B., & Keller, E.J. (1995, Summer). *Architectural anatomy*, Department of Computer Science, School of Architecture. New York: Columbia University, 10027. Journal presence: Teleoperators and virtual environments archive, *4*(3), 318–325, MIT Press, Cambridge, MA.
2. Willers, D. (2006). *Augmented reality at Airbus,* International Symposium on Mixex & Augmented Reality, http://ismar06.tinmith.net/data/3a-Airbus.pdf.
3. *Groundbreaking augmented reality-based reading curriculum launches*, "PRweb", 23 October 2011.
4. Keerthi, K., *Using virtual reality and augmented reality to teach human anatomy*, The University of Toledo Digital Repository, May 2011, http://utdr.utoledo.edu/cgi/viewcontent.cgi?article=1625&context=theses-dissertations

5. Hoffelder, N.. *Augmented reality shows up in a Japanese textbook (video)*, April, 2012, http://the-digital-reader.com/2012/04/08/augmented-reality-shows-up-in-a-japanese-textbook-video/

6. Bajura, F., Ohbuchi Bajura, M., Fuchs, H., & Ohbuchi, R. (1992). Merging virtual objects with the real world: seeing ultrasound imagery within the patient. *ACM, 26*(2), 203–210. doi:10.1145/142920.134061.

7. Zhu, E., Hadadgar, A., Masiello, I., & Zary N.. *Augmented reality in healthcare education: An integrative review*, http://www.ncbi.nlm.nih.gov/pmc/articles/PMC4103088/

8. Boud, A. C., Haniff, D. J., Baber C., & Steiner S. J.. *Virtual reality and augmented reality as a training tool for Assembly Tasks*, Proceedings of the IEEE International Conference on Information Visualization, 1999, pp. 32–36. Grubb, Howard, *A new collimating-telescope gun sight for large and small ordnance*, The Scientific Transactions of the Royal Dublin Society March 20 1901.

9. Lee, K. (2012, March). *Augmented Reality in Education and Training*, (PDF). Techtrends: Linking Research & Practice To Improve Learning 56(2). Retrieved 2014-05-15.

10. Davies, P. *How to measure enterprise AR impact*, https://www.youtube.com/watch?v=P-qJ6U-ixX0&feature=youtu.be&list=PLV7deeu6k7SjpDldZJT91sKQg2qyEBYzV

11. Babb, G. *Augmented reality can increase productivity*, AREA blog » Analysis, http://thearea.org/augmented-reality-can-increase-productivity/

12. Papagiannis, H. *Augmented reality applications: Helping the blind to see*, Tech Innovation, Intel, February 10, 2015. https://iq.intel.com/augmented-reality-applications-helping-the-blind-to-see/

13. Ortiz-Catalan, M., Guðmundsdóttir, R.A., Kristoffersen, M.B., et al. *Phantom motor execution facilitated by machine learning and augmented reality as treatment for phantom limb pain: a single group, clinical trial in patients with chronic intractable phantom limb pain*, published online in the medical journal The Lancet on December 2016, http://www.thelancet.com/journals/lancet/article/PIIS0140-6736(16)31598-7/fulltext

14. http://www.loyalreview.com/www-hallmark-comextra-watch-hallmark-webcam-greetings/

15. Retail Data: 100 Stats About Retail, eCommerce & Digital Marketing, https://www.nchannel.com/blog/retail-data-ecommerce-statistics/

16. Peddie, J. (2013) *The history of visual magic in computers*. London: Springer. ISBN 978-1-4471-4931-6.

17. Augmented reality Tennis. https://www.researchgate.net/publication/29488914_AR_tennis. December 2005.

18. *The Invisible Train*. https://www.youtube.com/watch?v=CmZhCUhDtRE

19. First augmented reality game for a console. http://www.guinnessworldrecords.com/world-records/first-augmented-reality-game-for-a-console [Edition 2010]

20. How Pokémon, G. O. (2016, July 21) Took Augmented Reality Mainstream. http://knowledge.wharton.upenn.edu/article/how-Pokémon-go-took-augmented-reality-mainstream/

21. Brian D. Wassom, *augmented reality eyewear & the problem of Porn*, http://www.wassom.com/augmented-reality-eyewear-the-problem-of-porn-from-the-archives.html

22. Hartley, A. (2010, January 10) *Pink technology develops augmented reality porn*. http://www.techradar.com/news/world-of-tech/future-tech/pink-technology-develops-augmented-reality-porn-662635?src=rss&attr=all

23. Rampolla, J. (2015, March 12). *Virtual/augmented reality adult porn bridges gap to augmented child porn .... Not if, but when*. http://www.ardirt.com/general-news/virtual-augmented-reality-adult-porn-bridges-gap-to-augmented-child-porn-not-if-but-when.html

24. Wassom, B. (2014, December 10). *Augmented reality law, privacy, and ethics*. Elsevier. ISBN-13: 978–0128002087

25. http://augmentedtomorrow.com/augmented-reality-glasses-helping-students/

26. Jarrett, D. N. (2005). *Cockpit engineering* (p. 189). Ashgate Pub. ISBN 0-7546-1751-3. ISBN 9780754617518. Retrieved 2012-07-14.

27. *Falcon 2000 Becomes First Business Jet Certified Category III A by JAA and FAA*; Aviation Weeks Show News Online September 7, 1998.

28. *Head-up guidance system technology—A clear path to increasing flight safety,* http://www.mygoflight.com/content/Flight%20Safety%20HGS%20HUD%20Study%20Nov%202009.pdf

29. *NASA develops Augmented Reality headset for commercial pilots.* http://phys.org/news/2012-03-nasa-ar-headset-commercial.html.

30. Crain, D.W. TV Object locator and image identifier. US Patent 4,084,184.

31. *Bioengineers Create Sensor That Measures Perspiration to Monitor Glucose Levels.* http://www.utdallas.edu/news/2016/10/13-32235_Bioengineers-Create-Sensor-That-Measures-Perspirat_story-sidebar.html?WT.mc_id=NewsHomePage

32. https://www.colloquy.com/latest-news/passing-fad-or-cool-nerdy-colloquy-research-shows-63-of-u-s-consumers-wary-of-wearable-prices/

Software Tools and Technologies

7

Abstract

Several companies are offering tool kits to aid developers in creating applications that work well in an augmented reality environment. A few of the most popular tools and APIs are covered in this chapter.

Large companies will usually have an advantage by offering partners advanced hardware and accompanying software tools. Nonetheless, the technology has demonstrated it does not love closed gardens especially at times when innovation is required to help nascent industries find their potential. Open standards will eventually win out to make room for new ideas and approaches.

Several companies are offering tool kits to aid developers in creating applications that work well in an augmented reality environment. I have listed a few here to give the reader a flavor of what is involved in such tools, which can be very esoteric and technical—I have tried to avoid that, but we will have to get a little technical in this section.

The companies listed in the following sections do not represent all of the suppliers of toolkits and development programs, and do not necessarily represent the best or most popular, just ones that I picked at random or had some familiarity with. So, apologies to all those I missed, but once again, this was not meant to be a buyer's guide.

An augmented reality system is basically a computer with sensor input (camera, microphone, etc.), processors, and output (display, earphones, etc.). To bring all those components to life and make them useful there have to be applications. The applications communicate with the processors and sensors via an operating system (OS) (e.g., Android) and a specialized software layer known as the application program interface (API) which in turn requires the processor supplier to create specific software for the processor known as a driver (device-driver) to communicate with

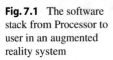

Fig. 7.1 The software
stack from Processor to
user in an augmented
reality system

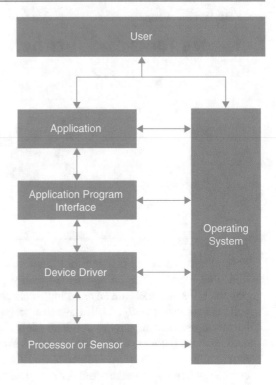

the API. The generalized relationship between these elements is shown in the following diagram (Fig. 7.1).

The software toolkits in an augmented reality, or any computer-based system have, as you might imagine, an even deeper segmentation, which consists of the API, libraries of specialized functions, and in the case of development systems, developer user-interfaces, as illustrated in the following diagram (Fig. 7.2).

Software toolkits are a set of utility programs, a set of software routines or a complete integrated set of software utilities that are used to develop and maintain applications and databases.

A software development kit (SDK or "devkit") is typically a set of software development tools that allow the creation of applications for a certain device. SDKs are employed to enrich applications with advanced functionalities, advertisements, push notifications and more. Most application developers implement specific software development kits for an application type (e.g., augmented reality) or a device. Some SDKs are critical if the developer wants to create an application for a specific operating system (e.g., iOS, Android, Windows, etc.) and/or applications unique to that operating system. For example, the development of an Android application requires an SDK with Java, for iOS apps an iOS SDK with Apple's Swift, and for MS Windows the .NET Framework SDK with .NET.

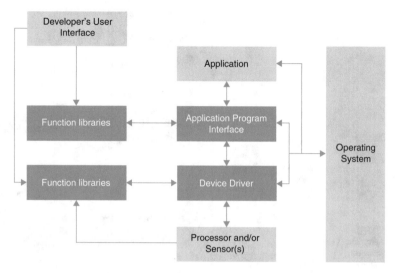

Fig. 7.2 Software toolkits consist of libraries and device drivers

The block diagram of an augmented reality system will look something like the illustration in (Fig. 7.3). The specific function blocks, sensors, radios, and output devices will vary by manufacturer and application. However, the basic configuration will include a camera, location sensors (GPS, Magnetometer), communications (at least Wi-Fi), and a display. It should be recognized that a fully robust augmented reality system is akin to having a supercomputer on your head.

There are very few standards in augmented reality so having the ability to reprogram an augmented reality system in the field is extremely important to extend the useful life of a system, as well as to prototype and develop, and test a new product.

One of the most critical elements in an augmented reality system is the sensor hub. The sensor hub accommodates all types of sensors and in a complex software driven manner allocates the sensor data to the processors (i.e., DSP, GPU, and CPU). Several sensors need real-time access to the processors (e.g., the camera sensors), while others can be sampled less often (e.g., compass). Since there are several sensors, radios, and output devices in an augmented reality system, several device drivers are needed, as well as process or flow drivers and APIs.

Some augmented reality device builders have developed their own proprietary APIs and device drivers, as well as their own dedicated hardware for certain functions within their augmented reality device. However, for the most part augmented reality device suppliers use commercial off-the-shelf (COTS) heterogeneous processors such as the type found in smartphones, tablets, and embedded systems. Those COTS processors however, also vary depending on what components they contain. For example, some have one image signal processor (ISP), some have two, and some have none. Some COTS processors have a sensor hub while others do not, and some have a DSP while others do not.

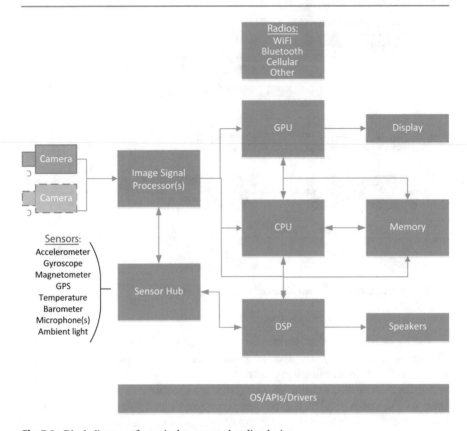

Fig. 7.3   Block diagram of a typical augmented reality device

The easier and preferred way to design and develop a system, almost any system, is to use open standards. Open standards spread the development costs among several companies and individuals (the members of the standards body), and insure interchangeability as well as the most up to data versions of the software.

7.1   Khronos Group

One such body that creates royalty-free, open standards is the Khronos Group [1]. Established in 2000 to stabilize and harmonize APIs for graphics processors (GPUs), the organization has steadily grown to encompass parallel-processing program languages (OpenCL), inter-processor communications (EGL), new generation 3D graphics (Vulkan) and several vision-processing APIs. The organization has been at the forefront in developing APIs for both augmented and virtual reality.

Khronos has a broad plan for open standards to address all parts of the camera, vision, and sensor fusion pipeline. OpenVX is the key API for vision processing acceleration and was launched in 2013. At the time of writing the need and direction

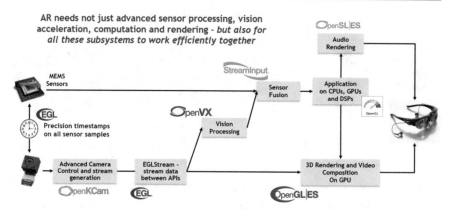

Fig. 7.4 Khronos APIs for augmented reality (Khronos)

Fig. 7.5 OpenVX is an
API for low power vison
acceleration (Khronos)

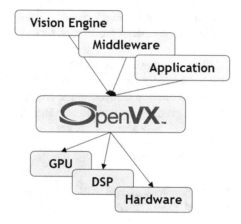

for OpenKCAM for advanced camera control, and StreamInput for sensor fusion, were still under evaluation.

Figure 7.4 shows the Khronos APIs for augmented reality and the interconnections of those APIs.

Fast and power efficient vision processing is key for compelling augmented reality. The landscape of vision processing APIs is quite encompassing and so different APIs are used to access different types of processors for vision processing.

OpenCL provides general purpose computes acceleration and so can be used for vision processing, including neural network acceleration. However, Khronos also has a specific vision processing API, called OpenVX that is targeted at vision acceleration in real-time, mobile and embedded platforms. OpenVX has a higher level of abstraction than OpenCL for performance portability across diverse processor architectures such as multi-core CPUs, GPUs, DSPs and DSP arrays, ISPs and dedicated hardware—important for very lower power vision processing (Fig. 7.5).

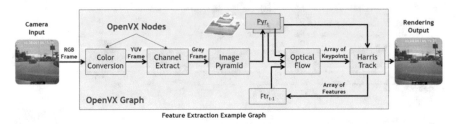

Feature Extraction Example Graph

Fig. 7.6 OpenVX graph about the needed processing before execution starts (Khronos)

An OpenVX programmer connects vision functions—OpenVX 'nodes'—into a graph with no assumption about the acceleration hardware. This enables the OpenVX silicon implementer to map the graph onto any processor—providing application portability to a very wide variety of acceleration architectures—including dedicated hardware for very low power consumption which can't be reached by programmable APIs Fig. 7.6).

On programmable processors, OpenVX is often accelerated by OpenCL if it is available.

Neural Network Processing is becoming essential for many vision processing tasks, especially including pattern recognition. The OpenVX Neural Network Extension enables Convolutional Neural Network topologies to be represented as OpenVX graphs—which can be mixed with traditional vision nodes.

7.1.1 OpenCV

In addition to standard APIs, there are various industry open libraries such as OpenCV. OpenCV (Open Source Computer Vision) is a library of programming functions for real-time computer vision. Originally developed by Intel's research center in Nizhny Novgorod (Russia) in 1999, it was later supported by Willow Garage and is now maintained by Itseez (http://itseez.com/). The library is cross-platform and free for use under the open-source BSD license (Fig. 7.7).

After a developer decides on which APIs and driver toolkits to use, the next step is to pick the applications development toolkit. There are several to choose from, open systems, and industry or proprietary systems. A few of the more popular ones are discussed, as well as a couple of examples of their use by developers.

7.2 ARToolkit

The ARToolkit developed by Hirokazu Kato of Nara Institute of Science and Technology is a software library for building Augmented Reality applications and was first released in 1999. These are applications that involve the overlay of virtual

OpenCV

- **Extensive and widely used open source vision library - written in optimized C/C++**
  - Free-use BSD license
- **C++, C, Python and Java interfaces**
  - Windows, Linux, Mac OS, iOS and Android
- **Increasingly taking advantage of heterogeneous processing using OpenCL**
  - OpenCV 3.X Transparent API; single API entry for each function/algorithm
  - Dynamically loads OpenCL runtime if available; otherwise falls back to CPU code
  - Runtime Dispatching; no recompilation!

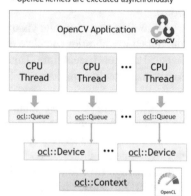

Fig. 7.7   OpenCV 3.X will transparently use OpenCL is available—see slide 16

Fig. 7.8   Seeing things that aren't really there (Courtesy the HIT Lab, University of Washington)

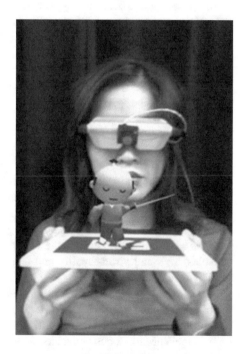

imagery on the real world. For example, in the image to the right a three-dimensional virtual character appears standing on a real card. It can be seen by the user in the head set display they are wearing. When the user moves the card, the virtual character moves with it and appears attached to the real object (Fig. 7.8).

One of the key difficulties in developing augmented reality applications is the problem of tracking the user's viewpoint. To know from what viewpoint to draw the virtual imagery, the application needs to know where the user is looking in the real world.

ARToolKit uses computer vision algorithms to solve this problem. The ARToolKit video tracking libraries calculate the real camera position and orientation relative to physical markers in real time. This enables the easy development of a wide range of Augmented Reality applications. Some of the features of ARToolKit include:

- Single camera position/orientation tracking.
- Tracking code that uses simple black squares.
- The ability to use any square marker patterns.
- Easy camera calibration code.
- Fast enough for real time augmented reality applications.
- SGI IRIX, Linux, MacOS and Windows OS distributions.
- Distributed with complete source code, by Daqri

In the spring of 2015, the augmented reality startup Daqri, which was working on a HoloLens-style augmented reality helmet and already offering a number of augmented reality software tools, acquired ARToolworks, the company behind the popular open-source ARToolKit libraries. As part of the acquisition, Daqri will make ARToolKit's commercial Pro tools available for free under an open source license. The company said it will continue to invest in ARToolKit, too.

7.2.1 Vuforia

One of the best-known augmented reality tool sets, with over 300,000 developers globally, and as mentioned previously, used in more than 35,000 applications which have driven more than 300 million app installs. In 2016 Parametric Technology company (PTC), owner of Vuforia, announced a partnership with Unity to integrate the Vuforia platform into Unity's popular game engine and development platform. Unity is a cross-platform game engine that runs on 21 platforms from PCs to game consoles, TVs and virtual reality and augmented reality systems, and counts 5.5 million developers.

Vuforia enables 3D content to be placed in physical environments. The core of the offering is the Vuforia Engine, which provides computer vision functionality to recognize objects and reconstruct environments. One of Vuforia's recognition features is the VuMark, a customizable visual code that can be affixed to any product or machine—either manually using a decal, or automatically printed during the manufacturing process. It is intended to visually indicate to a user that an augmented reality experience is available, such as step-by-step instructions for assembly, use, cleaning, repair, inspection, etc.

Vuforia enables 3D content to be placed in physical environments. The core of the offering is the Vuforia Engine, which provides computer vision functionality to recognize objects and reconstruct environments.

Vuforia's image targets allow developers to recognize and track images that are printed on a planar surface. Vuforia can recognize up to one-thousand images stored locally on a device or millions of different images stored in the cloud. Image targets are commonly used to place content on products such as books, magazines and product packaging.

Vuforia's 3D reconstruction stack, Smart Terrain, provides developers with access to the surfaces and objects found in the environment. With Smart Terrain, developers can create AR games that can interact physical objects in the world.

One of Vuforia's recognition features is the VuMark, a customizable visual code that can be affixed to any product or machine—either manually using a decal, or automatically printed during the manufacturing process. It is intended to visually indicate to a user that an AR experience is available, such as step-by-step instructions for assembly, use, cleaning, repair, inspection, etc.

The VuMark Designer allows Adobe Illustrator users to create VuMarks from existing graphics and brand assets such as logos. This allows them to create VuMarks that are visually appealing, while capable of encoding any kind of data, such as a serial number or URL.

Creation of new 3D content remains complicated, labor-intensive, and is cost prohibitive for many augmented reality deployments at scale. Yet there are existing repositories of 3D content created with CAD tools, and PTC is in the process of unlocking them.

The goal is to make development simpler. Vuforia is a fine tool for people who write code. But many people such as those who create technical drawings and instructional content, don't write code. They could build augmented reality experiences if they had the right tools. ThingWorx Studio, was developed from the Vuforia platform and from PTC's 3D background.

ThingWorx Studio will enable a content creator to build an augmented reality experience from existing 3D content—whether created with PTC or 3rd-party tools. And with just a few clicks, it can be published to the cloud. Once published, the ThingWorx View application can scan a "ThingMark" to present the user with relevant experiences to download and launch.

Additionally, ThingWorx Studio enables IOT solution builders to create virtual dashboards for connected products. Because it's integrated with PTC's ThingWorx IOT platform, developers can create virtual gauges and attach them to sensors that will deliver real-time data. They can be published and launched from ThingWorx View.

The Vuforia 6.1 release includes full support for Microsoft HoloLens. Some of the things it can be used for are listed here: https://library.vuforia.com/

Other tool sets (such as Augment, ScopeAR, and ViewAR) are built on Vuforia.

7.2.2 Augment

Founded in October 2011, and based in Paris France, Augment has become one of the leaders in augmented reality product visualization. The company offers brands, retailers and manufacturers its augmented reality eCommerce SDK for native mobile app and web (javascript) integrations.

Fig. 7.9 Augment places a 3D of a coffee pot on the counter and lets the customer selects the color of the tank (Source: Augment)

The idea of Augment came from Co-founder & CEO Jean-Francois Chianetta's online shopping experience. He was reading reviews that described a product as the biggest of its type. "With photos, you couldn't really see that," he said. The mechanical engineer then came up with a solution—the first application with which you could visualize 3D models in the real world (Fig. 7.9).

The SDK offers retailers the ability to personalize their customer's shopping experience by embedding augmented reality product visualization into their existing eCommerce and mobile commerce platforms. Tapping the visualization button on a smartphone or tablet launches the augmented reality viewer, displaying a rendering of the product in the customer's environment in real time, at scale.

The SDKs include Augment's centralized product database, which includes various 3D models of products. If Augment has the product available in their database, the Augment button appears on the product page. If not, it's not displayed. When the 3D model does become available, the button appears.

The company claims hundreds of product models are being added monthly. However, If the user needs a product model immediately, Augment has an add-on 3D design service available to create the model.

7.2.3   Infinity AR

Founded in 2006, in Petach Tikva, Israel.

Infinity AR says their engine uses basic and affordable hardware: 2D stereoscopic cameras, and inertial measurement units (IMU), in order to provide an

Fig. 7.10 Infinity AR engine overview (Infinity AR)

accurate digital 3D scene representation of one's current physical environment: That in turn enabled an intelligent understanding of the mapped 3D scene by creating a depth map and 3D reconstruction.

Information about a broad series of essential factors that influence the environment and are crucial for building high quality real-life augmented reality experience such as light sources, reflections, transparency, shadows, etc., and recognition of real world objects, their physical characteristics and how they affect the scene (Fig. 7.10).

The company's software augmented reality engine performs six functions:

- Image matching
- Position and orientation

- Physical world digitization
- Control and gesture NUI
- 3D model tracking
- Face to face interaction

Ongoing analysis of user orientation and position in the environment sensing and presenting the environment from the user's point of view is needed because it keeps moving.

InfinityAR's computer vision algorithms are optimized to run on the central augmented realityFo glasses application processor, resulting in low power consumption.

7.2.4   Intel RealSense

Intel's RealSense technology combines hardware and software and the company has been acquiring companies to expand its technology and add capabilities to attract developers. The basic RealSense includes camera streaming capability, essential interfaces, and tools. Additional components can be added on according to the requirements of the application being developed.

Cursor Mode: enables UIs that depend on hand accuracy and stability. Intel offers specific gestures to use for multiple AI purposes.

3D Scan: Captures stationary objects from a sequence of images taken from various viewing angles. The object can then be converted into a 3D triangle mesh and used for simulation, editing/printing, or analysis.

User Background Segmentation: RealSense segregate objects and people from the foreground to enable different backgrounds to be used.

Face Tracking & Recognition: Faces identified and tracked. Intel says it supports 78 landmark points for accuracy, 3D face detection, and roll, pitch and yaw.

Hand Tracking and Gesture recognition: Supports multiple hand gestures such as thumbs up, etc., but is not intended for applications that require accurate hand tracking.

The RealSense SDK can be downloaded at https://software.intel.com/en-us/intel-realsense-sdk/download.

7.2.5   Kudan

Kudan was founded by Tomo Ohno (CEO) in Bristol UK, in 2011, the company started working on augmented reality in 2011 when most people were not very aware of it, and there wasn't much technology available. The company spent four years developing augmented reality tools that it used for various brands and agencies, while it kept on building and enhancing its own engine. After an accumulation of four years of client work and R&D, the company decided its tool set and engine was ready for the big time, and they would offer it to the world at large. It has many unique features targeted at mobile devices.

Like so many other companies in an emerging market (if augmented reality having been started in the 1960s can be considered emerging) the lack of technology and quality in third-party augmented reality and computer vision engines led the company to forge their own. At the time their assessment of the industry was that the existing tools had limited usability and technical applicability in mobile, and that was a roadblock in the evolution of augmented reality and its associated computer vision needs.

Today the company is offering an augmented reality SDK with a 2D/3D recognition engine enabled by proprietary tracking CV technology (e.g., SLAM) and can support marker recognition and marker-less operation.

Kudan says their SLAM engine enables real-time 3D and position tracking from 2D images without depth sensor or stereo camera, by capturing feature points and calculating a real-time trajectory of view point with six-degrees of freedom tracking (6DOF).

7.2.6   GoogleTango

Google's Tango technology is capable of mapping its surroundings and enabling the creation of 3D maps for navigation. The technology allows objects to be correctly placed within a space and can be used for games and tasks such as interior design and real estate. It has applications for first responders. Through its working relationship with Qualcomm and the support for Tango in Qualcomm's snapdragon chips the first AR phones on the market, the Lenovo Phablet 2 Pro and Asus ZenFone AR have support for Tango. These are just the first, more are in the pipeline. Companies are watching the success of these devices but their availability in the market will spur development.

7.2.7   Hololens

Microsoft's Hololens has the potential to define the market after the fact. The company has laid back and observed what has been emerging, and, with Hololens has introduced what it believes is the best headset possible given the potential and restraints of the technology. As one of the main platforms in personal computing, Windows is assured of a leading position in business and industrial applications. Microsoft does not offer a specific Hololens SDK but rather includes it as part of its developer portfolio in Visual Studio. It's part of a continuum of capabilities for the Windows ecosystem. Microsoft is gathering partners from industry, gaming, and consumer applications to create a Windows environment for AR.

Fig. 7.11 Using augmented reality on tablet as a training device (Scope AR)

7.2.8 Scope AR

Founded in 2011 in Edmonton, Alberta Canada, Scope AR is a developer that builds augmented reality products that support industrial customers, by applying the organizations with expertise when and where needed. The company claims to be the creator of the first-ever true augmented reality smart instructions and live support video calling solutions—WorkLink and Remote AR. Through WorkLink, the company provides a set of tools to allow subject matter experts (SME's) to create rich animated, step-by-step augmented reality instructions. The users become their own experts, learning to assemble, repair or troubleshoot problems wherever they are.

Using the information contained in existing CAD files, SME's (not developers or programmers) will be able to create complex motions and clarity that has not been possible before. By adding layers of text description, photographic or video reference imagery, and simple intuitive effects, almost anyone can create an unprecedented quality of instruction without extensive training or previous experience.

Finished modules can be published in real-time, giving employees access to the most current essential work instructions, while also ensuring version control is managed at all times (Fig. 7.11).

Scope AR also provides an augmented reality-based remote assistance application, Remote AR, which is used by companies such as Caterpillar, Assa Abloy and Sealed Air. Remote AR is like Facetime plus augmented reality allowing for an expert to support a technician with annotations and 3D models overlaid on a video from the technician, from anywhere in the world. The latest version of Remote AR now features:

- Depth camera support to eliminate the requirement for markers
- In-application audio for support calls, which eliminates the need to have a separate phone connection in order for the technician and expert to have voice contact
- A low-bandwidth mode so workers can function and receive support even in the most challenging of network conditions
- A Windows Desktop Expert to enable Windows users to provide support to mobile users

Scope AR believes augmented reality will allow everyone in an organization to instantly access the expert guidance needed to perform even the most complex tasks with ease for any device, and easily updated. Additionally, they offer individual's performance measurement, and training—augmented reality makes all this a reality—today, says the company.

7.2.9   ViewAR

Founded in 2010, in Vienna, Austria, ViewAR describes itself as a provider of 3D visualization apps for use in mobile business solutions. At the time the company's founder, Markus Meixner, was working on a gaming project that utilized augmented reality and became convinced that augmented reality's capabilities could and should be expanded from gaming applications into more practical business use. At that time, augmented reality toolsets for businesses were rudimentary so Meixner began ViewAR as a project to combine a front-end that featured 3D design and rendered augmented reality experiences, with a back-end that drew upon database and server infrastructure.

Europe's furniture industry responded to the advantages that augmented reality visualization solutions could offer, and from there the company grew to create custom applications for architects, construction companies, interior designers and more.

The ViewAR SDK comes with a customizable HTML, Javascript, and CSS interface that provides material options for models and their individual parts. Object snapping is available for model manipulation and customization, and the SDK supports tracking systems like Vuforia, Metaio, Pointcloud, RealityCap, and indoo.rs. Depth cameras, Bluetooth gamepads, laser distance meter, common HMDs and other peripherals are supported, the SDK runs on iOS, Android, Windows and WebGL(Browser).

7.3   An Augmented Reality Operating System

In 2013, in Osaka, Japan-based Brilliant Service introduced a new operating system (OS) named Viking, designed for use in augmented reality glasses. The company's goal is to completely replace the cellphone. In 2016 the company changed the name of the OS from Viking to Mirama.

Fig. 7.12 Brilliant Service demonstrating their augmented reality headset (Source: Brilliant Service)

Built using Objective-C programming language, the OS initially offered only basic functions (phone, navigation), but has been expanded to include most of the features found on smartphones today, and more. The company also plans to open up Viking to developers, so they can write applications for the OS.

In addition, the company developed an augmented reality headset, they are calling simply, Glass. The headset was constructed using off-the-shelf parts just for testing purposes. The company used Vuzix STAR 1200XL glasses, a generic RGB camera and a PMD CamBoard nano depth camera to make the demo headset (Fig. 7.12).

The headset was able to perform some very basic facial recognition. When we looked at Johannes Lundberg, the senior engineer responsible for the OS, a box appeared around his head which correctly showed his name. However, when we looked at another booth-goer who was not listed in the system, the software incorrectly identified him as someone else, rather than simply reporting that he was not in the database.

7.4   The Role of Augmented Reality Interfaces

As people in industry and consumers begin to grasp the impact of augmented reality often the question is asked, will it replace common communications-interface tools, such as keyboards, mice and monitors, even smartphones?

Using augmented reality smart glasses can indeed replace the interaction devices we use today such as keyboards, mice and monitors, but not universally or in all situations. In a private, or even semi-private office or cubicle, an office worker, engineer, or manager could lean back (feet on the desk optional) and through voice recognition dictate memos, answer email, write blogs, and fill out forms. The transaction, document, or web page would appear in the user's augmented glasses.

In many instances, it will be more efficient and easier to use, and provide freedom from being anchored to a desk and computer in an office. However, the old technology will hang on when it still works—the balance will shift toward augmented reality, but the adoption will vary based on need.

Obviously one wouldn't (or shouldn't) want to sit in a chair talking to his or her virtual screen on their augmented glasses. However, we've all had the pleasure of being in a public place and listening to half a discussion by some inconsiderate person on the phone, or some want to be big shot showing off just how important he or she is.

7.4.1 Who Will Define Augmented Reality?

Initially manufactures will define what augmented reality is, and isn't. That is because they will have to put something out into the market as a trial. There will be, as in all emerging markets, the pioneers. Each will have unique operating systems, applications, user-interfaces, and security, etc. Then independent developers will introduce applications and those applications will bring new features, which will in turn inspire users. The users will then then drive the market by expecting and demanding improvements, new features, and changes. And slowly, evolutionarily, broad industry standards will emerge that allow and support interoperability between different manufactures, just as we have today with PCs and (for the most part) smart phones.

Augmented reality will be part of, and enable both a utopian future, and in some cases a dystopian future. With the power of enablement to do new things and existing things more efficiently, there will be those who use it to cause harm to people, to take advantage of the weak, and even to start and fight wars. Diversity in goals and needs is the nature of humanity, and augmented reality, like the disruptive technologies of the steam engine, dynamite, PCs and the web before it, will be used for good and evil.

7.5 Summary: Players and Platforms

As is always the case the large companies, Apple, Intel, Google, Microsoft, Qualcomm have an inside track with their ability to present partners with hardware and accompanying SDKs. However, the technology world does not love closed gardens especially at times when innovation is required to help nascent industries find their potential. Open standards will eventually win out to make room for new ideas and approaches.

I did not mention Apple in this section. It's always risky to speculate what Apple might do but Apple has acquired one of the creative drivers in augmented reality with the acquisition of Metaio, and in 2013, Apple acquired one of the leading makers of 3D mobile cameras PrimeSense of Israel. PrimeSense had fostered a strong developer community with OpenNI. That work has not been lost, it has dispersed to other platforms and is going on within Apple's developer network. With the release of the iPhone 7, a phone with dual cameras, Apple has already fielded a platform for AR products. There is obviously more to come. And as pointed out earlier, Apple CEO Tim Cook thinks augmented reality is a larger opportunity than virtual reality. Cook has been dropping hints about Apple's interest in augmented and virtual reality since the beginning of 2016.

The large companies with strong hardware and software positions are going to have a defining role in AR. They already have that role, but the other communities described in this section are going to have much to add. They will contribute to the larger ecosystems.

Reference

1. https://www.khronos.org/

Technology Issues

8

Abstract

In this section, some of the key technical issues in building an augmented reality device are discussed. The number of sensors, and the technology associated with them, combined with the need to operate at low power and be lightweight, is an on-going challenge for the device builders.

Augmented reality systems (headsets, helmets, HUDs, etc.) must interact with our eyes and brain, and the eye-brain connection is a very powerful, amazingly complex and capable system.

Knowing where you are is one of the most critical functions in augmented reality. How can a system identify things and deliver potentially mission critical information in a timely manner if it doesn't know where you are? But how does it know where you are?

The concept of voice control, like augmented and virtual reality, are terms that have been in our vocabulary for so long, many think they know what they are and how they work.

The use of hand gestures as a means of communicating and controlling the information provided by augmented reality systems provides an attractive alternative to cumbersome interface devices for human-computer interaction (HCI); hand gestures can help in achieving the ease and naturalness.

Eye tracking is the process of measuring either the point of gaze (where one is looking) or the motion of an eye relative to the head. Eye-tracking is an old concept developed in the 1800s made using direct observations.

If ever the statement, "one size does not fit all," was appropriate, it would be in the case of a user interface.

© Springer International Publishing AG 2017
J. Peddie, *Augmented Reality*, DOI 10.1007/978-3-319-54502-8_8

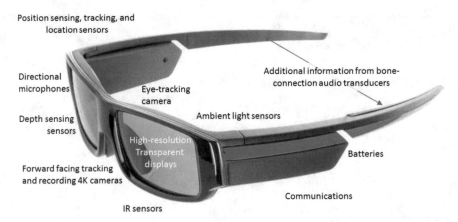

Position sensing, tracking, and
location sensors

Directional
microphones

Eye-tracking
camera

Additional information from bone-
connection audio transducers

Depth sensing
sensors

Ambient light sensors

High-resolution
Transparent
displays

Batteries

Forward facing tracking
and recording 4K cameras

Communications

IR sensors

Fig. 8.1 An augmented reality headset uses a broad range of sensors and technologies that have
to be low power and lightweight

In this section, some of the key technical issues in building an augmented reality
device are discussed. The number of sensors, and the technology associated with
them, combined with the need to operate at low power and be lightweight, is an on-
going challenge for the device builders (Fig. 8.1).

Ten or more sensors can be found in a high-end set of augmented reality smart
glasses or helmet. The number of sensors as well as the resolution and size of the
display will depend on the application for which the device is designed.

In the following sections the various sensors, display technologies, and associated software, as well as some of our physiological characteristics which determine
how and why a sensor or display should behave, will be examined. As you will
discover, a great deal of work has to go on to have a fully functional augmented
reality headset.

8.1   Our Amazing Eyes

Augmented reality systems (headsets, helmets, HUDs, etc.) must interact with our
eyes and brain, and the eye-brain connection is a very powerful, amazingly complex
and capable system. Because the eye-brain is so capable, it can make up for our
blind spot and make us think 30 Hz interlaced displays are smooth and continuous.

The eye is about 25 mm (~1 inch) diameter and filled with 2 fluids of refractive
index 1.336. The iris expands and shrinks from around 1–8 mm to regulate light.
The cornea and bi-convex lens with focal length around 20 mm focus the light on
the retina. This lens changes shape to focus between infinity and around 100 mm to
accommodate focus on the fovea.

The fovea has a visual area of only two-degrees wide, about the width of your
thumb when you stretch your arm at full length in front of you. Everything outside
of that area we interpret as indistinct and vague.

Our eyes are also very fast, and able to scan at up to 900-degrees per second, making them the fastest moving body part. Evolution developed that capability so we could interpret the dangers in our environment. To do that efficiently we needed to be able to see what is coming and quickly.

8.1.1   Rods, Cones, and Fovea

There are two types of photoreceptors in the human retina, rods and cones. Rods are responsible for vision at low light levels (scotopic vision). They do not mediate color vision, and have a low spatial acuity. Our eyes contain about 100 million rods which are used for achromatic vision.

For a wavelength of 550 nm (yellow near green) and a pupil diameter of about 2 mm, we get an angular resolution of 1/3600 in radians or, more commonly written, 1 arcmin. This corresponds to visual acuity, or resolving power, that is "the ability to distinguish fine detail" and is the property of the cones in our eyes [1]. We have about six million cones and they are concentrated in the center of the eye in the fovea. Cones are active at higher light levels (photopic vision), are capable of color vision and are responsible for high spatial acuity.

A resolution of one arcmin is possible with 100% contrast at best, and two arcmin are at least sufficient. The exact crispness requirements are a complex function of contrast, focus of attention, and other factors [2]. When viewing extended lines, the visual system aggregates activity across groups of photoreceptors, to achieve super-resolution of 0.13 arcmin. This is known as Vernier acuity. Vernier acuity sometimes requires cortical processing and "pooling" to detect it. This phenomenon is also known as hyperacuity. Vernier acuity is resistant to defocus, motion, and luminance, but is subject to practice effects and changes in attention. After training, observers' thresholds have been shown to improve as much as sixfold [3].

8.1.2   Resolution

From the standard lens resolution equations [4], if one is good at math they can derive the theoretical resolution of the human eye. Generally speaking, our eyes have a lens diameter between 1 and 9 mm and a focal length of about 20 mm with the larger pupil diameters occurring in young people who still have a very flexible iris tissue. Most people have upper lens diameters of 4–6 mm. Given that and under fairly good lighting conditions, we can assume about our pupil diameter is about 2 mm or less. That's a useful number to remember.

Resolution is usually measured in cycles per degree (CPD) which measures an angular resolution, or how much an eye can differentiate one object from another in terms of visual angles. Resolution in CPD can be measured by bar charts of different numbers of white/black stripe cycles. This value is what physiologists have found for the best resolution a human eye can deliver, and this is also what TV standards consider to be "crisp," i.e., acuity.

8.2   What We See

Computer and augmented reality screens are expressed in pixels per inch (PPI), whereas printers are expressed in dots per inch (DPI), they are for practical purposes the same.

The average reading distance is 305 mm (12 inches), if a pixel is projected at 0.4 arc minute that is 35.5 microns and at 305 mm away that is about 720 ppi/dpi. A pixel projected at 1 arc minute will be 89 microns or about 300 dpi/ppi. Magazines are printed at 300 dpi, fine art/photo printers are 720 dpi, which is considered as good as needed.

The PPI and the distance from the eye determine the acuity realizable by the viewer. In humans, 20/20 vision is the ability to resolve a spatial pattern separated by a visual angle of 1 min of arc (a 20/20 letter subtends 5 min of arc total). If the PPI or DPI is below 70 the text is not readable.

8.2.1   Blind Spot

Looking at the diagram of the eye (Fig. 8.2, Sect. 8.1) the retina which contains the rod and cones is where the light that is focused by the lens falls. However, the information from the retina must get to our brain, and it does that via the optic nerve. However, the connection of the optic nerve to the retina removes retina area and that creates a blind spot. If light falls on the blind spot we will not be aware of it. And yet we see perfectly, there is no visual spot, no missing information in what we see. That is because our eyes are never still, not even when we sleep.

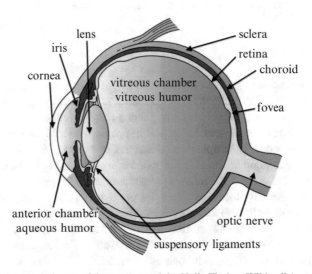

Fig. 8.2 The three main layers of the eye (artwork by Holly Fischer, Wikipedia)

8.2.2   Eye Movement

Our eyes are moving all the time, darting left, right, up, down. We aren't usually aware of it. The movements are called eye saccades ('jerking movement': from French, literally 'violent pull'). The result of the saccade is our brain fills in the missing spot based on all the other neighboring information it is getting, due to the saccade. Humans and many animals do not just look at a scene in fixed steadiness; instead, the eyes move around, locating interesting parts of the scene and building up a mental, three-dimensional 'map' corresponding to the scene. A saccade is also an involuntary consequence of turning of the head to one side or the other in response to a startling noise off to the side, or a sudden motion detected in the visual periphery.

Saccades are different from physiological nystagmus, which are small involuntary tremors of the eyeballs; when nystagmus is eliminated by stabilizing the image on the retina, visual perception fades rapidly from fatigue of the retinal receptors. Nystagmus is a condition of involuntary (or voluntary, in rare cases) eye movement, that may result in reduced or limited vision. Due to the involuntary movement of the eye, it is often called "dancing eyes."

8.2.3   Interlaced TV and Motion Perception

Persistence of vision is the phenomenon by which an afterimage seemingly persists for approximately 40 milliseconds (ms) on the retina of the eye. This is used to explain why we don't see black flicker in movie theaters or (usually) on CRTs.

Persistence of vision, which is popularly taught as the reason for motion illusion, is merely the reason that the black spaces that come between each "real" movie frame are not perceived, which makes the phi phenomenon the true reason for motion illusion in cinema and animation, including the phenakistoscope [5] (the first widespread animation device that created a fluent illusion of motion), zoetrope (one of several pre-film animation devices that produce the illusion of motion by displaying a sequence of drawings or photographs showing progressive phases of that motion), and others (Fig. 8.3).

Fig. 8.3 A zoetrope
animation wheel
(Wikipedia)

The phi phenomenon is the optical illusion of perceiving a series of still images, when viewed in rapid succession, as continuous motion [6]. The phi phenomenon and persistence of vision together form the process of motion perception.

Motion perception is the process of inferring the speed and direction of elements in a scene based on visual, vestibular, and proprioceptive inputs. Although this process appears straightforward to most observers, it has proven to be a difficult problem from a computational perspective, and extraordinarily difficult to explain in terms of neural processing.

The human eye/brain system can sometimes process out flicker. This was particularly noticeable in the days of CRT Televisions in Europe that only ran at 50 Hz. compared to televisions in North American (and much of South America) that ran at 60 Hz. When traveling from the U.S. people would notice flicker when they first arrived but then the flicker becomes less noticeable over time.

However, when generating digital imagery, it can be important in include blur with moving objects because the eye/brain expects it or else the image will appear to stutter. Including motion blur was a major subject in computer generated imagery in the mid 1980's. Interestingly, even though a moving object is blurred, it will still be perceived as relatively sharp. Doing motion blur incorrectly is also known to cause headaches.

And eye saccades may cause other issues like rainbow effects with single chip digital light processing (DLP) projectors, striping in electronic blend zones, or RGB cross-talk in diffraction optical waveguides. The colors might shift with waveguides and eye saccades due to the limited eyebox (small shifts in eye location could shift the colors). Some people that were very sensitive to DLP "rainbow effects" were not sensitive to flicker and vice versa. This suggests that the eye/brain mechanism for rainbow and flicker are different.

8.3   Latency Issues in Augmented Reality Displays

Researchers [7] have found that for virtual reality (where the observer cannot see the normal world), the end-to-end latency (or, perhaps more descriptively the difference between perception to motion) should be below 40 ms (milliseconds). For augmented reality, the requirements are even higher. The displacement of objects between two frames should not exceed 15 arcmin (0.25 degrees), which would require a maximal latency of 5 ms even when one rotates their head at a moderate speed of 50 degrees-per-second. Several other researchers using some similar approaches have arrived at similar maximal latency times. In some special situations, just as fighter pilots, speeds of up to 2000 degrees-per-second have been reported. However, it is unlikely people rotating their head that fast will notice slight object displacements. Most researchers suggest that 10 ms will be acceptable for augmented reality [8].

To avoid the discomforting effects of virtual reality (what is commonly known as simulator sickness, or VR sickness), it is necessary to keep the system response to head motion ("photon-to-motion latency") as fast or faster than the vestibule-ocular reflex (VOR),[1] one of the fastest reflexes in the human body at 7 ms–15 ms [9], which stabilizes the retinal image at the current fixation point by rotating the eye in response to head motion.

In 2004, NASA's Aviation Safety Program, Synthetic Vision Systems Project conducted research in advanced flight deck concepts, such as Synthetic/Enhanced Vision Systems (S/EVS), for commercial and business aircraft [10]. Part of the project included the development of spatially-integrated, large field-of-regard information display systems. Head worn or helmet-mounted display systems were proposed as a method in which to meet the objective. From the research, the researchers concluded that commonplace head movements of more than 100 degrees-per-second would require less than 2.5 ms system latency.

One technique explored at the University of North Carolina was to deliberately (but randomly) modulate the image data turning binary pixels into perceived gray scale. From the image generator when the viewer's pose changed this created a pseudo motion blur effect, and engaged the viewer's eye (and brain) to integrate the results. The researchers claimed to have realized an average latency of just of 80 μs of end-to-end latency (from head motion to change in photons from the display) with a 50-degee-per-second panning speed [11].

---

[1] The vestibulo-ocular reflex (VOR) is a reflex, where activation of the vestibular system causes eye movement. This reflex functions to stabilize images on the retinas during head movement by producing eye movements in the direction opposite to head movement, thus preserving the image on the center of the visual field(s).

8.3.1   Field-Sequential Color System and Latency

A field-sequential color system is one in which the primary (RGB) color information is sent to the display in successive images, and which relies on the human
vision system to integrate or fuse the successive images into a color picture (see
Fig. 8.18 Field sequential color technique, section "Field sequential color—
LCoS"). Obviously, the transfer speed has to be fast, at least 10 ms per primary
color (see previous, "Interlaced TV and Motion Perception," Sect. 8.2.3). The
field-sequential color system dates back to 1940 when CBS tried to establish the
concept as the color TV standard for the U.S. The Federal Communications
Commission adopted it on October 11, 1950 as the standard for color television
in the United States, but it was later withdrawn [12].

High resolution LCoS and DLP displays use field sequential color where they
have a single set of mirrors that display a single-color plane at a time (see LCoS,
Sect. 8.7.3.5). To aid the eye/brain in integrating the color planes designers repeat
the same colors multiple times per frame of an image. However, some designs that
propose using field sequential color use different images to generate what is known
as sequential focus planes (where each focus plane is focused at a different point in
space). This is done in augmented reality systems to satisfy the vergence-
accommodation conflict issue (see Fig. 4.2: Accommodation distance vs. Vergence
distance in 3D viewing, Sect. 4.1.2) in a simple 3-D stereo image with objects near
the eyes. The two eyes will point/verge at the point in space where the object appears
to be, but the eye's focus will typically be far away; this sets up a conflict between
where the eyes are aimed and where they are focused [13] (Fig. 8.4).

The result of this compromise is that the images get color rings around their
edges (called "fringing").[2] This effect is particularly noticeable in one's peripheral
vision which is more motion/change sensitive. That means the problem tends to get
worse as the FoV is increased. The provision of sequential focus planes gives the
eyes a more comfortable focus zone.

Karl Guttag [14] who has worked many years with field sequential display
devices, specifically LCoS, thinks the human vision system will have difficulty
"fusing" the colors if a slow color field update rate is employed, and he expects
people will see a lot of field sequential color breakup (fringing) particularly when
objects (in the image) move.

"In spite of all my background and supposed bias toward field sequential color
LCoS," said Guttag, "I really have a hard time seeing it as a long-term solution for
head mounted displays due to color breakup and latency."

Field sequential color also inherently has more latency since an image is usually
generated at a whole color image and then must be broken into the three (or more)
component colors. For the colors to line up to reduce color breakup the image can
move between the various colors. Supporting "focus planes" would only add to this

---

[2]Chromatic Aberration, also known as "color fringing" or "purple fringing", is a common optical
problem that occurs when a lens is either unable to bring all wavelengths of color to the same focal
plane, and/or when wavelengths of color are focused at different positions in the focal plane.

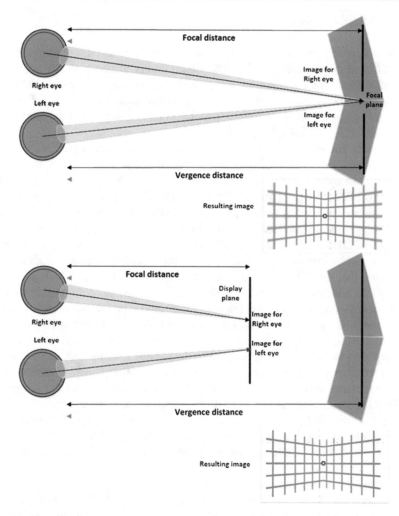

Fig. 8.4 Vergence and focal distance differences result in sharp or blurry images (Note the grid at the top is blurrier especially at the edges)

delay. Thus, trying to solve vergence-accommodation with focus planes only trades one bad effect for another.

Vergence-accommodation is a real issue but only for objects that get close to the user's eyes. Guttag thinks a better solution is to use sensors to track the eye's pupils and adjust the image accordingly, and as the eye's focus changes relatively slowly it should be possible to keep track. In other words, move the problem from the physical display and optics domain (that will remain costly and problematical), to the sensor and processing domain (that will more rapidly come down in cost).

8.3.2   Display Issues

The virtual reality and augmented reality/mixed reality head display markets use very different display technologies. The virtual reality market typically uses large flat panels which are less expensive and make it easy to support very wide FOV (but with greater than 4 arcmin per pixel angular resolution). The augmented reality/mixed reality "see-through" markets (with the notable exception of the large Meta 2) use microdisplays (DLP, LCoS, OLED).

The most common display technologies used in augmented reality are LCD, OLED flat panel on glass, OLED microdisplays on silicon, DMD (digital micromirror device, an optical semiconductor on which DLP technology is based), LCoS, and micro LEDs. Larger flat panel (LCD and OLED) displays have been sold (to augmented reality headset developers) as stand-alone modules, and in some cases, use industry standard interfaces such as DVI, HDMI, or DisplayPort. The microdisplays (LCoS, DLP, OLED) are generally sold as chipsets with controllers with various input. While these interfaces allow easy interconnections, they impose certain restrictions that are difficult to work around. Specifically, they deliver display data sequentially, a technique derived from the raster scan method (developed in the late 1930s for cathode ray tube (CRT) television sets), and it introduces almost an entire video frame of latency in the display device itself or worse in the case of field sequential color. The processing algorithms for DLP's sometimes trade some loss of image quality for lower latency, but even so the latency is more due to field sequential color. Since the display interface is raster-scan-based, a display device must receive an entire image before it can start to display a single pixel of that image.

Field sequential color is at a huge disadvantage in terms of latency. DLP compounds this with all the dithering and other processing needed, which takes time. If the extra processing is turned off, then the latency increases. FSC LCoS is better in terms of latency but it still has to wait for a frame to be totally received before it can display its first color.

And on devices that accept scan-line data, the display of the bottom of the image occurs much later than the display of the top of the image. Therefore, raster scan is inherently unsuited for low-latency applications, unless the output of the scan (to the display) is performed at very high rates, which can create memory access and high-power utilization issues.

The most common display technologies used in augmented reality are LCD, OLED, DMD, LCoS, pico-projectors, and micro LEDs. Historically these displays have been sold (to augmented reality headset developers) as stand-alone modules, and in some cases, use industry standard interfaces such as DVI, HDMI, or DisplayPort. While these interfaces allow easy interconnection, they impose certain restrictions that are difficult to work around. Specifically, they deliver display data sequentially, a technique derived from the raster scan method (developed in the late 1930s for cathode ray tube (CRT) television sets), and it introduces almost an entire video frame of latency in the display device itself. Since the display interface is raster-scan-based, a display device must receive an entire image before it can start to display a single pixel of that image. And on devices that accept scan-line data, the display of the bottom of the image occurs much later than the display of the top of the image. Therefore, raster scan is inherently unsuited for low-latency applications, unless the output of the scan (to the display) is performed at very high rates, which can create memory access and high-power utilization issues [15].

Head-worn (headset or helmet) augmented reality systems optically combine the computer-generated image with the user's direct view of the surroundings (known as "optical see-through"), in contrast to smartphone and tablet-based augmented reality applications, which combine the computer-generated image with video imagery from the device's camera (known as "video see-through").

For head-worn displays (headsets and helmets), optical see-through with its direct no latency view of the viewer's local environment is desirable and likely indispensable for extended use.

However, optical see-through comes with a built-in problem. Any optical technology that combines a computer image with the real world is going to have at least some negative effect on the real-world view. At a minimum, it is going to dim the real world and it can be worse as the real world passes through the optical structures that direct the computer-generated image toward the eye. Unlike video see-through displays, which allow synchronization of real and processor generated (virtual) images by deliberately delaying the video stream an optical see-through augmented reality must present synthetic imagery at the speed of "reality" to keep virtual and real objects aligned. Therefore, it must rely on minimal latency or on prediction techniques when computing synthetic imagery [16].

Unfortunately, latency effects accumulate throughout all the stages in the video pipeline of an augmented reality system (tracking, application, image generation, and scanned output to the display), so if special techniques are not employed (e.g., minimizing latency or predictive techniques) the debilitating effects of an optical see-through multiply. However, in the worst case, predictive techniques do the opposite of what they should do if the motion changes direction.

There is not just the magnitude of the offset between the intended and the achieved location of the computer-generated object, but also the change in the offset as a function of time—the synthetic object appearing to wander or swim about the real scene [17]. While predictive tracking can significantly reduce the misalignment between synthetic and real imagery, errors are still present, especially during rapid changes in head pose.

Direct addressing of the display from the image generation section of the augmented reality system is possible in matrix-like devices such as OLED, LCD, microLED, LCoS, DMD and, laser-beam scanning (LBS). Pico projectors which use a LCoS chip are assembled subassemblies which take serial data and therefore, are inherently latent.

As augmented reality systems develop, the developers of such systems have to get deeper into the display technology and drive it directly. Here the industry encounters the classic chicken-and-egg problem. Until augmented reality system builders have sufficient volume of sales, the cost of displays with the necessary exposure of their construction will be high because they will be treated as special class devices. That will keep the cost of augmented reality head-worn systems high in price, which will keep the sales volume down.

8.4   Eye-Box

The eye-box is the volume of space within which an effectively viewable image is formed by a lens system or visual display, representing a combination of exit pupil size and eye relief distance. The term was first used by John Flamsteed (1646–1719), an astronomer in the late seventeenth century.

The eye-box is often equivalent to the exit pupil (a virtual aperture in the optical system) and consists of the range of eye positions, at the eye relief distance (distance between the vertex of the last optic and the exit pupil), from which the entire image produced by the display is visible. This includes both angular and lateral movement of the eye.

The exit pupil is important because only the light rays which pass through the virtual aperture can exit the system and enter the wearer's eyes.

The eye-box is also shared with the FoV (see Fig. 8.5, Sect. 8.5). the effective eye-box of a smart glass can be much larger than the real optical eye-box when various mechanical adjustments of the combiner may be used to match the exit pupil of the combiner to the entrance pupil of the user's eye. However, for any position of the combiner, the eye-box has to allow the entire FoV to be seen unaltered, at the target eye relief. It may happen that for a specific position of the combiner, the entire display might be seen indoors (large pupil), hut the edges of the display might become blurry outside due to the fact that the eye pupil diameter decreases [18].

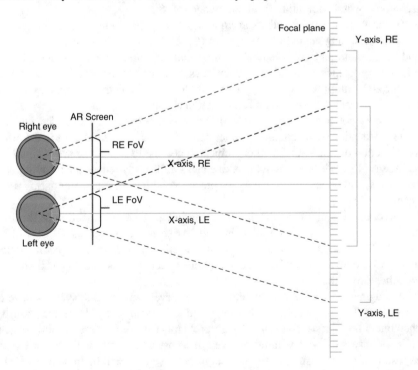

Fig. 8.5 Determination of field of view

8.4.1   Head Motion Box

In a head-up display, the head motion box, or eye-box, is a three-dimensional region in space surrounding the cockpit eye reference point (ERP) in which the display can be viewed with at least one eye. The center of the head motion box can be displayed forwards or aft, or upward or downward, with respect to the cockpit eye reference point to better accommodate the actual sitting position of the pilot. The positioning of the eye reference point is dependent on a number of ergonomically related cockpit issues such as head-down display visibility, the overmixed reality. The-nose down look angle, and the physical location of various controls such as the control yoke and the landing gear handle. In many cases, the cockpit eye reference point and where the pilot actually sits can vary by several inches. The head-up display head motion box should be as large as possible to allow maximum head motion without losing the display information [19].

It is also referred to as the design eye reference point (DERP) where a pilot is at the optimum location for visibility, inside and outside the cockpit, as well as the correct position for access to the cockpit switches and knobs.

8.5   Field of View

The field of view (FoV) (FoV) of an augmented reality device is one of the most important and controversial aspects of the device.

The calculation of field of view is basic trigonometry, the subtended angle derived from the horizontal distance to the focal plane and the vertical distance covered (seen), as illustrated in the following diagram.

However in practice outside of the laboratory, it can sometimes be difficult to judge. In principle, to measure the augmented reality field of view, one holds a ruler at a known distance from one's eyes, and then marks down where the apparent left and right edges of the display area fall on the object. Knowing the distance X between the left/right markers and the distance Y between the eyes and the object, the FoV is calculated via simple trigonometry: FoV = 2 × tan-1(X / (Y × 2)).

Some people mistakenly believe that a small FoV is a result of the augmented reality device's limited graphics processing power, or display, and therefore easily improved with a more powerful GPU or higher resolution display. The reasoning is that increasing the field of view of a 3D graphics application leads to a proportional increase in the number of pixels displayed, and if more pixels are displayed, then the GPU has to do more processing, and the display has to have more pixels. In the case of games, without explicit frustum culling, that would be a correct conclusion. However, with modern GPU programs that can cull complex geometric objects automatically, the effect is usually small (as long as the final rendered image size in pixels stays the same).

Some suppliers, or companies who say they will be suppliers, try to use FoV as a marketing differentiator. It is misguided and inconsiderately confusing to consumers and sophisticated users as well.

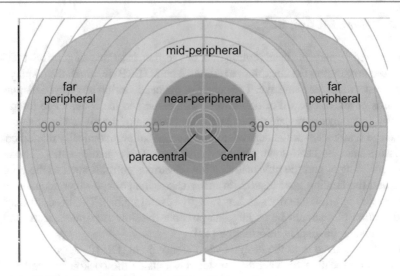

Fig. 8.6 Field of view of the human eye (Wikipedia)

The approximate field of view of an individual human eye (measured from the fixation point, i.e., the point at which one's gaze is directed) is 60-degrees [20]. (It's actually a bit more complex than that because human vision is not a perfect cone, but 60-degrees is an accepted range; we actually have a small area in focus, the rest of our FoV comes from eye and head movement (Fig. 8.6).

The 60 degrees is an illusion of focus. If human vison is 60-degrees FoV, then what value is there in building an augmented reality system with greater than 60-degrees FoV. In the case of augmented reality, our attention is drawn to the data being displayed. It would seem logical that we do not need, nor would we benefit from, a wider view which would incorporate our high-speed peripheral vision.

However, we don't just stare straight ahead. Our eyes are never completely at rest. They make fast random jittering movements even when we are fixated on one point. Saccades are the rapid movement of eyes that is used while scanning a visual scene. In our subjective impression, the eyes do not move smoothly across the printed page during reading. Instead, our eyes make short and rapid movements called saccades [21].

Therefore, a limited FoV has been likened to looking at the world through a cardboard tube, and requiring the viewer to move his or her head about to see the whole world.

Ron Padzensky, a noted commentator on augmented reality said, "But image overlay use cases promise to be so much more than that and the experiences will feel more natural when visual information flows from the far peripheral to the paracentral as our gaze moves about. I also believe that an expanded FOV will serve to more naturally draw attention to activity needing to be attended to in one's periphery. This more natural experience will be critical to mass adoption."

Optics engineer, and CEO of IMMY, an augmented reality optics supplier, Doug Magyari, points out that, "The key is the number of neurons stimulated—that is the goal of everything we, as humans, do. The biggest point that everyone in this field is missing is that these devices, augmented reality or virtual reality, are a unique communication tool that connect people to content unlike anything ever created. People are understanding this in general, but not in specifics, and it is from the specifics comes the magic these new communication tools offer—in other words, not by accident.

> To communicate any message properly requires an integration of the structure of the content, with specific human centric mechanics, this is especially true in the AR/VR environment where you have taken over someone's eyes and ears. This means understanding the message you are trying to convey, and reaching, or communicating to all of the parts of the brain simultaneously, the conscious, the subconscious & the autonomic brain, with both visual and audio content. There is a real art to doing this correctly, but the short answer is that if you only occupy ~ 30-degrees of the vision system you cannot reach the needed neurons to engage the viewer emotionally, which is where all learning and enjoyment reside. This is true in augmented reality as much as it is in virtual reality, even though the use or message is radically different. We as humans still function the same way. It is because of the lack of understanding of this issue; how, and why, people are so enthralled by what they are experiencing with this medium, that so many major companies have failed so often.

So then, assuming the size of the display (i.e., what the user actually sees) stays fixed, then increasing the resolution, the pixels per inch (PPI) will result in increasing the acuity and therefore the size of the pixels will get smaller, which will increase the FoV.

The following chart shows the general relationship between screen resolution, size, and FoV.

As Fig. 8.7 indicates, increasing the display's resolution (assuming a fixed display size) will increase the FoV as the pixels get smaller and fit better in our natural fovea view. This suggests the display technology will be the limiting property in FoV due to pixel size.

Unlike most displays, eye resolution is not constant—it varies over the retina (Fig. 8.8).

Depth of field is another factor that has to be taken into consideration when designing an augmented reality system. Depth of field is the distance between the nearest and the furthest objects that give an image judged to be in focus by the viewer and the headset's camera. The system must allow clear viewing of both the image presented by the display and the real objects (in an augmented reality display).

The field of view of the device's camera must align with the FoV of the virtual camera in the rendering tool otherwise the virtual images will be disproportionately sized, or possibly located out of view.

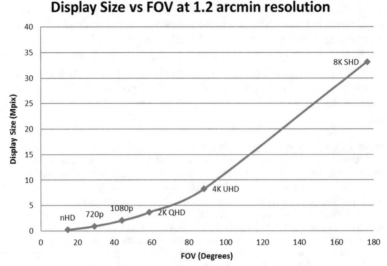

Note: Above the curve you would not be able to see the individual pixels on the display.
Below the curve you would be able to distinguish between the pixels (screen door effect).

Fig. 8.7 FoV as a function of screen resolution and size

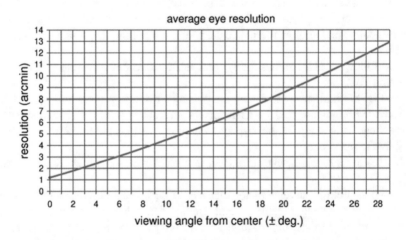

Fig. 8.8 The average resolution of the human eye (y) with respect to the visual field (x)

8.5.1   Pixel Pitch

The issue of resolution and FoV is insidiously complicated because so many variables are involved. One discussion that gets attention is pixel pitch.

Pixel pitch (sometimes called dot pitch, line pitch, stripe pitch, or phosphor
pitch) directly correlates your display resolution and optimal viewing distance. The
smaller the pixel pitch number, the more pixels used to make up the image on your

Fig. 8.9 When the display is close to the viewer's eyes the minute distances between the pixels becomes visible crating what is known as the "Screen-Door" effect or Fixed Pattern Noise (Image source Wikipedia)

display, thus improving the resolution and optimal viewing distance. Dot pitch describes the distance between dots (sub-pixels) on a display screen. In the case of an RGB color display, the derived unit of pixel pitch is a measure of the size of a triad (RGB dots) plus the distance between triads. Dot or pixel pitch can be measured horizontally, vertically, or diagonally, and can vary depending upon the aspect ratio of the display.

The screen-door effect (SDE) or fixed-pattern noise (FPN) is a visual artifact of displays, where the distance between pixels (or subpixels) become visible in the displayed image to the viewer, usually as a black line or border (Fig. 8.9).

The screen-door effect can be seen in digital projector images and regular displays under magnification or at close range. Increasing display resolution reduces it; however, with displays very close to the eye as in a virtual reality headset the screen door effect has been an issue because the display is a single display across the viewer's entire field of view. In augmented reality systems, the display occupies a smaller portion of the viewer's total field of view so the screen-door effect is not as noticeable.

The pixels per inch (PPI) are seldom published by the augmented reality headset manufactures.

Smartphones, for example, with a 5.5-inch screen and 1080 × 1920 resolution have a PPI of 400, and at that resolution, near your eyes, the screen door effect will be noticeable. The PPI should be greater than 500, if close to the eye. A HUD for example is far enough away it can use a smaller resolution. However, as the PPI is increased, within a fixed display space, the FoV will be reduced.

The display area in worn augmented reality devices (glasses and helmets) is typically to the right of the right eye, and either slightly above or below the center of vision. Factory-installed head-up displays in automobiles are typical at the bottom of the windscreen, and in an airplane either near the top or at the bottom of the windscreen. After-market head-up displays can be almost anywhere. Some augmented reality glasses put information on the far edge of both lenses. Advocates and critics argue about the location, the distraction to focus (and taking your eyes off the main object); there is no right answer, and in most cases, it's a matter of learning to accommodate the augmented reality device. That accommodation is one of the limiting factors in consumer acceptance of augmented reality.

8.6   Displays

Displays are our main source for information and often interaction. Augmented reality and associated technologies are delivered to the user through a display or projection device of some type, and at some distance. It can be (is) different for all cases.

8.6.1   Proximity

Displays can be in three different locations, far (signage, billboards, annunciators, command and control, conference rooms, CAVEs, (Cave Automatic Virtual Environments [22]), etc.), near (computers, in-vehicle dashboard/cockpit, TV, etc.), and close (wearables—e.g., head-mounted displays, watches, etc.). Near-displays are sub-divided into lean-back and lean-forward. Lean-back is TV viewing, and lean-forward is computer viewing. Cockpit and in-vehicles displays are lean-forward, because like a computer they are typically involved with some form of interactivity.

8.6.2   Close

Close displays are sub-divided into four primary categories, Virtual reality (virtual reality) head-mounted displays (HMDs), augmented-reality displays (helmets, and glasses), handheld devices such as a smartphone or tablet, and personal media player (PMP) or devices (PMD) primarily for entertainment, although can also be used for business. A fifth category could be contact lenses and implants.

8.6.3   Virtual Reality

As mentioned earlier, virtual reality-head-mounted displays, are categorized as close HMDs and sub-divided into those with an integrated or built-in dedicated display (e.g., Oculus, HTV Vive), and smartphone display (e.g., Samsung Gear). A VHMD completely occludes the user's view of the outside world and immerses him or her in the virtual world.

8.6.4 Augmented Reality

Likewise, augmented reality-head-mounted displays, which are close HMDs, are sub-divided into data and graphics. Data augmented reality head-mounted displays are those devices that only deliver information in the form of data (i.e., text and very primitive graphics objects such as a box or triangle) and graphics. Graphics augmented reality-head-mounted displays deliver complex computer-generated graphics data, such as engineering drawings, maps, or entertainment.

Augmented reality-head-mounted displays come in the form of helmets, can be data-only or graphics capable, and glasses (also known as smart-glasses). Augmented reality can also be delivered to tablets and smartphones that have forward-facing cameras. When augmented reality is used on such handheld devices, (which could include notebook computers), they are sometimes referred to as see-through or "Windows on the World" (WOW) systems.

Traditional user interfaces (UIs) for "off-the-desktop" applications display the digital information on flat 2D surfaces. Spatially augmented reality (SAR) uses projectors to display on walls, or a table top that a user can interact with without a head-mounted display or handheld device. It is like a CAVE (Cave Automatic Virtual Environment—a virtual reality environment consisting of a cube -shaped room in which the walls are rear-projection screens) but lacks the physical 3D aspect of a CAVE.

8.6.5 Mixed

Unlike augmented reality, mixed reality has the advantage of being able to integrate and interact with your surroundings, it tries to combine the best aspects of both virtual reality and augmented reality. Mixed reality is a marketing term being promoted by Magic Leap, Microsoft, and a few smaller firms (Fig. 8.10).

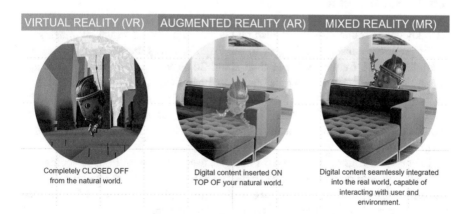

Fig. 8.10 Comparison of realities (Courtesy Magic Leap)

Mixed reality (MR), also called hybrid reality, is the merging of real and virtual worlds to produce new environments and visualizations where physical and digital objects co-exist and interact in real time. It tries to combine the best aspects of both virtual reality and augmented reality.

The good news, bad news is that augmented reality is, or will be, in everything and as such there is the need to identify which implementation you are referring to.

8.6.6   Ambient Light

When images and information are superimposed on one's view of their surroundings, the amount of the environment's light will affect the viewability of that information. Therefore, an ambient light sensor is necessary to measure that background light and drive the brightness of the augmented reality device's display when there is more light and dim them when there is less.

The ambient light conditions vary widely from indoor to outdoor use. This can have a profound effect on the display requirements so the image will show up against the real world.

8.6.7   Color Depth

The number of colors producible by the display known as color depth is of importance to the viewer, depending on the type of data being displayed. The human eye can discriminate up to ten million colors. However, if only text, or simple maps are being displayed, the image generator used does not need to provide such a wide color depth. If on the other hand complex images of mechanical devices, or human anatomy are being displayed, the color depth is critical for discrimination.

8.6.8   Refresh Rate

Also known as frame rate, the refresh rate is the frequency at which an image generator produces consecutive images to the display, and is measured in frames per second (FPS). A frequency lower than about 20 FPS is perceived as flicker, and below 12 fps is considered separate images to the individual while faster rates create the illusion of motion. 24 is the current minimum video standard which would be the expectation for HMD display refresh, however, as mentioned elsewhere, to avoid latency refresh rate can run as high as 120 fps. Frame rate is also expressed as Hz in some cases.

Twenty-four frames per second (or more) is used for movies. Film projectors use a double gate and display the same frame twice to get the flicker rate up to 48 Hz. Flicker is more of an issue when there is blanking (no image) between frames such as with film or a CRT that have blanking at or below 60hz.

Today's displays generally update from 60 to 120 Hz. Going to higher frame rates reduces any perceived jitter with fast moving images.

8.6.9 Summary

Obviously, we couldn't experience augmented reality without a display device of some type, and as is so often the case, no one solution can (or will) satisfy all requirements. There is more on displays in the chapter, "Displays," (Sect. 8.6).

Augmented reality is the next, major, mobile computing platform, and everything we've learned from smartphones will be used for augmented reality. That will include how to squeeze incredible performance out of processors while using minimal power which lets the weight be reduced. The mass production of smartphones drove down the price of sensors and display screens, and augmented reality device builders are benefiting from that.

Scientists have a lot to work to do given the capabilities of human vision. In some cases, our vision is good enough to make accommodation for slower displays and a certain amount of latency. And, on the other hand, the increasing power of processors will also enable sharper images integrated into reality, easier to read text, and richer colors. When improvements come, our eyes are ready for it (Fig. 8.11).

At the same time, Moore's law, has continued to enable semiconductors to get smaller, denser, and more powerful. Semiconductor manufacturing of screens such as OLEDs and microLEDs has also benefited augmented reality. And whereas some people think the consumer version of augmented reality, when it arrives, will replace the need for a smartphone, augmented reality will forever be in the debt of the smartphone industry. Like smartphones, the augmented reality evolution will take years but has the potential to be huge. My personal forecast/hope is that by

Fig. 8.11 Smartphone technology will enable the development of consumer and commercial augmented reality devices (Qualcomm)

2020–2025 we will use augmented reality as casually and commonly as we do a smartphone today. And some people have predicted it's only a matter of time before we trade in our smartphones for smart-glasses.

8.7   Augmented Reality Displays

As mentioned earlier, the first augmented reality display was the teleprompter developed by Hubert Schiafly in 1950 and based on the concept of Pepper's Ghost.

The first wearable augmented reality device was the Philco head-mounted remote surveillance system developed in the early 1960s [23]. The portable display used in augmented reality devices has been a challenge and often the limiting component (due to size, weight, cost, power consumption, heat, brightness, resolution, reliablity and durability) for a wearable device. As a result, multiple solutions have been developed, offered, and tried, and we have learned that there is no panacea, no "one size fits all."

This section will discuss wearable augmented reality device displays and not the displays found in mobile devices such as smartphones, notebooks, tablets, and HUDs. Those devices are capable of providing an augmented reality experience, they just aren't (easily) wearable.

Also, most augmented reality headsets (helmets, glasses, add-ons, etc.) only employ one display (usually over the right eye). When two displays are employed the challenge of generating a projected stereo 3D (S3D) image is added to the workload of the image generator and content, which is challenging, and one of the reasons single displays are the primary model. That doesn't mean you can't view 3D objects with an augmented reality headset, it just means the objects will be flat. However, because the object will be effectively stationary, you can move around it and get the effect of stereo.

Stereoscopic viewing is one of the distinctions between augmented and virtual reality. Virtual reality headsets present two separate views to create the pseudo stereoscopic image (using two flat displays) and your brain creates the three-dimensional image. Mixed reality headsets, which are basically virtual reality headsets with a forward-looking camera, also generate a quasi-stereoscopic 3D image.

Work on lightweight display devices or schemes will go on for some time, perhaps until we have implants such as those developed at Monash University in Clayton, Victoria's work [24] or the Alpha IMS developed by University of Tübingen, Germany [25].

In the meantime, there are developments ranging from adaptation of organic light-emitting diode (OLED) screens produced for smartphones, to experimental contact lens. In this section the leading display techniques will be briefly discussed for survey purposes. Display technologies are quite complex, and volumes have been written about them. It is beyond the scope of this book to replace, compete, or even approach those tomes. However, a knowledge and awareness of the many display types is appropriate. The technologies listed here are not exhaustive, and are listed alphabetically, not in terms of popularity or the most promising.

There are various ways to approach the taxonomy of displays used in augmented reality systems.

8.7.1   Transparency

One approach is transparency. Using that approach, there are two main head-worn display technologies developed in the industry today:

- **Non-Transparent:** Most of the display choices are non-transparent. The display device generates an image and then the image is reflected or routed to the user's eye. Examples in this category include projectors, retinal image lasers, liquid crystal displays (LCDs), ferroelectric liquid crystals on silicon (FLCoS), and liquid crystal on silicon (LCoS). There are also direct-view OLED microdisplays.
- **Transparent:** Transparent displays are OLEDs and possibly contact lens with micro light-emitting diodes (LEDs).

8.7.2   Technology

Another approach is by the type of technology used. For example, microdisplays and flat panels and/or reflective versus emissive. Most augmented reality see-through headsets use microdisplays and most virtual reality headsets use flat panels. The exception is the Meta 2 which uses a large OLED flat panel and then very large optics (essentially dual spherical combiners like are used in some HUD displays).

Even OLED that could be see-through are used as non-see-through devices. Therefore, his distinction may not get the reader anywhere.

8.7.2.1 Emissive or Reflective

LCDs are transmissive (an LCD screen that uses a backlight, as discussed later, section "Back lighting vs. transparency"). What most effects the optical design is whether the module is emissive or reflective. The optical design for an OLED micro-display or high temperature poly-silicon (HTPS) LCD are essentially the same even though the LCD has a backlight.

DLP and conventional LCoS optics are more complicated because you have to route light into them to illuminate that panel and then back out. Himax came up with front lit LCoS with a module that acts a lot like a transmissive LCD by using a waveguide to illuminate the LCoS device (see next section).

8.7.2.2 Optical Path

However, what counts more to the optical design is the optical path. In this regard, an OLED micro-display, HTPS LCD, and Front-Lit LCoS act the same.

A big advantage on non-emissive displays (and critically important to diffractive and holographic waveguides, is that you can control the wavelengths of light by the

The EyeTap Principle

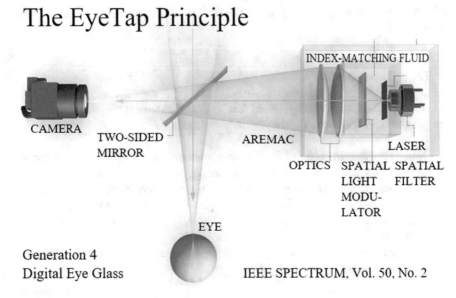

Fig. 8.12   Steve Mann's EyeTap optical path to establish collinearity (Mann)

emission source (LED or Laser). OLEDs output broad spectrum light which does not work.

8.7.2.3 Eyetap vs. Offset

Steve Mann, inventor of the EyeTap, and pioneer in augmented reality, states that the virtual image must be collinear with what the wearer is seeing in the real world. Mann's criterion for mitigation predicts any resulting mismatch between viewfinder image and the real world would create an unnatural mapping. Mann points out that anyone who has walked around holding a small camcorder up to his or her eye for several hours a day will obtain an understanding of the ill psychophysical effects that result. Eventually such adverse effects as nausea, and flashbacks, may persist even after the camera is removed.[161]

To mitigate that problem, EyeTap is designed with as near as possible perfect collinearity, and illustrated in Fig. 8.12 (Sect. 8.7.2.3).

The embodiments of the wearable camera system sometimes give rise to a small displacement between the actual location of the camera, and the location of the virtual image of the viewfinder. Therefore, either the parallax must be corrected by a vision system, followed by 3D coordinate transformation, followed by re-rendering, or if the video is fed through directly, the wearer must learn to make this compensation mentally. When this mental task is imposed upon the wearer, while performing tasks at close range such as looking into a microscope while wearing the glasses, there is a discrepancy that is difficult to learn, and it may give rise to unpleasant psychophysical effects.

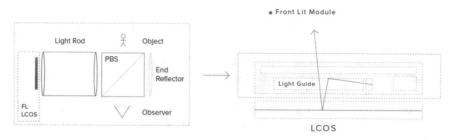

Fig. 8.13 Front-lit LCoS module is capable of delivering more than 5000 cd/m² high brightness, which is a perfect candidate for see-through head-mounted display application (Himax)

8.7.3   Direct Emissive and Modulated Displays

Display technologies can also be divided into two principal types of image generation—direct emissive, and modulated.

Transparent direct emissive image generators, which include OLED and micro LED.

Non-transparent modulated image generators are technologies such as liquid-crystal displays (LCD), Liquid Crystal on Silicon (LCoS) and microelectromechanical systems (MEMs) displays such as a digital micromirror device (DMD) or digital Light Processing device (DLP).

Founded in 2001 and headquartered in Tainan, Taiwan, Himax has somewhat blurred the line between emissive and modulated displays with their front-lit technology where they use waveguides to illuminate an LCoS panel so it can be used optically similar to an OLED or transmissive LCD device (Fig. 8.13).

This front-lit concept is probably going to find its way into quite a few designs for augmented reality headsets and helmets.

Modulated displays generally incorporate three primary components:

- External light source
- Combiner optics
- Pattern generator

In modulated displays the light is first directed to the external pattern generator. The image is then formed by either switching on or off each pixel in the array. For this type of non-emissive system, light must always be incident on every pixel.

8.7.3.1 Non-transparent Modulated Displays

The following sections will briefly discuss non-see-though displays that are being or have been used in augmented reality head-mounted display and helmets. Display in mobile devices like smartphones and tablets are not included (although such devices do get used in augmented reality applications), nor will micro miniature cathode-ray tubes (CRTs) be discussed, even though they were the first display devices used in augmented reality systems. CRTs are now considered obsolete. Nor will the scanned vertical array of LEDs be discussed that was used in the pioneering Private Eye head-mounted display that created a visual monochrome field (screen) using a vibrating mirror.

Non-transparent displays are just as their name implies, light is emitted from, or obscured by them and not through them. Although some of the active elements in a non-transparent display may be semi or fully transparent (depending upon their composition, and the voltage applied to them) or the emitting elements are so small they appear to be transparent, they will usually have a substrate and/or a back-panel lighting system.

8.7.3.2 Color Generation

Non-transparent displays are often monochromatic in nature and some scheme must be employed to make them into a non-monolithic-appearing color display.

8.7.3.3 LCDs with Color Filter

The LCD itself is only a light valve and does not generate light; the light comes from a backlight that is either fluorescent or a set of LEDs. LCDs use three sub-pixels with RGB transmissive color filters (CF). The pixels must be relatively large and let through only 1–1.5% of the light. Scaling down is limited by the colors bleeding together ("leaking colors," LC effects) and light throughput. Although the panels don't use much power, they do not make very efficient use of the (back-panel) illumination light which is the primary power consumer. LCDs also have restrictive off-angle viewing. However, in the case of augmented reality that is not much of a problem.

Also, color can be created in an LCD without a color filter—via the field sequential color processes. This may be an appealing approach for near-to-eye solutions as it enables much higher resolutions. FSC is covered later (section "Field sequential color—LCoS") with other technologies (LCoS and DMD), but it can certainly be used with LCD as well.

LCDs are an electronically modulated optical device made up of any number of segments controlling a layer of liquid crystals and arrayed in front of a light source (backlight) or reflector to produce images in color or monochrome.

8.7.3.4 LCD Screens

Although studied since the late 1880s, it wasn't until 1972 that the first active-matrix liquid-crystal display panel was produced in the United States by T. Peter Brody (1920–2011) and his team at Westinghouse, in Pittsburgh, Pennsylvania [26]. There are several suppliers of liquid crystal micro-displays that are currently available and that have been integrated in different headsets. Kopin's transmissive LCD on single crystal silicon transistors has been utilized in smart-glasses from Vuzix and Recon, as well as in the company's own brand headset, the Solos.

Note that "transmissive" means it can be backlit. The completed display module with backlight is not transparent. In Fig. 8.14, you can see through the display because it is monocular and will be out of focus if the user is focused past it.

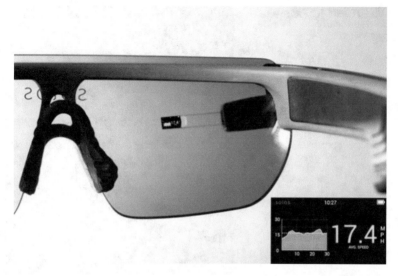

Fig. 8.14 Kopin's 4-mm module Pupil, behind the rim and almost invisible from the outside (Source: Kopin)

LCDs are used in a wide range of applications including computer monitors, televisions, instrument panels, aircraft cockpit displays, and signage. They are common in consumer devices such as DVD players, gaming devices, clocks, watches, calculators, and telephones, and have replaced cathode ray tube (CRT) displays in nearly all applications.

Back Lighting vs. Transparency
LCDs are inherently transparent, although the polarizing solution generally blocks almost half the light, or more. They are referred to as light-valves, which can pass or block polarized light. In the construction of LCD displays for mobile devices, PCs, dashboards, and signs, a bright light back panel is placed behind the LCDs. It is the back-panel light that makes an LCD non-transparent. There are also edge-lit, and front-lit solutions, as well as reflective LCDs used in monitors and industrial systems, but not augmented reality headsets.

Early LCD displays used a reflective back panel because at the time the cost, size, and power requirements of an emissive back panel was prohibitive (and still today, large numbers of passive matrix display, clocks/calculators/etc., are reflective). Since then the panels have been made very thin using cold cathode fluorescent lamps (CCFLs), and since about 2010, LEDs have been used for back panel lighting.

Presumably, an augmented reality display being used in nominal ambient light could be a native LCD panel mounted in the lens of the headset or helmet. However, it wouldn't work well at night or in dark areas, or smoke-filled areas.

However, a 'guilty little secret' of many transparent LCDs is that the transistor arrays can act as diffraction gratings and don't give a clear view of anything that's distant. That's why they are often used in showcase applications where the object being viewed is closer to the display than the viewer.

Fig. 8.15 Syndiant's
LCoS moduel (Source
Syndiant)

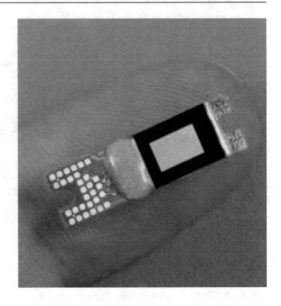

8.7.3.5 LCoS

Liquid-Crystal on Silicon (LCoS) is a technology used to create micro-displays by sandwiching a layer of liquid crystals between a cover glass and a highly reflective, mirror-like surface patterned with pixels on top of a silicon chip. These layers form a micro-display that can be used in projection displays such as large-screen, rear projection TVs and head-mounted displays for augmented reality headsets and helmets.

Liquid Crystal on Silicon (LCOS) microdisplays are not emissive and therefore require a separate illumination source which is modulated by the micro display giving full color and grayscale. As the luminance is not linked to the display technology itself, the luminance options can be considered to be customizable for the application (Fig. 8.15).

Developed by General Electric in the early 1970s [27], it wasn't until the late 1990s that a number of companies attempted to develop products for both near-eye and projection applications. LCoS, is also called micro-displays by some manufacturers. There are many types of microdisplays—the category is not limited to LCoS.

Over $2 billion has been spent going back to the late 1970s, trying to develop the technology and infrastructure behind LCoS displays. After a fitful start, the technology has finally matured. As mentioned, General Electric was the first company to develop LCoS in the 1970s according to Armitage, Underwood, and Wu.[139] In the late 1990s IBM, in conjunction with Philips and Nikon, developed the first three-panel projection systems based on an LCoS engine [28]. The technology was first employed in projection TVs, and brought to market by JVC, Sony, Olevia (Brillian) and others (like Spatialight, MicroVue, Micro-display, and Colorado Micro-display).

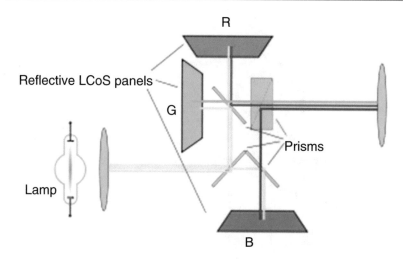

Fig. 8.16 Conceptual diagram of an LCoS projector (Wikipedia)

In 1997, JVC reported development of a 1365 × 1024 Digital Direct Drive Image Light Amplifier (D-ILA). Around the same time, IBM reported development of a 2048 × 2048 LCoS panel, which they used in a three-panel engine to demonstrate a 28- inch diagonal rear-projection computer monitor prototype. Many people credit IBM with having developed LCoS. Later commercial implementations of LCoS technology included Sony's Silicon X-tal Reflective Display (SXRD) and JVC's D-ILA.

As mentioned above, LCoS is a miniaturized reflective active-matrix liquid-crystal display or "micro-display" that uses a liquid crystal layer on top of a silicon backplane. It is also referred to as a spatial light modulator. LCoS was initially developed for projection televisions but is now used for wavelength selective switching, structured illumination, near-eye displays and optical pulse shaping. By way of comparison, some LCD projectors use transmissive LCDs, allowing light to pass through the liquid crystal.

The first versions used three reflective color panels as shown in Fig. 8.16.

Over time engineers figured out how to use a polarization beam-splitter (PBS) to condense the optics and eliminate the reflective panels, as shown in Fig. 8.17.

In a LCoS display, a CMOS chip controls the voltage on square reflective aluminum electrodes buried just below the chip surface, each controlling one pixel.

Most companies have abandoned the LCoS technology development after many years of R&D and investment including Intel and Philips. The technology found new opportunities in the micro projector (pico-projector) markets for head-mounted displays.

In Google's early prototype Glass, they used a color filter LCoS and then they switched to field sequential LCoS. This seems to suggest that they chose size over issues with the field sequential color breakup. Field sequential LCoS pixels are less than 1/3rd the size (and typically closer to 1/9th the size) of any of the existing 3-color devices (color filter LCD/LCoS or OLED).

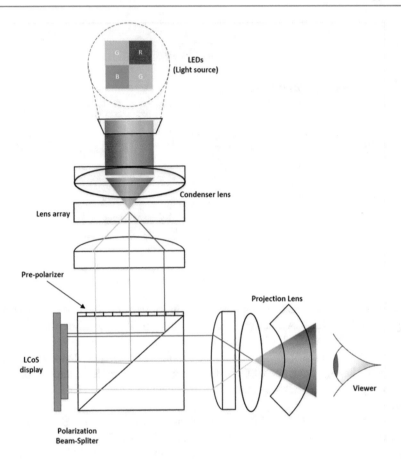

Fig. 8.17 LCoS with polarization beam-splitter for color (Panasonic)

Color Filter Reflective—LCoS

Color filter reflective (LCoS) is similar in function to an LCD color filter but the sub-pixels (color dots) can be physically smaller; however, they are still limited in how small they can be made (scaling down) due to needing three sub-pixels and color bleeding. Light throughput is better, about 10%. LCoS also requires more complicated optics (such as a beam-splitter) than transmissive LCDs, but share the low power benefit. Himax says they can support "Front-Lit" for both field sequential and color filter LCoS.

Field Sequential Color—LCoS

Field sequential color (FSC) can also be used by LCoS displays. However, FSC can suffer from color breakup due to the sequential fields, and will often produce a rainbow effect, but the pixels can be very small (less than 1/3rd that of a LCD color filter). However, color breakup is significantly reduced by going to 360 color fields per second (two each of red, green, and blue) per 1/60th frame today as modern light sources can be switched on/off so quickly and LC response times are so much faster.

Fig. 8.18   Field sequential color technique (Source: Syndiant)

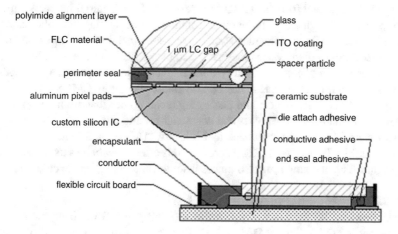

Fig. 8.19   FLCoS micro-displays

Light throughput is higher, in the order of 40% (assuming a 45% loss in polarization) (Fig. 8.18).

A field-sequential color LCoS requires higher power to the panel due to changing fields. The optical path is like Color filter reflective LCoS, but to take advantage of the smaller size requires smaller but higher quality optics. Field-sequential color LCoS potentially mates well with lasers for very large depth of focus so that the augmented reality image is in focus regardless of where the user's eyes are focused. However, that is not always a good thing due to vergence/accommodation issues.

8.7.3.6 FLCoS

Ferroelectric liquid crystals (FLCoS) were first proposed in 1980 by Noel A. Clark (1940–), and Sven Torbjörn Lagerwall (1934–) [29]. and have made a wide impact on applications as diverse as optical correlation and holographic projection.[3] They are inherently faster switching than other liquid crystals (Fig. 8.19).

---

[3] FLCOS was contemplated for holography due to its high speed, but never implemented because the pixels were too big. To display a holographic interference pattern, you need large arrays of very small pixels.

FLCoS micro-displays are differentiated from other micro-displays by their use of ferroelectric liquid crystals (FLC) which can switch in less than 100 μsec, as compared to conventional nematic liquid crystals found in LCDs which switch in the 1 ms range. LC switching speed is roughly proportional to the square of the thickness. For the same LC, an LCoS reflective panel needs to be half as thick and thus is 4X faster. There have been a lot of advances in Tn LC "blends" that are much faster and even some Van LC blends, therefore it's possible to have Tn LC 1 ms or faster.

The fast switching speed of FLCoS enables a single complementary metal-oxide-semiconductor (CMOS) silicon die whose surface is coated with FLC to produce full color displays. The CMOS circuitry interfaces to a standard video input and creates the image on the pixilated reflective mirrors that are implemented using the top layer of metal from the CMOS process. The FLC material interacts with the light passing through the material either rotating or not rotating the polarization of the light based on the voltage placed on the pixilated metal by the CMOS circuitry. The FLCoS micro-display uses the fast speed of the FLC to generate a high frame rate sequence of red, green and blue (RGB) images which the human eye integrates into full-color images. Because the FLCoS micro-display is CMOS-based, it can use high-volume interconnect and packaging technologies that are inherently consistent with small size, low power and consumer pricing models.

However, FLC has the drawback that it has to "DC balance" with the illumination off (unlike Tn and VAN LC). Therefore, this effectively halves its speed advantage again. The blanking time also makes it somewhat more prone to color breakup.

8.7.3.7 Digital Light Processing (DLP)

Developed in 1987 by Dr. Larry Hornbeck (1943–) of Texas Instruments (with significant R&D funding by DARPA), DLPs consist of millions of optical, micro-electro-mechanical technologies, that use digital micro-mirrors, they are also known as digital mirror devices (DMDs). A DLP uses Field Sequential Color and can go to higher field rates than LCoS to reduce the color bleeding effects. Device and control is comparatively high powered and has a larger optical path. The pixel size is bigger than FSC LCoS due to the physical movement of the DLP mirrors. Light throughput in the order of 80% (does not have the polarization losses) but falls as pixels get smaller (gap between mirrors is bigger than LCoS). (Fig. 8.20)

The diagram shows the mirror mounted on the suspended yoke with the torsion spring running bottom left to top right (light grey), with the electrostatic pads of the memory cells below (top left and bottom right).

DLP is used by Avegant Glyph and Vuzix among others for near eye displays and it dominates in pico projectors and large venue and theater projectors.

TI is still promoting it for near to eye use and it has some design wins. It is also being considered for future HUD displays (Navdy and other aftermarket HUDs use DLP).

Fig. 8.20   Diagram of a
Digital micromirror
(Source: Wikipedia)

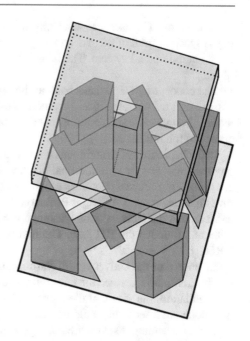

8.7.3.8 Laser Beam Scanning

An alternative to pixelated displays is a MEMs-based scanner coupled with a red, blue, and green micro-laser. Based on the laser beam scanning (LBS) methodology pioneered by the University of Washington and commercialized by MicroVision under their Nomad brand, QD Laser more recently has been demonstrating near eye laser scanning glasses.

When used in near eye applications, the laser scanning is drawn right on the retina, known as a retinal scanning display (RSD). A remarkable feature of RSD is that the image will be in-focus for users that require glasses even without their glasses.

The current drawbacks of RSD include the high cost of the lasers, relatively high power consumption of the drive and control electronics, flicker effects due to the scanning process (affects a few people severely), and the comparatively low resolution compared to other technologies.

The primary focus by Microvision for many years has been Pico Projectors. Brand named PicoP, this is pico-projector scanning technology and can combine projection and image capture in a single, tiny scanning engine. However, the image capture is low resolution and has temporal aliasing issues compared to camera based technologies.

Retinal Scanning and Virtual Retinal Displays

Retinal scanning displays (RSD) or a retinal projector (RP) projects a pattern of photons directly onto the retina of the eye. This pattern may be in the form of a raster scan, as in the case of a television picture, or a vector or line graphic representation. The user sees what appears to be a conventional display image float-ing in space in front of them even though there is no original object or intermediate image in the optical system. The image is only formed on the retina by the pattern of light.

The concept for VRD dates back to the 1980s when scanning laser ophthalmos-copy (SLO) was developed as a method of examination of the eye. It uses the tech-nique of confocal laser scanning microscopy for diagnostic imaging of retina or cornea of the human eye.

In the beginning of experiments with direct eye display techniques, the terminol-ogy used was simply virtual retinal display or VRD. The VRD manipulated coher-ent light to introduce a photon stream through the pupil of the eye to the retina. The investigations started at Wright Patterson Airforce base in the late 1970s, and were carried on at the University of Washington when Tom Furness joined the faculty in 1989 and founded the HIT Lab. The first patents for retinal scanning were named VRD.

Licensees of the University of Washington's patents, wanting to establish prod-uct differentiation, created the term retinal scanning displays. In addition to product differentiation, the vision at the time was that other sources of light, besides scan-ning coherent laser light, could be used.

Retinal scanning displays are more generic and can use different types of photon generators. A subset of the category, known as virtual retinal display (VRD) only uses lasers.

Frame or screen-based HMDs, include devices where the object plane (or the place where the images are formed) is located in a spatially adjacent way close to the eye. The original object is made to appear at a distance by optics that collimate or make parallel the light rays coming from the display object. The image forming devices are typically by LCDs, DLP/DMDs, OLEDs, LCoS, and microLEDs and use raster-line or matrix element approaches for producing a pattern of light on the faceplate or two-dimension plane. (Raster-scanning was originally used by CRTs in TVs). The completed (fully scanned) image is presented as an image frame, several times (e.g., 60) a second so as to appear as a continuous image by the human visual system (Fig. 8.21).

Retinal scanning displays can operate in either see-through (augmented reality) or non-see through (virtual reality) modes. Matrix element devices suffer from not having sufficient luminance (light intensity) to compete with the ambient light in many see-through applications such as superimposition of virtual graphics over an outside daylight scene. Alternatively, direct retinal scanning produces a sufficiently bright beam that can compete with the outside light streaming into the eye.

Other advances of direct retinal scanning are that the resolution of the display is not limited to the number of matrix elements or the physical size of the image object and can paint as many elements across any field of view depending on the configu-ration of the light modulation and scanning elements of the photon beam. The limit of resolution of a scanning laser light source into the eye will be a function of the scanning speed (how fast the mirror is moved), and the number of scanning lines—the same basic principles as used in TV CRTs. However, with microscopic coherent

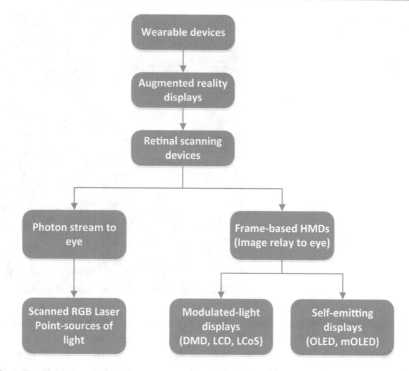

Fig. 8.21 Head-mounted displays taxonomy

light from a laser, the dot size (the pixel) can approach the resolution of the eye itself (the rods and cones). Similarly, the field of view can be almost anything desired, depending upon the configuration chosen for the scanning mechanism.

As mentioned, the VRD was conceived by Thomas Furness in 1985 while working at the Armstrong Laboratory at Wright-Patterson Air Force Base as a means of providing a higher luminance helmet-mounted display for pilots. About the same time in 1986, Kazuo Yoshinaka (1916–2001) while working at Nippon Electric Co also developed the idea [30]. In November 1991, Furness and his colleague Joel S. Kollin completed the development of the VRD at the Human Interface Technology Laboratory at the University of Washington and filed a patent in 1992 [31].(Fig. 8.22)

The VRD technology was licensed by the University of Washington to the new startup, Microvision in 1993. Commercial applications of the VRD were developed first at Microvision Inc. in the early 2000s in their Nomad Augmented Vision System using their PicoP scanning technology, an ultra-miniature laser projection and imaging solution based on the laser beam scanning methodology. Later, at Expo 2005, Brother Industries demonstrated a stationary-type of its Imaging Display that focused light onto the retina and in 2011 introduced their AirScouter using what they called a retinal imaging display (RID). NEC later adopted Brother's technology and announced in Japan the Tele Scouter.

Fig. 8.22 Thomas Furness
viewing the color VRD
optical bench. (Courtesy,
Thomas Furness, Univ. of
Washington)

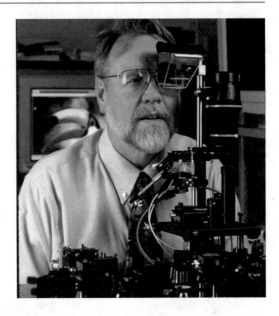

Retinal scanning displays that use lasers as photon sources (as in the case of the virtual retinal display) exhibit high brightness. The color reproducibility can also be excellent due to the high color saturation of the laser light. However, modulation (turning off and on) of the laser light at high rates, is more challenging in the devices that are used today (such as acoustic-optical modulators and Kerr cells). The field of view of the perceived scene is a function of the subtended angle of the optics combining the outside scene with the display scene. Hypothetically, retinal scanning displays can reach every receptor in the retina. If a waveguide is used there are the same FOV issues.

Due to the small exit pupil in some configurations of retinal scanning displays, there is the added advantage of the display always being in focus regardless of the accommodation (focus the eye) or the use of corrective lenses. This is the case when the exit pupil of the optics is substantially smaller than the entrance pupil of the eye. For example, a light adapted eye in a high luminance environment is typically 4 mm in diameter. A display exit pupil of 1 mm would be like a pinhole camera through which display light enters the eye. In this case, even though the light is collimated (as if coming from the distance) it is always focused on the retina. This is like reducing the aperture stop of a camera. The smaller the aperture, the larger the depth of focus. One of the big advantages of laser scanning is that the image is in focus whether or not there are corrective lenses for the user's vision (Fig. 8.23).

While the idea sounds intriguing, it is complicated to achieve. There is the need to precisely combine three separate lasers which can be challenging to make compact. At this point in time green lasers are expensive and difficult to manufacture. Similar to field sequential color, there can be breakup effects of having a raster scan (and with no persistence like a CRT) on a moving platform (as in a head mount display). While there are optics still involved to relay the scanning point of light on

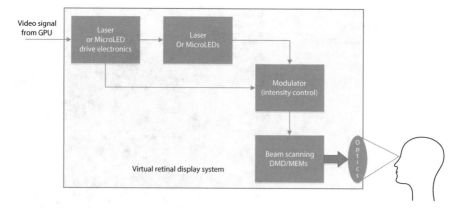

Fig. 8.23   A diagram showing the workings of the virtual retinal display

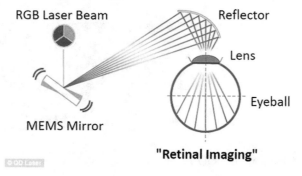

Fig. 8.24   Laser retinal imaging using a rotating mirror (Source: QD Laser)

the retina, it could have a large depth of focus due to the small exit aperture of the optics. Due to its higher luminance, the retinal scanning approach may become a good long term solution for augmented reality, but there are a lot of technical and cost issues that keep this from being a serious display alternative immediately (Fig. 8.24).

Although a laser retinal system can have excellent brightness, it is no better or worse for eye safety than DLP and LCOS.

The one BIG advantage of laser scanning is that the image is in focus whether or not there are corrective lenses for the user's vision. However, a downside is that things like "floaters" in the user's eye will cast shadows on the retina that are visible. (see, "Smart Contact Lenses: Ocumetrics Bionic Lens," section "Smart contact lenses: Ocumetrics bionic lens", for further discussion).

In June 2014, QD Laser (Kawasaki, Japan) and the Institute for Nano Quantum Information Electronics at the University of Tokyo announced the development of a wearable, transparent, head-worn display called Laser Eyewear (LEW) based on laser retinal imaging optics. QD Laser showed the glasses at the Society for Information Displays (SID) in San Francisco in May 2016 (Fig. 8.25).

Fig. 8.25 Mitsuru
Sugawara, CEO of QD
Laser (Credit: QD Laser)

Fujitsu (which spun out QD Laser, and retains a close relationship) has developed smart-glasses that project imagery directly onto the user's retina with a laser, instead of using small LCD screens like other wearables. The glasses house a small laser projector that projects imagery from a front-facing camera or a mobile device onto a user's retina. The glasses could help people with vision loss.

The prototype was shown at a Fujitsu technology expo in Tokyo in May 2015, and could be linked to a mobile device or a camera mounted on the glasses.

8.7.4   Optical Routing

In non-transparent displays, how the image gets from the display device to the eye is a function of optical routing (plumbing), and is done with mirrors (regular and half silvered), optical waveguides, light pipes, diffraction gratings or micro-prisms, and light-guides. For reasons known only to the marketing people and a few professors, these optical routing techniques sometimes get categorized as unique display technologies—they have nothing to do with display or image generation.

The first serious work and patent [32] was done in 1987 by Juris Upatnieks (1936–) while at the University of Michigan, and uses the basic principle of any diffractive light guide principle.

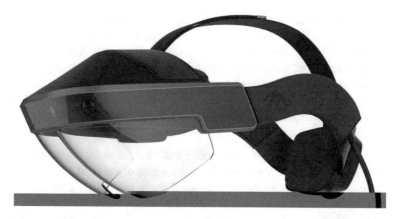

Fig. 8.26   An example of an augmented reality headset using half-silvered curved mirror, the Meta 2 (Source: Meta)

The work done later uses volume holographic layer by Sony and surface diffraction grating by Nokia. Microsoft is using Nokia technology and the former Nokia team to develop HoloLens, The recent work done in the UK and Europe is about optimizing holographic material and configuration to reduce the color issues.

Since then, various techniques have been developed for augmented reality headsets, also known as see-through video wearable displays. Most of these techniques can be summarized into two main categories: curved mirror based and waveguide based. A "see-through" augmented reality display is redundant; all augmented reality headsets are see-through—that's the whole idea behind augmented reality. Curved mirrors and waveguides can cause some amount of distortion which needs to be corrected optically or electronically and which could add cost and/or reduce image resolution. (Fig. 8.26)

Waveguide or Light-guide techniques reduce the cumbersome display optics of a curved half-silvered mirror in front of the wearers face, but also restricts the field of view and generally hurts the image quality. Each have their merits and drawbacks, and application segments.

Various waveguide techniques have existed for some time for see-through wearable displays. These techniques include diffraction optics, holographic optics, polarized optics, and reflective optics. In the following sections I will briefly discuss some of the optical routing systems being offered.

One of the main advantages of diffraction grating is that power consumption is orders of magnitude better than some of the other techniques (including other reflective techniques such as Google Glass). This is a key success factor since most devices are battery powered and are targeting "mobile" use cases.

8.7.4.1 Display Devices Versus Waveguide Compatibility

Karl Guttag has 37 years of experience in Graphics and Image Processors, Digital Signal Processing (DSP), memory architecture, display devices (LCOS and DLP) and display systems including Heads Up Displays and Near Eye Display (augmented reality and virtual reality). For the last 35 years was generally the lead technical person on the design and/or system product rising to TI Fellow at Texas Instruments and being the CTO at three startups. He is named inventor on 150 issued U.S. Patents including key patents related to display devices, graphics/ imaging processors, graphics interface circuits, microprocessors, signal processing (DSP), Synchronous DRAMs, and Video/Graphics DRAM. Billions of dollars of yearly revenue have been attributed to products using these inventions.

Karl Guttage

Flat thin optical waveguides give the sleeker look that industrial designers want but they work on optical principles that restrict the nature of the light.

To begin with, all waveguides as input need the image light "collimated" which means the light rays are all parallel to each other which makes the image appear to focus at infinity. If the light is not collimated it will not have total internal reflection (TIR) in the waveguide properly and leak. It is generally easier to collimate the illumination light used for reflective microdisplays (DLP, LCoS, or Laser Scanning) than it is to collimate light from an OLED. OLEDs have been used with freeform optical (thick) waveguides with one or two TIRs where flat waveguides require many more TIRs, but there are not any examples of them working with flat waveguides (this could in part be due to other issues with the character of the OLED light). Magic Leap's Patent Applications 2016/0011419 (shown in Fig. 8.27 Sect. 8.7.4.1) show a straight forward way to achieve field sequential focus planes using a Spatial Light Modulator (SLM) such as DLP, LCoS or OLED micro-display.

Waveguides that use diffraction gratings or holographic elements usually require that the various colors have narrow "line width" (tight spectrum) primary colors. The amount they bend the light depends on wavelength and if the colors don't have a narrow line width, the image will spread and blur. Importantly, this effectively eliminates OLED microdisplays from working with diffractive/holographic waveguides because OLEDs emit broader spectrum primaries. For this reason, the diffractive/holographic waveguides have used reflective DLP, LCoS, and laser scanning

Fig. 8.27 Field sequential focus planes using a Spatial Light Modulator (U.S. Patent Office)

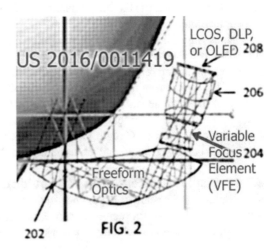

microdisplays where the illumination spectrum can be controlled by the illumination source of LEDs or lasers.

Lumus, for example, uses light polarization to control the exiting of the light with its prisms. This tends to make it favor LCoS microdisplays that already require polarized light.

Most flat waveguides only route a small percentage of the light from the display device to the eye (sometimes less than 10%). This is another major reason why LCoS and DLP devices tend to be used with waveguides as they can crank up the brightness by having brighter LEDs illuminating them. When used outdoors in sunlight, it can be desirable to have over 3000 nits[4] to the eye. If a waveguide is only delivering about 10% to the eye the image source would have to be on the order of 30,000 nits. A typical OLED micro-display only outputs between 300 and 500 nits or roughly two orders of magnitude less than would meet this requirement (eMagin as demonstrated some that have 4500 nits but are not known to be in volume production). Generally reflective optical combiners with either flat and/or curved reflective element(s) don't have problems with broader spectrum primary colors and work with light that is not highly collimated. This allows reflective combiners to work with OLEDs and with simpler optical systems before the optical combiner.

8.7.4.2 Eye Relief

Karl G uttage is the COE and founder of KGOnTech which provides independent technical and market consulting in the areas of display and graphics devices and systems. KGOnTech also provides support for intellectual property (IP) litigation including being a technical expert, prior art research, and investigations of infringement.

A major issue with the various waveguide technologies is "eye relief" and often as a practical matter this comes down to "will it work with a person wearing their own glasses." On some optical designs, there is no provision for eyeglass wearers while others require that prescription lenses be installed.

The greater the eye relief, the larger and more complex the optics become. At a minimum the optics get bigger and more expensive based on the angle of the horizontal and vertical FOV and the distance from the eye. Providing eye relief can also cut into the FOV as the optics are further from the eye, so generally as the FOV increases the eye relief is reduced.

8.7.4.3 Optical Waveguide

There are different types of waveguides, only some of which are diffractive. A waveguide means that the image reflects via Total Internal Reflection (TIR) which is guiding the image. An optical waveguide is a transparent sheet that lets light (from the image source—display, projector, etc.) be transmitted from the source to the user's eye. Since it is glass the user can also see through it.

---

[4]Nit (nt) is a unit of luminance. It is a non-SI name used for candela per square meter (1 nt = 1 cd/m2). The candela per square meter (cd/m2) is the derived SI unit of luminance. The unit is based on the candela, the SI unit of luminous intensity, and the square meter, the SI unit of area.

For TIR to work the light must be at about 42 degrees (depends on the index of refraction) or more from the normal. The simplest way to get light to enter (in-couple) at this angle is to have the entering optical surface at the entry angle (for example Vuzix). The diffraction grating or holograms can make light entering perpendicular to the surface of the optics turn at the desired angle for TIR (examples of this are Hololens and Vuzix).

The diffractive techniques use deep slanted diffraction gratings (i.e. the Nokia technique which has been licensed to Vuzix and is used by Microsoft for its Hololens project), and Magic Leap. This technique uses slanted gratings to in-couple collimated light entering the waveguide at a particular angle, then the light travels through the waveguide using the principle of total internal reflection or "TIR", and finally, the light is extracted to the eye with another set of slanted gratings.

Lumus simply has an angle edge to the waveguide for the in-couple and then they use prisms to change the angle to the image light to make it exit.

The concept was first introduced in the late 1980s, but the devices weren't very good. The dispersion of the image due to chromatic path differences was pretty bad. When the ability to correct digitally by pixel image offsets came together, it improved. But you can't correct for "error/scatter" and you can't correct for change in focus. Even the best of the waveguides available hurt the image quality compared to simpler and cheaper optics, but they give a thin form factor.

Confusing the matter can be the issue of optical see-through and video see-through. Here again, these are not display device discussions, but again applications. Optical see-through is augmented reality. Video see-though is an attempt to use an occluding VR HMD with a front-facing camera in augmented reality applications. That is not a display discussion, and video see-through in my opinion is not augmented reality.

The whole purpose for a waveguide is to provide information overlaid with the real world, with regard to focus point, while still providing an unobscured view of the real world in a flat "glasses like" form factor. That is another major difference between augmented reality and virtual reality—the focal length. In virtual reality there basically isn't one. In augmented reality it is absolutely critical.

Also, OLED are incompatible optically with the use of a diffractive waveguide because OLEDs output very wide bandwidth light that is incompatible with waveguides. Diffractive waveguides work best with LCoS devices.

8.7.4.4 Holographic Waveguide

The holographic technique, developed in the early 1990s by Kaiser Optical Systems [33], is quite close to the diffraction grating technique described above with the exception that a holographic element is used to diffract the light [34, 35].

One of the ways to improve both see-through transmission and reflectance is to take advantage of high-reflectance holographic notch filters and V-coats (V-shape anti-reflection coating) [36]. The problem is that while these special coatings reflect more of a specific display color, they transmit less of that same color, which can alter perceptions of cockpit display color as well.

In June 1997, DigiLens was founded by Jonathan D. Waldern, and developed and marketed switchable Bragg grating nano-composite materials for the optical

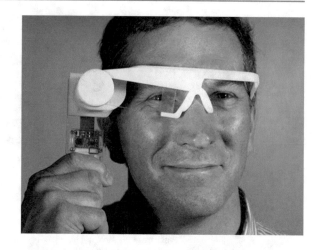

Fig. 8.28 Simon Hall in 2014 with a prototype of the waveguide fitted into a frame with an input. (Courtesy: National Physical Laboratory)

telecommunication and wireless micro-display markets. In January 2000, the company demonstrated the DL40, a compact, lightweight monocular eyewear display with a see-through and RGB color capabilities based on holographic polymer-dispersed liquid crystals technology [37]. Later DigiLens changed its business model to focus its R&D on fibernet switching chips rather than HMDs. In October 2003, DigiLens was acquired by SBG Labs. Nowadays SBG Labs produces head-up displays based on their switchable waveguide technology.

Developed in 2014 by UK-based TruLife Optics, with researchers from the adaptive-optics group at the National Physical Laboratory (NPL) near London, it overcame the overlay problem for augmented reality displays. It was an optical component that consisted of a waveguide (a rectangle of high-quality glass or plastic that acts as the lens) that contained two postage-stamp-sized holograms overlaid onto it. (TruLife Optics was a spin-off from Colour Holographic—a company with expertise in producing holograms.) (Fig. 8.28)

Holograms reflect visible wavelengths of light such that the incident light is reflected at an angle with regard to the hologram. Holograms are intrinsically limited when used in a waveguide due to the fact that the reflected light loses intensity with angular variation s (e.g., off-plane grating couplers and in-plane distributed Bragg gratings for guided-wave optical filtering). Therefore, only limited angles are possible in order not to lose too much light and to keep good image uniformity. Therefore, this technique is intrinsically limited in FOV.

This technique has color issues known as the "rainbow effect," usually due to field-sequential color, and also suffers from limited FoV. Holographic elements reflect only one wavelength of light so for full color, three holograms are necessary; one that reflects Red, Green, and Blue respectively, and are sandwiched together Each wavelength of the light is slightly diffracted by the other color hologram which causes the color cross-talk in the image. (Some people that were very sensitive to DLP "rainbow effects" are not sensitive to flicker and vice versa. This suggests that the eye/brain mechanism for rainbow and flicker are different.) They can also suffer from chromatic aberrations because the light not getting bent and routed properly.

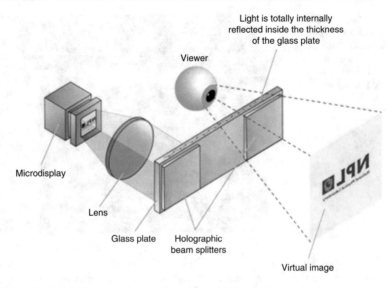

Fig. 8.29 Holographic waveguide (Courtesy: National Physical Laboratory)

A key point is that in this example the red has to pass thorough the green and the blue and it is going to be affected. There is also some error/scatter of light at each hologram or diffraction grating which leads to what Guttag has dubbed "waveguide glow."

Some of the color non-uniformity can be corrected electronically but there are limits to this as the human eye is extremely sensitive to this phenomenon. This technique is used by Sony and Konica-Minolta and is schematically shown in Fig. 8.29 (Sect. 8.7.4.4).

Variations of this technique have come from Trulife Optics, developed in partnership with the National Physical Laboratory in Teddington, London, and Dispelix, Finland. Dispelix, which is commercializing the technology developed by VTT Technical Research Centre of Finland, claims their waveguide is rainbow effect free, provides exit pupil expansion,[5] and is compatible with LCoS, LCD, LED and laser image sources.

In military systems, applying optical waveguide technology to a head-mounted display (HMD) has the key goal of providing the user with improved tactical situational awareness by providing information and imagery. It also maintains compatibility with night vision devices (Fig. 8.30).

BAE Systems presented one such technology in 2009 and this is now in production for a range of Helmet Mounted Display products. Holographic Optical Waveguide reduces size and mass and eliminates many of the constraints inherent in conventional optical solutions [38]. This technology is basically a way of moving light without the need for a complex arrangement of conventional lenses. BAE

---

[5] In optics, the exit pupil is a virtual aperture in an optical system. Only rays which pass through this virtual aperture can exit the system.

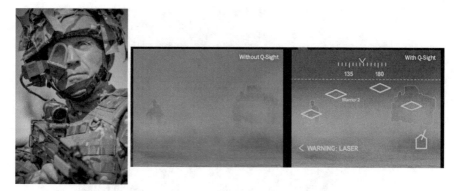

Fig. 8.30   BAE's Q-Sight HMD using holographic waveguide optics (BAE Systems)

Fig. 8.31   Holoeye
Systems' binocular
holographic waveguide
visor display (HWVD)
with holographic
waveguide (Holoeye
Systems)

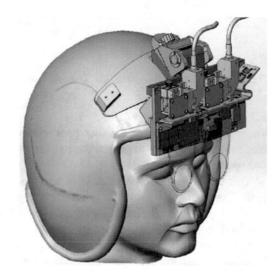

Systems has exploited this technology in their Q-Sight family of scalable Helmet
Mounted Displays (Fig. 8.31).

Holoeye Systems expanded the concept of Q-Sight in a binocular holographic
waveguide helmet visor (HWVD) display, that obtained the following
characteristics:

- 40-degree horizontal field of view
- See through configuration with 80% transmission
- 1460 × 1080-pixel resolution LCoS displays, 6.5 μm pixel pitch, 0.48-inch
  diagonal
- BAE Systems monoblock Gen 2 holographic waveguides

The significance of this work is the design, development and prototyping of a
rugged, compact binocular HMD based on-state-of-th- art wide FOV planar holographic waveguide technology and a high resolution LCoS image generation [39].

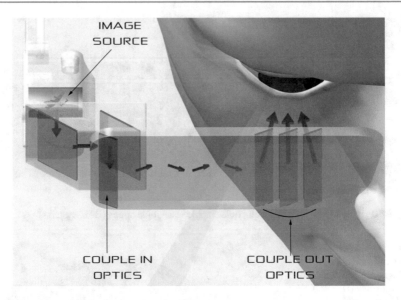

Fig. 8.32 Polarized optical waveguide (Courtesy Lumus)

8.7.4.5 Polarized Waveguide

The polarized waveguide technique uses multilayer coatings and embedded polarized reflectors in order to extract the light towards the eye pupil. The concept has been patented by Lumus.

This technology allows wider FOV and the eye motion box can also be quite large. The light guide uses various numbers of reflectors, having reflectivity that is modified to maintain uniform illumination across the field of view and eye-box. The modified reflectivity is generated by layered polarized coatings on glass plates as currently plastic is not an optimal waveguide substrate. These innovative coatings have various number of layers that reflect uniformly all the relevant spectrum at specific polarization. The coated plates are glued together, cut, and polished in order to make the waveguide (Fig. 8.32).

One of the criticisms about the design is that the system and reflectors are polarized and therefore when used with an OLED display, nearly 60% of the light is lost when it is reflected [40]. Also, the color aberration of non-uniformity of color can exist due to polarization states, but Lumus thinks they have overcome these artifacts.

LCoS and other LCD based image projectors are inherently polarized. By orienting the polarization of the projector to that of the reflective coating, the light loss is minimized.

As for un-polarized OLED sources, at present they are not as bright as needed and suffer from brightness degradation with time. Furthermore, their angular light distribution doesn't overlap the required projection distribution (substantial light loss on top of the 50% polarization loss). Therefore, at present Lumus and others don't find the OLED to be a mature technology for augmented reality applications.

Fig. 8.33 Optinvent's ORA-X-1 headset with augmented reality eyepiece (image courtesy Optinvent)

Lumus has demonstrated waveguide optics which achieve a 55-degree field of view from optics less than 2 mm thick, potentially enabling a truly glasses-sized augmented reality headset. The method is achromatic therefore excels in maintaining color composition of the projected image. The image generator (LCoS for example) is oriented optimally relative to the waveguide reflectors to eliminate polarization loss.

8.7.4.6 Surface Array Reflector Waveguide

A surface array structure is made up of several reflecting structures which makes it possible to have a thinner light guide while maintaining a large eye motion box as well as a large FOV. This technique is used by Optinvent, and branded as Clear-Vu.

The surface structure allows a molded monolithic light guide (out of one piece of plastic) to be used which is coated with a semi reflective coating. A cover plate is glued to the piece of plastic in order to protect the structure and to assure the optical see-through function. This cover plate component does not need to be precise since it is not used to generate the virtual image. It only assures the see-through function by compensating the prismatic effect when the eye pupil looks through the structure of the light guide. The Clear-Vu technology therefore benefits from the reflective waveguide techniques (no color issues, molded plastic substrate, traditional coatings, better efficiency, large eye box and FOV). Moreover, it has the additional benefits of a thinner waveguide made out of one monolithic piece of plastic:

Optinvent has incorporated Himax's LCoS micro-display panels in its design. Microsoft also uses Himax's waveguides in its HoloLens, and Magic Leap has investigated it too (Fig. 8.33).

Optinvent offers the ORA-X claiming it to be a new device category that incorporates a headphone with an augmented reality eyepiece, which they are branding as the Smart AR Headphone. The arm on the ORA-X can pivot 180° so that it can

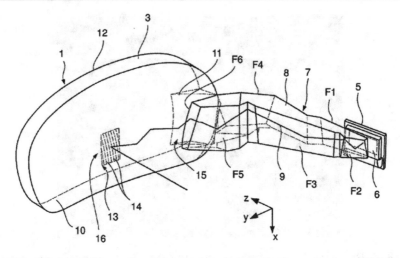

Fig. 8.34 Zeiss' optical uses a Fresnel lens to place the image in the vergence zone (U.S. Patent Office)

be used as a right eyed or left eyed product. There is a sensor which will automatically detect the position so that the sound and image can be flipped accordingly.

Khaled Sarayeddine, Optinvent's CTO, said, "Low cost see-through technologies for wearable augmented reality displays have been an elusive key element to enable the market for consumer oriented mobile augmented reality. Of the various waveguide technologies discussed, the reflective type seems to be the most promising for large scale consumer deployment. The main advantages are the lower cost, plastic substrate, and lack of color issues. Optical technologies are finally emerging that will enable consumer oriented wearable augmented reality display products to become a reality in the near future."

8.7.4.7 Zeiss Uses a Combo

Zeiss uses a form of a light-pipe/waveguide approach to their design to get the image from display (item 6) to along the optical path (item 9) to the Fresnel lens (item 14) in the spectacle lens (Item 3), as shown in Fig. 8.34 (Sect. 8.7.4.7), U.S. Patent 2016/0306171 A1.

The Fresnel lens reduces the amount of material required compared to a conventional lens by dividing the lens into a set of concentric annular sections. An ideal Fresnel lens would have infinitely many such sections (Fig. 8.35).

Zeiss has used eMagin's OLED with free form optics and a waveguide built into glasses. This suggests one could have prescription glasses made with their special exiting structure, the Fresnel surface. Other large consumer electronics companies are developing a similar design.

Fig. 8.35 Cross section of a spherical Fresnel lens (1), compared to the cross section of a conventional spherical plano-convex lens (2)

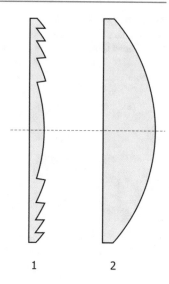

1   2

8.7.4.8 Single Beam-Splitter

To make a pair of consumer augmented reality smart glasses that don't look conspicuous, you would want to make them look as much like a normal set of spectacles as possible. Laforge Optical thinks they have done this, and can even make the spectacles with a person's prescription. One of the most ambitious companies was LA-based Optical, which introduced Shima prescription augmented reality eyewear. Laforge Optical promised attractive consumer style augmented reality glasses, describing itself as a California dream, made in Italy. Ironically, the company was not named after the character Geordi La Forge from *Star Trek* who was blind and used augmented classes to see Fig. 6.71 (Sect. 6.1.4). Laforge places a small display near the hinge of the specials, and projects the image to a beam-splitter embedded in the lens, as shown in Fig. 8.36 (Sect. 8.7.4.7), from their patent application (2016/0231577 A1).

That is a tricky optical manufacturing process. In the half-tone image in Fig. 8.16 (Sect. 8.7.3.5) you can see the beam-splitter in the lens (item 200), and the location of the display (item 400) (Fig. 8.37).

Laforge's design is one of the most straightforward (other than the tricky inclusion of the beam-splitter), which will keep size and weight down. Laforge's display features are minimal to keep the power required and the display complexity down, but it will pair with a smartphone and offer positional information. No camera is included in the first-generation glasses.

A fundamental issue when making augmented reality smart glasses is that they must have optics to locate the image in focus in front of the wearer, as one cannot focus on anything as close as a pair of glasses (or contact lenses, which has to do with the nodal point of the eye). If a transparent display was put on the surface of a person's glasses, it would be totally out of focus (there are also issues of size and resolution because it would not be a virtual image).

Fig. 8.36 Laforge's
beam-splitter lens system
(U.S. Patent Office)

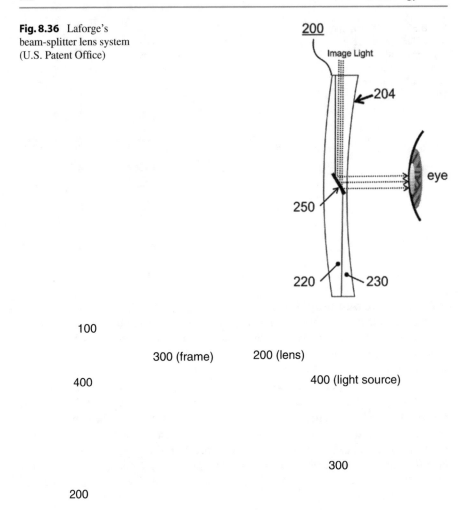

Fig. 8.37 Laforge's glasses with beam-splitter and display element (U.S. Patent Office)

8.7.4.9 HUD Displays

Synthetic vision head-up displays for aircraft pilots was developed by NASA and
the U.S. Air Force in the late 1970s and 1980s in support of advanced cockpit
research. The first use of a head-up display in a consumer vehicle dates back to
1988.

The illustration in Fig. 8.38 (Sect. 8.7.4.9), is a good example of how the first
devices worked. They used a waveguide (not called that at the time) and a very
bright display device (a CRT at the time).

The illustration is from a 1985 patent application submitted by the Environmental
Research Institute of Michigan (4,711,512). Low cost, retro-fit automotive HUDs
use a display device that simply shines up to the windshield—no optics at all.

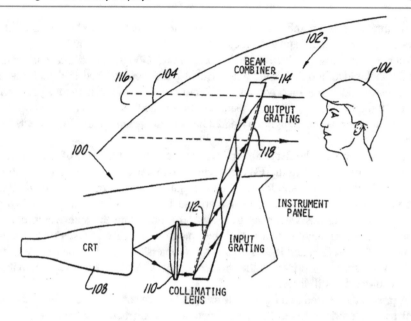

Fig. 8.38 An aircraft HUD using a waveguide (U.S. Patent Office)

8.7.4.10 Reflective

Reflective techniques are not waveguides, they use reflective optical components and don't rely on exotic components or multilayer coatings. They do not suffer from the color non-uniformity issues because they use semi reflective mirrors and reflect white light with minimal degradation. (To be a "waveguide" they need to reflect based on TIR.)

The possibility to use a molded plastic substrate is an advantage in terms of cost, weight, and eye safety (often they use shatter resistant polycarbonate plastics) of this technique as often there is a large lens-like combiner. As with the other waveguide technologies, an optical collimator magnifies the image generated by a microdisplay and injects it into the light guide. As a result, any type of micro-display can be used in this system since there is no polarization or color spectrum issues (LCD, LCoS, DLP, OLED), although those using polarized light may leverage polarizing beam-splitters in their designs.

Reflective systems can be enhanced by combinations of optical systems from reflective, refractive, and diffractive along with Fresnel optics. One popular configuration that aligns the image with the pupil well when looking straight forward is a simple flat beam-splitter, and curved semi-mirrored combiner that also acts to optically enlarge and change the apparent focus, or a combination of beam-splitter and curved combiner.

A simple flat beam-splitter (either exposed or encased in glass) requires all the optics for changing the apparent focus to be done in optics external to the beam-splitter. Epson uses a reflective beam-splitter, and Google use single flat beam-splitter embedded into their solid glass structure that does not use TIR (and thus is not a waveguide) and incorporates a reflective optical element (using polarized light, the light passes through the beam-splitter on the first pass to a curved optical mirror and after its polarization is rotated back to the beam-splitter that directs the light toward the eye).

The problem with the flat beam-splitter approach is that the size of the reflector is directly proportional to the FOV and eye box dimension, therefore the volume consumed by the beam-splitter can become quite large. In both the Google and Epson cases the light guide thickness is around 1 cm. Both Epson and Google use "side shooter" designs where the image is projected from the side which corresponds to the horizontal dimension of the image. In the case of Osterhout Design Groups R-6, R-7, R-8, and R-9 they use "top shooters" and the diagonal dimension of the beam-splitter is driven by the shorter vertical size of the image which makes it a bit compact if still large.

A prism can be used as a light guide as light bounces off the sides of it, with one wall usually partially mirrored or modified with a diffractive optical element or polarizer, all of which only move a fraction of the light, with non-polarized, or non-reflected light lost, reducing brightness. Google used a prism, what's known as a "birdbath" design, and according to Kohno, et al., "suffer from a concerning amount of display leakage." [41].

The term birdbath is used to refer to the combination of a beam-splitter and a curved combiner (the bowl of the bird bath). Google Glass might be considered a modified birdbath as normally the curved surface is the one you look through/at.

Normally this configuration is used with a non-see-through display with a non-see-through curved mirror, since see through displays would be too close to the eye for focus without optics, and if they are out of the visual path, they don't need to be see-through.

All see-through systems waste a lot of display image light, often 80–90% or more of the image light is wasted. If the beam-splitter is 50% transmissive, only half the image passes through to the corrective optics, and only half of that passes through to the pupil, losing 75%. Similarly, only half of the room light is passed to the pupil making the room appear darker. Decreasing the reflection to transmission ratio brightens the room, but with a 75% transmissive beam-splitter only 6% of the display would reach the eye. Generally, the more transparent the view of the real world is, the more light is lost. Waveguides are also extremely wasteful of the image light. The Lumus waveguide for example, needs a bright projector to drive it because it's less than 10% efficient.

Consider a simple mirror combiner that is 90% transmissive, then it is only 10% (nominally, there are other losses) reflective and will lose 90% of the image light reflecting off of it.

It has been estimated by some that a see-through headset could drive up the cost of the display and optics by at least 2X. The reason is that the optics cost more and the display engine has to be a lot brighter (usually by 5–15X or more).

This is particularly a problem for use with OLED displays that can't drive up the brightness without decreasing the life of the display. Some OLED-based systems block about 95% of the outside light. IMMY and Elbit avoid the roughly 75% loss of the beam-splitter but they still have the loss through the front curved combiner. Therefore, the vast majority of augmented reality headsets use LCoS and DLP because they can drive up the illumination brightness. There are some in the industry that feel it is the only way to support a highly transparent augmented reality display because you have to start with a very bright display to get the light out. IMMY is using an external shutter which may work for some applications.

In Google's case, the light is already polarized as part of the operation of the LCoS display, so there is not an additional loss for going through the beam-splitter twice (it causes a little loss but more like 10%, not 50%) because the light on the first passes is already polarized the right way. It then goes through a quarter wave-plate film before hitting the curved mirror that then sends it back through the same quarter wave to complete a full half wave change in polarization so that the light will then reflect on the second pass. There are losses going through the polarized beams splitter and minor losses from the film, but nowhere near 50% (Fig. 8.39).

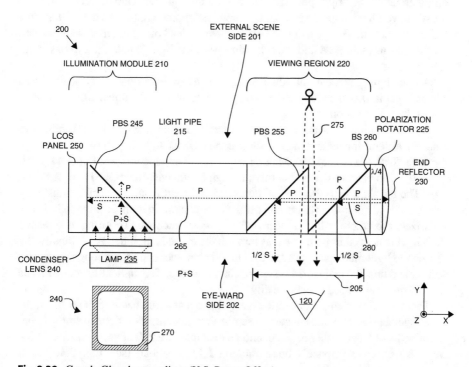

Fig. 8.39   Google Glass beam-splitter (U.S. Patent Office)

Fig. 8.40 Phase Space's
Smoke Combination AR
and VR HMD using
reflective optics (Source:
Phase Space)

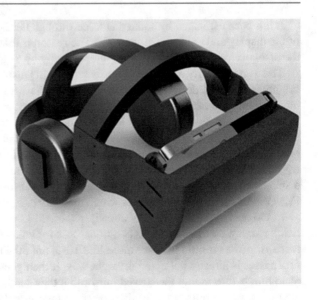

There is a polarization loss to get the light polarized before it goes to the LCoS device. So you take the big hit of 50 + % to get polarized light on the panel, but you only take the big hit once. The light coming off the panel that is meant to be light is all polarized to the "right polarization" to pass through the beam-splitter.

When you have unpolarized light, there is no choice but to take a 50% loss in a "birdbath" design. But by using the well-known "trick" of a quarter waveplate, both on the transmission pass and the reflection pass, the light is polarized to pass with minimal loss.

A thick light guide can introduce a higher level of distortion for the see-through vision. That is why the Google Glass display is located in the upper right hand corner of the user's vision.

Another common variation uses a flat plate combiner that first sends the light to a spherical semi-mirror and then on the second pass the light goes through to the eye (see Fig. 8.40, Sect. 8.7.4.10), Magic Leap's patent application (see Fig. 8.41, Sect. 8.7.4.10), and others such as Osterhaut Design Group with their ODG R-6, R-8, and R-9. The problem with this optical design is that light from the display must pass through the beam-splitter twice and off the curved combiner once. If the light is unpolarized, then there will be at least a 50% loss on each pass resulting in at least a 75% light loss in addition to the loss through the curved combiner. Additionally, the real-world light much pass through the curved combiner and then through the beam-splitter and thus the real world is significantly dimmed. This optical structure makes it problematical for augmented reality.

There are also examples of reflective systems that avoid needing the beam splitter altogether and only have a curved semi-mirror, the most obvious example being Meta's Meta2 HMD (see Fig. 8.26, and an example of a half silvered mirror HMD, Sect. 8.7.4), Phase Space's dual function HMD, Smoke (see Fig. 8.40, Sect.

Fig. 8.41 Magic Leap's
U.S. patent application for
a beam-splitting combiner
optical system (U.S. Patent
Office)

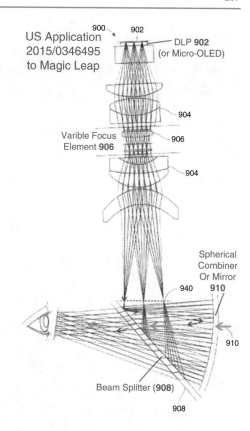

US Application 900
2015/0346495
to Magic Leap

902

DLP **902**
(or Micro-OLED)

904

Varible Focus
Element **906**

906

904

Spherical
Combiner
Or Mirror
940 **910**

910

Beam Splitter (**908**)

908

8.7.4.10), Magic Leap's patent application (see Fig. 8.41, Sect. 8.7.4.10), and others such as examples of microdisplays by Elbit with their Everysight bicycle HUD, and Skyvision aviation HUD, as well as IMMY.

A good example of a schematic representation of the optics used in a beam-splitter and curve reflective comber display can be seen in the illustration in Osterhout Design Groups patent 9,494,800 shown in Fig. 8.41.

A beam-splitter-combiner is a proven design used for years. The splitter-combiner mixed lenses with a spherical combiner partial mirror. The merits of this design are that it often turns out that mixing refractive (lenses) with mirror optics can lead to a more compact and less expensive design.

Osterhout Design Group (ODG) uses a beam-splitter in their R-8 smart-glasses. The beam-splitter moves the image away from the eye and into a curved mirror in a beam-splitter and curved mirror combination, as shown in Fig. 8.42 (Sect. 8.7.4.10).

There are also free form optics waveguides such as Kessler Optics which use curvature to control how the light exists. Kessler has also designed a birefringent eyepiece for augmented reality near-eye systems, as illustrated in Fig. 8.43 (Sect. 8.7.4.10).

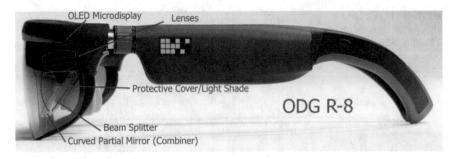

Fig. 8.42 Osterhout Design Group's R-8 augmented reality smart-glasses uses a beam-splitter and curved mirror to reduce size (Source: ODG)

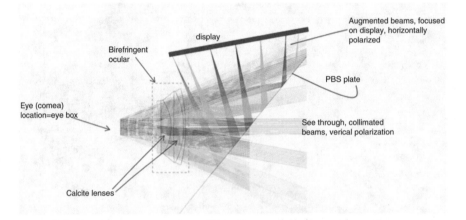

Fig. 8.43 Kessler Optics birefringent eyepiece design (Source: Kessler Optics & photonics Solutions)

The two channels, the see-through channel and the augmenting channel are orthogonally polarized and are combined using a polarization combiner. The eyepiece is made of birefringent elements. It has essentially no power for polarized light in the vertical direction used for the see through and has significant power between 30 and 60 mm focal length for polarized light in the horizontal polarization used for the augmenting channel.

The polarizations for the see through and augmented channels can be reversed. The choice for vertical polarization for the see-through is to provide the function of polarized sun glasses in reducing glare from, say, wet surfaces. The see-through is shown as collimated but can be designed also to focus on objects about 0.5 m or other distances considerably larger than the focal length of the augmented channel.

Reflective systems with beam-splitters, curved lenses, polarizers, and other combiners show great promise and opportunity in augmented reality glasses, as well as helmets.

8.7.5 Transparent Direct-Emissive Displays

As mentioned in the introduction of this section displays can be emissive, or modulated, and transparent, or non-transparent. The previous sections have covered non-transparent. In this section, transparent displays will be discussed.

8.7.5.1 MicroLED

Following LCD and AMOLED, microLED has emerged as the next-generation display technology that is expected to be deployed widely for smart wearable devices. MicroLED offers significant improvements in many areas, including brightness/contrast, energy efficiency and response time.

Light-emitting diodes (LEDs) offer extraordinary brightness, efficiency, and color quality, but due to manufacturing issues were only used in displays as backlights or in modules (typically 512 × 512 pixel arrays used in large-area conference halls or billboard displays).

Light-emitting diodes is a well-known technology, used in everything from street lamps to power lights smartphones. Work using micro-miniature semiconductor techniques to create microLEDs began in the early 2000s, and by 2012–13 results were being shown that demonstrated the feasibility and potential of these self-emitting, high-intensity displays.

Producing reliable, high-performance emissive displays in a smaller form required new microLED technology. Several approaches have been proposed to isolate microLED elements and integrate these microLEDs into active-matrix arrays. The use of microLEDs offer the potential for significantly increased brightness and efficiency, with high dynamic range, for augmented/mixed reality, projection, and non-display light-engine applications.

Before Apple acquired LuxVue in May 2014, microLED technology was relatively unknown. But now the display industry is paying close attention, and many believe microLED technology could disrupt current LCD screens, as well as OLED displays.

In late 2016, virtual reality headset maker Oculus (Facebook) acquired InfiniLED, an Irish startup specializing in low-power LED displays. Founded in 2010, InfiniLED was spun out from the Tyndall National Institute, a research hub specializing in photonics and micro/nanoelectronics that's aligned with University College Cork. They developed ILED (inorganic LED, also referred to as MicroLED) displays, which is a next-generation technology that could succeed OLED, plasma, and LCD through offering greater power efficiency at a lower cost.

Micro-LEDs benefit from reduced power consumption and have been demonstrated to operate efficiently at higher brightness than that of an OLED display and in that respect, can deliver an emissive, high brightness solution. The drawback of LEDs is that they are inherently monochrome—the phosphors typically used in converting color in LEDs do not scale well to small size—which leads to a requirement for more complicated device architectures and it is not yet clear how scalable these can be (Fig. 8.44).

Fig. 8.44 A schematic cross-section of a MicroLED construction (**a**), and a micrograph of an active matrix microLED assembly (**b**) (Source: Display Daily)

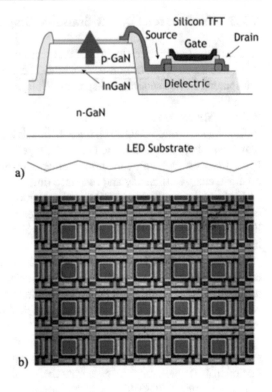

Micro-LED, also known as microLED, mLED or μLED, is an emerging flat panel display technology (mLED is also the name of a company that supplies microLEDs). As the name implies, microLED displays consist of arrays of microscopic LEDs forming the individual pixel elements. Compared to the widespread LCD technology, microLED displays offer far greater contrast, much faster response times, and would use less energy.

Along with OLEDs, microLEDs and ILEDs are primarily aimed at small, low-energy devices such as wearables like augmented reality headsets and smartwatches. Unlike OLED, microLED displays are easier to read in direct sunlight, while still significantly reducing energy demands compared to LCD. Unlike OLED, microLED is based on conventional GaN LED technology, which offers far higher total brightness than OLED products, as much as 30 times, as well as higher efficiency in terms of lux/W. It also does not suffer from the shorter lifetimes of OLED, although the multi-year lifespan of modern OLEDs has mitigated this issue in most roles.

ILEDs can reach a microscopic pixel size, as small as a 2-micron pixel. At such a size, a 1080p display is only .2-inches diagonal. It is expected iLED's will be half the cost of the OLED's.

8.7.5.2 OLED Screens

An Organic Light-Emitting Diode, is a thin-film semiconductor device based on organic materials that emits light when a current is applied. The concept and first

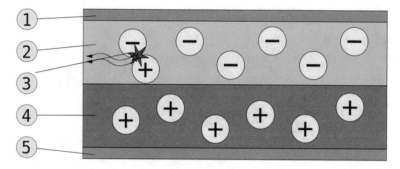

Fig. 8.45   Schematic of a bilayer OLED (Wikipedia)

observation electroluminescence in organic materials when stimulated by electricity was in the early 1950s by André Bernanose (1912–2002) and co-workers at the Nancy-Université in France [42].

The elements of an OLED, shown in Fig. 8.45, consists of: (1). Cathode (−), (2). Emissive Layer, (3). Emission of Radiation, and (4). Conductive Layer, (5). Anode (+).

Also called micro-displays by some manufacturers, non-emissive systems like LCoS, require an external light source with light always incident on every pixel, irrespective of whether said pixel is on or off, an undesirable trait for any portable application where battery life is paramount.

Emissive types of displays rectify that problem and can be more energy efficient, one of the main reasons there is a significant interest in micro-OLED displays (also called μ-OLEDs). Along with higher contrast, faster response time and a wider operating temperature range, micro-OLEDs have been used in prototypes such as the smart-glasses from Atheer Labs, with several companies developing products worldwide (e.g. eMagin, Yunnan OLiGHTECK, and Microoled).

OLEDs enable a greater artificial contrast ratio (both dynamic and static) and wider viewing angle compared to LCDs, because OLED pixels emit light directly. OLEDs also have a much faster response time than an LCD.

Unfortunately, current generations of micro-OLEDs are limited in brightness and experience and have short device lifetimes when run in high brightness conditions. As a result, there is significant research and development underway in making brighter, longer-lifetime OLEDs, with prototypes that use direct color emission rather than RGB color filter arrays showing significant promise in that respect.

Sony has been a leader in micro-OLED (m-OLED) using them in view-finders for their cameras, and their augmented reality smart glasses (Fig. 8.46).

Sony SmartEyeGlass Attach features a 0.23-inch OLED single lens micro-display, with a 640 × 400 resolution and a control board which contains an ARM processor, sensor hub, Wi-Fi and Bluetooth 3.0 connectivity. The display module is just 40 g. Sony has also developed a 1080p OLED with an 8.2-micron pixel.

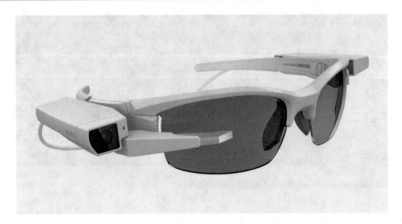

Fig. 8.46 Sony SmartEyeGlass Attach uses m-OLED display (Sony)

IMMY NEO System Resolution

Pixel Size (A)   • OLED Micro Display = 7.8 micron (0.0003")

Eye Distance to Display (B)   • 127mm (5.0")

Single Pixel Subtended Angle (C)   • C = tan A x B = 0.0034 Degrees = 0.2 arcmin

Optic System Magnifying Power (D)   • 8x Nominal

System Resolution (E)   • System Resolution (E) = C x D

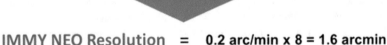

IMMY NEO Resolution   =   **0.2 arc/min x 8 = 1.6 arcmin**

Fig. 8.47 Display density realized from micro OLED display (Source: IMMY)

IMMY has developed an augmented reality headset using a proprietary micro OLED display and has realized the following display resolution in their Neo system (Fig. 8.47).

With a mirror, only optic IMMY says they are not diffraction limited by anything other than the human eye, which is ~1 arcminute.

Waveguides, diffractors and "holographic" optical approaches are approximately 10% efficient. So, you need 1000 nits to get 100 to the eye, which is quite bright. Mirrors are about 98% efficient, so, depending on how you set the combiner, the system is incredibly efficient. IMMY says they have 98% × 98% × 50% which equals 48% Therefore, with 200 nits to start times 0.48 they realize 96 nits into the eye, which is very efficient.

Table 8.1 Ambient light in various situations

Ambient Light in Candelas/Meter^2		
Movie Theater	0.15	0.50
Dim Room Light	3	7
Typical Room Light	100	200
Desktop for Reading	130	200
Room Indirect Sun	150	350
Room with Direct Sunlight	3000	17,000
Outdoor Daytime	10,000	35,000

Sony is moving to 5 microns, and will reach the limit of human vision at that point.

In 2017, Kopin demonstrate a small, fast, highest-resolution organic light emitting diodes micro-display with 2048 × 2048 resolution (four million pixels) in a one-inch diagonal size and that can operate up to 120 Hz with low power consumption.

A big issue for OLED with see though displays is brightness, measured in nits. For example, the Sony 1080p only goes to 200 nits nominal (which isn't much—a typical iPhone has 500–600 nits). Sony makes an XGA (1024 × 768) that goes to 500 nits with a bit larger (10.2-micron pitch) pixel. For augmented reality see-through a lot of the image light is lost. In a highly see-through display there is generally an 80–90% loss of the light; therefore, if you start with 200 nits for example, (and don't enlarge or shrink it much) you will only realize 20–40 nits at the output which pretty much limits the augmented reality device to being used in dimly lit rooms (a good movie theater (very dark) is supposed to have about 55 nits of the screen (SMPTE target)). For outdoor use one would want 3000+ nits and for an automobile HUD 15000+ nits would be needed (refer to Table 8.1: Ambient light in various situations, Table 8.1 (Sect. 8.6.6). This is why Microsoft (Hololens) and all the other transparent display supplier companies have chosen LCoS and DLP microdisplays so they can increase the nits.

eMagin has made claims for a prototype OLED microdisplay that offers up to 4500 nits.

8.7.5.3 Smart Contact Lens

At the moment, several companies are working on technology to make contact lens displays a reality. Google, Samsung and Sony are investing in the tech, for example.

However, I call your attention to a patent (CA2280022) Steve Mann got in Canada in 1999, titled, *Contact Lens for the Display of Information Such as Text, Graphics, Or Pictures* [43].

Sensimed (Lausanne, Switzerland) announced in March 2016, that its Triggerfish sensor-embedded contact lens was classified by the U.S. Food and Drug Administration (FDA) in the newly created category entitled Diurnal Pattern Recorder System, defined as: A diurnal pattern recorder system is a non-implantable,

Fig. 8.48 Contact lens with wireless pressure sensitive sensor (Source: Sensimed)

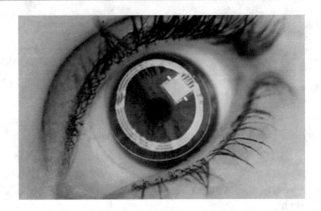

prescription device incorporating a telemetric sensor to detect changes in ocular dimension for monitoring diurnal patterns of intraocular pressure (IOP) fluctuations.

The Sensimed lens is a sensor-embedded contact lens system developed to improve the management of glaucoma. It has an integrated sensor and telemetry, and provides continuous wireless transmission of ocular dimensional changes over the course of 24 h. This is a first-of-a-kind wearable measurement system [44]. (Fig. 8.48)

I've included this device as a demonstration of the feasibility of building a device that is self-powered, can wirelessly transmit information for an extended period, and can be worn in one's eye. The following discusses some of the patents applied for contact lens-based displays—this is not science fiction.

Smart Contact Lenses: Google

On 16 January 2014, Google announced that for the past 18 months they had been working on a contact lens that could help people with diabetes by making it continually check their glucose levels. The idea was originally funded by the National Science Foundation and was first brought to Microsoft.

The Google X team has been working on contact lenses with Swiss drug maker Novartis, that will be able to detect blood glucose levels from your tears. This lens is medically focused, specifically for diabetics initially. There is another lens design that will help focus vision (Fig. 8.49).

The glucose lens will use miniaturized chips, sensors and hair-thin antenna to take measurements and transmit that data. Google is even working on LED lights that will notify a wearer of low blood sugar right in their field of view.

This is another example of embedding electronics in a contact lens. It has been suggested that a lens for the other eye could be an autofocusing camera to help a wearer with focus if that was a problem.

The project was announced in January 2014 at which point it had been underway for 18 months. Google owns two patents for smart contact lenses with flexible electronics and sensors that read the chemicals in the tear fluid of the wearer's eyes to determine if their blood sugar levels have fallen to potentially fatal levels.

Fig. 8.49 Contact lens for measuring glucose levels (Source: Google)

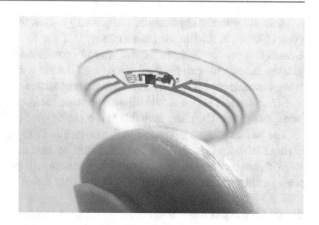

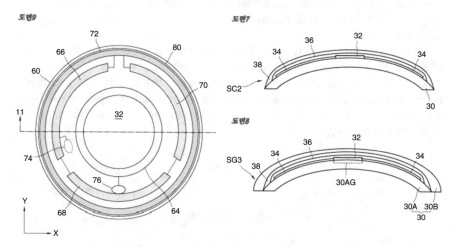

Fig. 8.50 Patent diagrams for Samsung's smart contact lenses. (Source: Samsung/Korea Intellectual Property Right Services)

Smart Contact Lenses: Samsung

Samsung applied for its smart contacts patent in 2014, and in April 2016, the South Korean government granted Samsung a patent for contact lenses with a display that projects images directly into wearer's eyes [45].

As shown in Fig. 8.50, a display unit (32) is in the center. A motion sensor (66) near the edge, and a radio (70), the CPU is below the center (78), and a camera (74) is the lower left. The motion sensor 66 may detect motion of the contact lens 30, that is, motion of an eyeball, or blink of the eyeball. The camera 74 may photograph an object or background on which the eyeball is focused. If the eyeball focuses on an object or background for a set period of time or the number of blinks is equal to or greater than a set value, the camera 74 may be operated. An external device, a smartphone, is needed for processing.

According to the application, the primary reason for the development of smart contact lenses is the limited image quality that can be achieved with smart-glasses. Lenses can provide a more natural way to provide augmented reality than smart-glasses, though we can imagine the privacy debate will reach entirely new heights when cameras are essentially hidden in contact lenses.

Smart contact lenses would allow augmented reality to be projected right into a person's eyes and be more invisible at the same time.

The blinking input is similar to the feature in Google Glass that lets users take pictures with a wink. Or a smartphone could be used to control the camera.

With contact lenses, instead of glasses, users will be able to enjoy augmented reality content more discreetly.

Smart Contact Lenses: Sony

Sony has also filed a patent for its own smart contact lens system [46]. Similar to Samsung the plan here is to incorporate cameras in order to allow for image and video capture.

The object of the patent is to provide a contact lens and storage medium capable of controlling an image pickup unit provided in the contact lens.

The design includes: a lens unit configured to be worn on an eyeball; an image pickup unit configured to capture an image of a subject, the image pickup unit being provided in the lens unit; and an image pickup control unit configured to control the image pickup unit (Fig. 8.51).

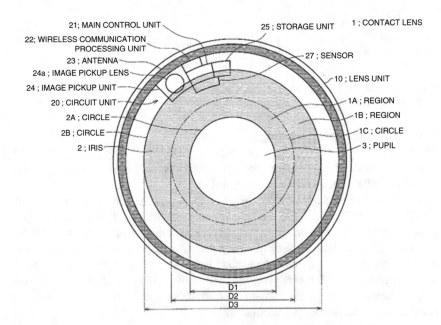

Fig. 8.51 Patent diagram for Sony's contact lens camera (Source: Free Patents on line)

Fig. 8.52 Ocumetics Bionic Lens to improve human vision (Credit: (Darryl Dyck/Canadian Press)

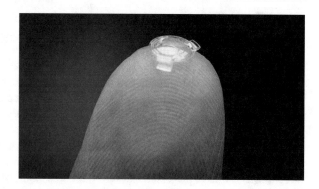

Sony also suggests in their patent that the camera would be (could be) activated by blinking. The patent doesn't say much about augmented reality and focuses on the physical workings of the device.

These lenses will be powered wirelessly but feature hardware to not only capture but also store the footage locally.

Smart Contact Lenses: Ocumetrics Bionic Lens

Dr. Garth Webb, an optometrist from British Columbia and the founder and CEO of Ocumetics Technology Corp, hopes to eliminate glasses and contact lenses forever. Webb and his team of visual scientists have invented the "Ocumetics Bionic Lens," a device that lets you see "three times better than 20/20 vision" without wearing any contacts or glasses at all. It is the product of 8 years of research and $3 million in funding, and has resulted in several internationally filed patents, according to the company.

These lenses are surgically inserted in an 8-min operation. The result would be immediate vision correction and the wearer would never get cataracts as the lenses would never wear away. Trials need to be carried out first. The first Ocumetics Bionic Lens could be available as soon as 2017, but it will only be an option for people over the age of 25 since eye structures aren't fully formed until that age (Fig. 8.52).

The Ocumetics Bionic Lens creator Dr. Garth Webb, says this is going to change the way the eye-care industry works. Even at 100 years old patients with this lens could have better vision than anything available right now can offer.

Unlike current contact lenses these bionic versions would need to be surgically inserted. This would mean the wearer will never get cataracts, a common problem, since their natural lenses would not decay due to lack of use.

Dr. Webb says: "If you can just barely see the clock at 10 f, when you get the Bionic Lens you can see the clock at 30 f away."

Since Webb's initial development, the design has been refined to a point where he is satisfied that it will be able to deliver upon a number of key features.

Some of these features provide a platform for fundamental performance and safety issues that are pre-requisite for what will be the final evolution of augmented reality.

Dr. Webb says the Bionic Lens can be tuned to deliver far better vision than is possible with eyeglasses/contact lenses/laser refractive surgery. This capacity will not be restricted to a few lucky people; it will simply become the new standard in eye care. The Bionic Lens helps to diminish degenerative change within the eye and is structured to absorb blunt force in situations of trauma.

The Bionic Lens serves as a docking station for replaceable intraocular treatment therapies such as vaccines/antibiotics/anti-inflammatory drugs and can be used alternatively as a docking station for digital projection systems. The human eye then, becomes the vehicle by which information is gathered and generated.

Normally the eye rotates upon its center of rotation to analyze details of an aerial optical image that is projected through the nodal point of the eye onto the retina. Since the center of rotation of the eye is coincident with the nodal point of the eye, the observer is able to gather and compare images without having to take time to recalibrate itself. This is an absolutely essential feature for survival in the real world as time delay could be fatal.

Light that projects from the Bionic lens emanates from the nodal point/center of rotation of the eye to generate a stabilized retinal image. Using advanced (but affordable) encephalography and electro-oculograms, stabilized retinal images can be made to become fluidly dynamic. In this way, the stabilized retinal image can be scanned over the surface of the retina from input collected from either brain wave patterns or eye movements. Rather than the retina moving to scan over a dynamic image, an image is guided over the surface of the retina by brain initiated activity.

Headsets and eye glasses used to project "virtual reality" images tend to have a number of restrictions and limitations in their ability to convey seamlessly augmented experiences. The arrival of contact lenses as projection systems might appear intriguing but these too are fraught with a number of unavoidable limitations that prevent the expression of seamless augmented experiences.

Similar to shortfalls normally associated with eye glasses and contact lenses in the real world, external eyewear will not be capable of delivering the versatility and seamless experiences that people will come to demand.

Also as part of the process the vitreous can be replaced. If that is done the vitreous obstructions that could interfere with light transmission using laser scanning could be eliminated for Bionic Lens recipients.

Removal of vitreous debris will assist then in everyday visual conditions as well. Once people become accustomed to having unobstructed and uncompromised vision, the naturally become less tolerant of any visual disturbance. As the vitreous is located posterior to the nodal plane of the eye, movement of hyaloid membranes, etc. are visible at all times. We as observers have "learned" to ignore these, except when visual conditions change.

Once the vitreous body begins to degenerate and decompose into movable sections, the eye is far less likely to suffer retinal detachment if the vitreous is replaced by sterile saline.

In summary, says Webb, the Bionic Lens will serve people with uncompromised vision as its default mode. In its augmented mode, it will likely become the ultimate connection for digitized communications.

Smart Contact Lenses: LED Contact Lens

In 2011, University of Washington researchers demonstrated a prototype device tested in the eye of a rabbit [47]. The contact lens device only had a single pixel of information, but the researchers said it was a proof of the concept that the device could be worn by a person. Eventually, they speculated at the time, it could display short emails and other messages directly before a wearers eyes.

In November 2014, researchers at Princeton University in New Jersey used a 3D printer to create a five-layered transparent polymer contact lens with quantum dot LEDs and wires hidden inside. One layer of the lens beams light into a wearer's eye [48]. The US Air Force funded the research and hopes that it could also be replaced with sensors that detect chemical biomarkers of fatigue in eye fluids to show pilots information and monitor their health and alertness.

The quantum dots go through the emissive layer to create a display of colors that are visible. The lens gets power wirelessly through an embedded antenna. It also stores energy via an integrated circuit and transfers energy to a chip containing one blue LED.

Also, keep in mind that researchers at the University of Washington are not the first to come up with a smart contact lens. Scientists at Oxford University are working on nanopixel lenses.

8.7.5.4 What Can You See?

I think contact lenses are probably the most far out because they're the most challenging with regard to miniaturization and providing power to them. But more importantly is the field of focus. Think about a contact lens. If I were to take a ballpoint pen, or magic marker, and put a dot, on your contact lens you wouldn't see it because it wouldn't be in your field of focus (see Sect. 4.1.2 "A few words about convergence conflict," Sect. 4.1.2).

Steve Mann, described as the father of augmented reality commented in an article about this, and said, "Google Glass and several similarly configured systems now in development suffer from another problem I learned about 30 years ago, that arises from the basic asymmetry of their designs, in which the wearer views the display through only one eye. These systems all contain lenses that make the display appear to hover in space, farther away than it really is. That's because the human eye can't focus on something that's only a couple of centimeters away, so an optical correction is needed. But what Google and other companies are doing—using fixed-focus lenses to make the display appear farther away—is not good." [49].

The concept of using a contact lens as a display device in an augmented reality concept is a little far-fetched in that it can't be a display. It has to be a projector. It has to put the image out in front of you somehow, so that you can focus on it.

Aids for the Visually Disabled

I don't think implants will be part of our normal lives for quite some time. Eye implants, that is. I think we'll have other implants, but not eye implants. I won't say not ever, but it would be a major, major challenge, because we take 95% of our information through our eyes and that's going to be the last frontier for experimenting with. However, there have been successful experiments with retinal implants.

People with the incurable genetic eye disorder retinitis pigmentosa due to genetic mutations that cause their photoreceptors to stop working and die, go blind. However, with the help of a retinal implant system brought to market in 2015, called Argus II, some patients with this rare disorder are regaining their sight. Electrodes implanted onto the retina at the back of the eye send electrical signals to the brain when the photoreceptors have stopped working.

The Argus II system has two separate components: a camera and visual processing unit a patient wears, and the surgically implanted receiving antenna and electrodes. The resolution is very low now, but it will improve, and the as it does, these systems will be able to add additional augmented information about the wearer's environment. Perhaps some people with normal or only partially limited eyesight will choose to get it.

8.7.5.5 Sound
Augmented reality devices must also produce correct sounds, and compensate for environmental noise. Creating virtual sounds based on the real world requires sound reflections to spread and interact with the environment appropriately. For example:

- Airports offer limited sound reflections, and have significant ambient sound.
- Hotel rooms have significant sound dampening.
- Conference rooms are enclosed room with reflective surfaces.
- Virtual people should sound like they are in the conference room.

To deal with all those different conditions the augmented reality system must employ noise cancelation and environment modeling, positional audio, noise filtering, and reverberation dampening.

Headphones
Headphones can be built into helmets, and earbuds are also an acceptable means of providing the user with audio input for either headsets, smart glasses, or helmets. Sound is a necessary capability for when the unit is to be used in loud environments.

Bone Conduction
Google Glass was one of the first augmented reality devices to employ bone conduction technology BCT which transmits sound through bones in your skull to the inner ear. BCT has a proven track record as it is used in the Military and medical world (Fig. 8.53).

This type of speaker does not have a moving membrane like traditional speakers, rather a small metal rod is wrapped with a voice coil. When current is pulsed through the coil, the magnetic field causes a piece of metal to expand and contract. When pressed against the jaw or skull it turns bone into a speaker. The effect is quality sound that seems to be coming from within one's head which others cannot hear, yet

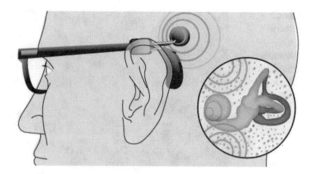

Fig. 8.53   Bone conduction sound device cannot be heard by others (Cochlea.org)

since the ears are not covered the user is not isolated from ambient sounds and therefore not vulnerable to the dangers of traditional earphones.

One commercial example is the Buhelusa's SGO5 headset that features a built-in bi-directional microphone, and provides bone conduction technology that allows one to listen to calls and music with no headsets or earphones.

8.7.5.6 Power and Other Issues

Projecting an image into one's eye, and/or capturing images from a camera sensor (in one's eye) may seem like a tall order. How would you power such things, how would you communicate with it?

Radio-frequency identification (RFID) [50] may be one way to activate such devices. (RFID) uses electromagnetic fields to automatically identify and track "tags". A tag can be attached to cash, clothing, and possessions, or implanted in animals and people. The wiring in the contact lens could be a tag, and when energized and activated by waves from an outside source, send its information [51]. This is known as reflected power (modulated backscatter) RFID tags, both passive and semi-passive, and was performed by Steven Depp, Alfred Koelle, and Robert Frayman at the Los Alamos National Laboratory in 1973 [52] (Fig. 8.54).

Alternatively, body heat might be used. North Carolina State University (NCSU) researchers developed a technique for harvesting body heat and converting it into electricity for use in wearable electronics as part of the U.S. National Science Foundation's Nanosystems Engineering Research Center for Advanced Self-Powered Systems of Integrated Sensors and Technologies (ASSIST) [53]. The lightweight prototypes conform to the shape of the body and generate more electricity than previous heat-harvesting technologies. The researchers also identified the upper arm as the optimal area of the body for heat-harvesting. The new design includes a layer of thermally conductive material that rests on the skin and spreads out the heat, and the material is topped with a polymer to prevent heat from dissipating to the outside air. The design forces the heat to pass through a tiny, centrally located thermoelectric generator (TEG); heat that is not converted into electricity passes through the TEG into an outer layer of thermally conductive materials, which rapidly dissipates the heat (Fig. 8.55).

Fig. 8.54 Small RFID chips, here compared to a grain of rice, are incorporated in consumer products, and implanted in pets, for identification purposes (Wikipedia)

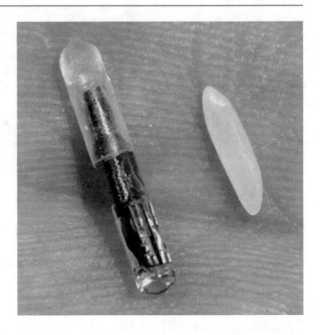

"The goal of ASSIST is to make wearable technologies that can be used for long-term health monitoring, such as devices that track heart health or monitor physical and environmental variables to predict and prevent asthma attacks," says NCSU Professor Daryoosh Vashaee.

Another approach may make use of some research done in 2016 at the University of California, Berkeley. They managed to reduce sensors into 1 mm cubes (around the size of a large grain of sand), and implanted them into the muscles and peripheral nerves of rats. Those cubes contained piezoelectric crystals that turn vibrations into electricity, which was used to provide a power source for miniature on-board transistors [54] (Fig. 8.56).

In their experiment, the UC Berkeley team powered up the passive sensors every 100 microseconds with six 540-nanosecond ultrasound pulses, which gave them a continual, real-time readout. They coated the first-generation motes—3 mm long, 1 mm high and 4–5-millimeter-thick—with surgical-grade epoxy, but they are currently building motes from biocompatible thin films which would potentially last in the body without degradation for a decade or more.

8.7.5.7 Contact Lens: In or Out?

One of the visions of augmented reality is the idea of eliminating glasses altogether and using contact lens. However, you can't use a contact lens as a display per se' because its beyond your focal plane. Therefore, for contacts to be used they'd have to project an image into your retina, as a laser rental scanning device does today in some headsets. I have no doubt this will be possible and the main obstacle I see (no pun) is powering the device. An ultrasonic stimulated piezo cell may well be the answer, if other concepts such as thermoelectric or accelerometer powered techniques are unsuccessful.

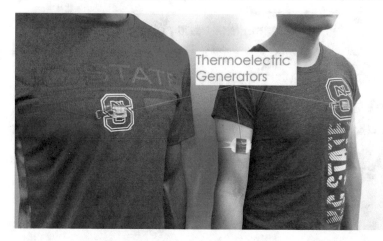

Fig. 8.55 TEG-embedded T-shirt (*left*) and TEG armband (*right*) (Source: North Carolina State University)

Fig. 8.56 Dust-sized sensor, 3 mm long and 1 × 1 mm in cross section, attached to a nerve fiber in a rat. Once implanted, the battery less sensor is powered and the data read out by ultrasound (Photo credit Ryan Neely)

8.7.5.8 The Ultimate Augmented Reality Display?

One can imagine a contact lens with display and camera (such as Samsung [55] and Sony proposed) combined with a corrective lens (such as Ocumetrics has proposed [56]) and containing health measuring devices (such as Google and Sensimed) have developed. Add to that night vison enhancement (such as the super-thin infrared light sensor researchers at the University of Michigan's College of Engineering created using graphene [57]) (Fig. 8.57).

The development of microLEDs implanted in contact lens will be the ultimate augmented reality display system. By 2035 we will look back at smart-glasses as quaint novelties of the times.

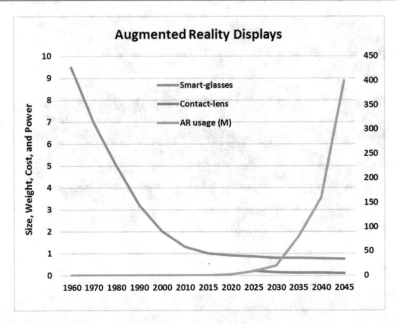

Fig. 8.57 Evolution of Augmented Reality display systems

8.8   Sensors

Augmented reality devices can have from as few as one to many depending upon the type of device, and the manufacturer's targeted market. (Refer to Fig. 4.1: Block diagram Augmented Reality system, Sect. 4.1.) A head-up display in an automobile for example would probably only have one sensor, an ambient light sensor to control the brightness of the projector. A powerful smart-glasses system could have a half dozen or more (light sensor, camera, (perhaps multiples) depth sensor, barometric, IMU, accelerometers, proximity sensors, and one or two microphones), plus up to four radios (Bluetooth, Wi Fi, GPS, and telephone network).

All the sensors are important or the manufacturer would have used the space, added the cost, or power consumption. However, sensor technology is a study in itself, and beyond the scope of this book. I will however give a cursory overview on the critical sensors.

8.8.1   Cameras

In order for augmented reality to work in all systems, with the exception of in-vehicle head-up displays, there has to be a camera to see what the user is seeing. Cameras vary in resolution, speed, color-depth, size, and weight. There is no single augmented reality camera sensor. Some systems have two forward-looking cameras to provide stereoscopic depth sensing. Some systems have multi-spectral cameras to see IR, and/or UV. The cameras can be used for recording.

An augmented reality's forward-facing camera can be used for image recognition to enable the device to identify an image in the real world based on its unique visual features. Image recognition is used to identify what has caught the user's attention so information about it can be displayed.

More advanced augmented reality devices will use advanced computer vision techniques as part of an artificial intelligence (AI) system. The goal of computer vision is for computers to achieve human-level understanding of images. Augmented reality is pushing the boundaries of computer vision and trying to achieve this goal with computer vision and related technologies.

8.8.1.1 Depth Sensing

Depth Sensing and 3D imaging techniques use cameras. Depth-sensing can be accomplished by photogrammetric stereo triangulation, or by emitting an IR or UV pulse, and timing how long it takes to be reflected which is a time-of-flight technique like RADAR, or by emitting a special pattern known as structured light. Once again, no single solution will serve all applications.

Using structured light a 3D camera has a projector that sends out an infrared dot pattern to illuminate the contours of the environment. This is known as a point cloud. As the dots of light get further away from the projector they become larger. The size of all the dots are measured by a camera algorithm and the varying sizes of the dots indicates their relative distance from the user.

8.8.1.2 Thin Photo Sensors, and Lenses Will Yield Skinny Lightweight Devices

Using a graphene sheet nanometers thick, South Korea's Institute for Basic Science (IBS) has developed the world's thinnest photodetector. Graphene is conductive, and thin (just one-atom thick), transparent, and flexible. However, it doesn't behave like a semiconductor, so its application in the electronics industry has limited use. To increase its usability, IBS researchers sandwiched a layer of the 2D semiconductor molybdenum disulfide (MoS2) between two graphene sheets and put it over a silicon base.

With a thickness of just 1.3 nm, 10 times smaller than standard silicon photodiodes, this device could be used in wearable electronics (i.e., AR), smart devices, Internet of Things (IoT), and photo electronics (Fig. 8.58).

The IBS researchers initially thought the device would be too thin to generate an electric current but, unexpectedly, it did. "A device with one-layer of MoS_2 is too thin to generate a conventional p-n junction, where positive (p) charges and negative (n) charges are separated and can create an internal electric field. However, when we shone light on it, we observed high photocurrent. It was surprising! Since it cannot be a classical p-n junction, we thought to investigate it further," explains Yu Woo Jong [58].

To understand what they found, the researchers compared devices with one and seven layers of MoS_2 and tested how well they behave as a photodetector, that is, how they are able to convert light into an electric current. The researchers found that the device with one-layer MoS_2 absorbs less light than the device with seven layers, but it has higher photoresponsivity.

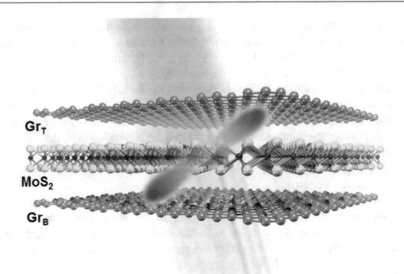

Fig. 8.58 Device with the MoS2 layer sandwiched between top (GrT) and bottom (GrB) graphene layers. Light (green ray) is absorbed and converted into an electric current. When light is absorbed by the device, electrons (*blue*) jump into a higher energy state and holes (*red*) are generated in the MoS2 layer. The movement of holes and electrons created by the difference in electronic potential (Source: IBS)

"Usually the photocurrent is proportional to the photo absorbance, that is, if the device absorbs more light, it should generate more electricity, but in this case, even if the one-layer MoS_2 device has smaller absorbance than the seven-layer MoS_2, it produces seven times more photocurrent," said Yu.

Why is the thinner device working better than the thicker one? The research team proposed a mechanism to explain why this is the case. They recognized that the photocurrent generation could not be explained with classical electromagnetism, but could be with quantum physics. When light hits the device, some electrons from the MoS_2 layer jump into an excited state and their flow through the device produces an electric current. However, in order to pass the boundary between MoS_2 and graphene, the electrons need to overcome an energy barrier (via quantum tunneling), and this is where the one-layer MoS_2 device has an advantage over the thicker one.

Because the device is transparent, flexible, and requires less power than the current 3D silicon semiconductors, it could accelerate the development of 2D photoelectric devices, say the researchers.

8.8.1.3 A Thin Sensor Needs a Thin Lens

The world's thinnest lens, one two-thousandth the thickness of a human hair, opening the door to flexible computer displays and a revolution in miniature cameras.

A group of researchers from the Australian National University (Canberra) and the University of Wisconsin (Madison) have discovered that a single molecular layer L of molybdenum disulfide (MoS_2) has a giant optical path length), is about 10 times greater compared to another monolayer material, graphene. Although this may seem like an esoteric result, it has a very practical consequence for photonics as the researchers have demonstrated, just a few monolayers of MoS_2 can be used to create what the researchers call the "world's thinnest optical lens," only 6.3 nm thick. With a diameter of about 20 μm, the concave MoS_2 lens the researchers fabricated has a calculated focal length of −248 μm at a 535-nm wavelength.

Lead researcher Dr. Yuerui (Larry) Lu from The Australian National University (ANU) said the discovery hinged on the remarkable potential of the molybdenum disulphide crystal.

"This type of material is the perfect candidate for future flexible displays," said Dr. Lu, leader of the Nano-Electro-Mechanical Systems Laboratory in the ANU Research School of Engineering.

We will also be able to use arrays of micro lenses to mimic the compound eyes of insects. "Molybdenum disulphide is an amazing crystal," said Dr. Lu. It survives at high temperatures, is a lubricant, a good semiconductor and can emit photons too.

The capability of manipulating the flow of light in atomic scale opens an exciting avenue towards unprecedented miniaturization of optical components and the integration of advanced optical functionalities."

Molybdenum disulphide is in a class of materials known as chalcogenide glasses that have flexible electronic characteristics that have made them popular for high-technology components.

Dr. Lu's team created their lens from a crystal 6.3-nanometres thick—9 atomic layers—which they had peeled off a larger piece of molybdenum disulphide with sticky tape.

They then created a 10-micron radius lens, using a focused ion beam to shave off the layers atom by atom, until they had the dome shape of the lens.

The team discovered that single layers of molybdenum disulphide, 0.7 nanometers thick, had remarkable optical properties, appearing to a light beam to be 50 times thicker, at 38 nanometers. This property, known as optical path length, determines the phase of the light and governs interference and diffraction of light as it propagates.

"At the beginning, we couldn't imagine why molybdenum disulphide had such surprising properties," said Dr. Lu.

Collaborator Assistant Professor Zongfu Yu at the University of Wisconsin, Madison, developed a simulation and showed that light was bouncing back and forth many times inside the high refractive index crystal layers before passing through.

Molybdenum disulphide crystal's refractive index, the property that quantifies the strength of a material's effect on light, has a high value of 5.5. For comparison, diamond, whose high refractive index causes its sparkle, is only 2.4, and water's refractive index is 1.3.

8.8.2   Localization, Tracking, and Navigation Sensors

Knowing where you are is one of the most critical functions in augmented reality. How can a system identify things and deliver potentially mission critical information in a timely manner if it doesn't know where you are? But how does it know where you are? There are several ways described in previous sections.

Just as a smartphone (which can also be an augmented reality device) can "know" where you, so can a dedicated augmented reality device. They do it with GPS radios, triangulation with cell phone towers, accelerometers, and compasses using magnetometers, and complex combinations of several of them.

In the case of seriously mission-critical military helmets, the location data comes from the complex and redundant sensors and radios in the airplane, ship, or tank.

Precision positioning requires accurate location fixes, and then high-resolution incremental measurements until the next accurate fix can be obtained. SLAM for example provides a stable measurement but suffers from error accumulation and scale ambiguity that introduce a less and less accurate localization over time. One concept to overcome that is to include constraints provided by a pre-defined 3D model of an object of interest (i.e., where the user is, in a general sense) a priori knowledge (e.g. model-based tracking). It results in a very accurate and stable localization. This is referred to as a model-based solution and relies on a prebuilt map of 3D features.

The combination of position and orientation is referred to as the pose of an object, even though this concept is sometimes used only to describe the orientation. The pose of the camera is estimated on-line by matching 2D features extracted from the images with the 3D features of the map.

8.8.3   Inertial Measurement Unit

An inertial measurement unit (IMU) is a sensor array that measures and reports a body's specific force, angular rate, and sometimes the magnetic field surrounding the body, using a combination of accelerometers and gyroscopes, sometimes also magnetometers. It is used to sense, calculate, and reports a body's specific force and angular rate. The sensors provide six degrees of freedom: three accelerometers are mounted at right angles to each other, so that acceleration can be measured independently in three axes.

Three gyroscopes are also at right angles to each other, so the angular rate can be measured around each of the acceleration axes (Fig. 8.59).

IMUs are necessary for augmented reality devices to track the movement, position, and gaze of the user so they can adapt dynamically to the images or information being presented to the user.

The IMU pays a critical role in getting the image the viewer sees in the right location and orientation. The camera is not in the exact same place on the augmented reality device as the IMU, so it "sees" the world from a slightly different location and angle. This difference, though small, might be enough to make the

Fig. 8.59 IMUs work, in
part, by detecting changes
in x, y, z, pitch, roll, and
yaw (Source: Wikipedia)

virtual objects in view look a bit misplaced, or possibly misshaped. Photogrammetric
software must compensate for this in real time. The distances between components
on the device are considered extrinsic parameters. which denote the coordinate system transformations from 3D world coordinates to 3D camera coordinates.

8.8.3.1 MEMs

IMUs built using micro-electro-mechanical systems (MEMs) are employed as gyroscopes, which are used to keep track of the device's movement (in 2-axis) from an
initially known location.

MEMs are made up of components between 1 and 100 micrometers in size (i.e.
0.001 to 0.1 mm). They usually consist of a central unit that processes data (the
microprocessor) and several components that interact with the surroundings such as
micro sensors. The types of MEMs devices can vary from relatively simple structures having no moving elements, to extremely complex electromechanical systems
with multiple moving elements under the control of integrated microelectronics.

Each type of MEMs gyroscope has some form of oscillating component from
where the acceleration, and hence direction change, can be detected. This is because,
as per the conservation of motion law, a vibrating object likes to continue vibrating
in the same plane, and any vibrational deviation can be used to derive a change in
direction. These deviations are caused by the Coriolis force, which is orthogonal to
the vibrating object.

MEMs-based IMUs are commonly found in smartphones and tablets, and some
augmented devices.

8.8.4   Haptic Feedback

Haptic is defined as of, or relating to, tactile sensations and the sense of touch as a
method of interacting with computers and electronic devices. Typically, it is a vibration or other tactile sensation received from a computer or electronic device.

Haptic feedback, often referred to as simply "haptics", is the use of the sense of
touch in a user interface design to provide information to an end user. This is usually
in the form of vibrations from the device. The device can be a game controller or a

touch screen on a mobile device such as a smartphone or tablet to denote that a touchscreen button has been pressed. In this example, the mobile device would vibrate slightly in response to the user's activation of an on-screen control, making up for the lack of a normal tactile response that the user would experience when pressing a physical button.

In computer and console games, there are haptic devices like force-feedback controllers. Similar controllers are used in virtual reality systems.

However, one of the criteria for a successful consumer augmented reality system is for it to be inconspicuous. How then does the user interact with its? As mentioned elsewhere ("Gesture Control," Sect. 4.1), hand gestures are one way, but that can be awkward in a public environment (imagine a crowded airport with people waving their hands about in front of their glasses).

Another approach is voice, as discussed elsewhere ("Voice Control," Sect. 8.10.1), and eye tracking ("Eye-Tracking," Sect. 8.10.3).

A haptic device made of thin film materials as described below have the quality of not only providing feedback, but also are capable of accepted input. Imagine a decorative, inconspicuous wrist band that the wearer could inconspicuously tap to change menus or direct queries.

8.8.4.1 Haptic Feedback Thin as an Eyelash

Qiming Zhang is a distinguished professor of Electrical Engineering and Materials Science and Engineering at Pennsylvania State University. He is the inventor of electroactive polymers and nanocomposites for applications such as artificial muscles, sensors and actuators, energy storage and conversion. Along with his partner Ralph Russo (formally at Apple) they founded Strategic Polymer Sciences in 2006 based on the proprietary technology developed at Penn State. Then they developed a film based actuator composed of 30–50 layers of film and electrodes—very similar to a capacitor, but with a magic property—it moves (Fig. 8.60).

The device has a frequency range from 0 Hz to 20 kHz with response time < 10 ms, and an operating voltage range from 100 to 212v. The company got overly ambitious, didn't have the right manufacturing capabilities, and in 2015 restarted, and renamed the company to Novasentis.

The company now has top tier supply chain and manufacturing partner in place.

The actual device can be made in almost any size and shape, but to get the product accepted and into production systems, the company settled on the 10 × 10 mm pad. The pad could be a button (or array of button, embedded in a game controller, an automobile steering wheel, the fingers of a glove in an augmented or virtual reality application, or embedded into a wrist strap for a wearable device.

The company thinks with clever waveforms they can produce hundreds of unique physical signatures, more likely their customers might choose 20 different notifications and dozens of different texture and other finer sensations. And because of the small mass of the device, and its ability to work at frequencies between 100 and 20 kHz, you can also have it make sounds when it gives feedback.

Similar work on polymers for haptic feedback have been done at the Korea Advanced Institute of Science and Technology (KAIST).

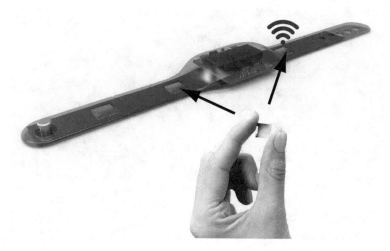

Fig. 8.60 One implementation of the actuator is 10 × 10 mm and only 150 μm thick (Source: Novasentis)

Researchers at KAIST have developed an electrode consisting of a single-atom-thick layer of carbon to help make more durable artificial muscles [59].

Ionic polymer metal composites (IPMCs), often referred to as artificial muscles, are electro-active polymer actuators that change in size or shape when stimulated by an electric field. IPMCs have been extensively investigated for their potential use in robotics inspired by nature, such as underwater vehicles propelled by fish-like fins, and in rehabilitation devices for people with disabilities.

An IPMC "motor", or actuator, is formed from a molecular membrane stretched between two metal electrodes. When an electric field is applied to the actuator, the resulting migration and redistribution of ions in the membrane causes the structure to bend. IPMC actuators are known for their low power consumption, as well as their ability to bend under low voltage and to mimic movements that occur naturally in the environment (Fig. 8.61).

The researchers acknowledge that there are still many challenges and more research is needed to realize the full potential of the graphene-based electrodes and their subsequent commercialization. They plan to further enhance the bending performance of the actuators, their ability to store energy and their power.

8.8.5 Earthquake Prediction Sensor

The emission of radon has been identified as a possible marker for earthquake prediction, for as much as 2–3 days in advance, and a paper published in 2015 by two Korean researchers suggests radon and thoron detection might be a precursor [60].

In 2017, at a consumer electronics conference (CES), a startup company, Rium, offered a pocket-sized radon detector. The company claimed its instrument will be able to differentiate not only the particle type (Gamma, Alpha, Beta) but also

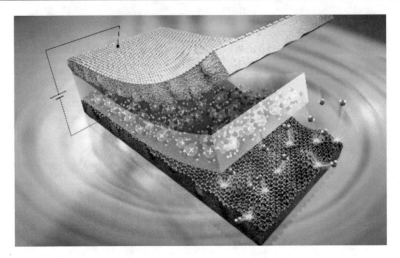

Fig. 8.61 Schematic of the ionic polymer-graphene composite (IPGC) actuator or "motor". When an electric field is applied, the redistribution of ions causes the structure to bend (Credit: Korea Advanced Institute of Science and Technology)

radioactive isotopes (radon, uranium, cesium, etc.). This information will trace the origin of exposure (natural, industrial, medical) and accurately calculate its impact on health in real time.

Radon is a naturally occurring sub-soil substance, and is harmful to health. Homes built over radon sources either must have special ventilation adapted to the situation or be abandoned.

In the study conducted in Korea, the researchers proposed placing radon-thoron detectors in caves (to block background interference). That could be tied into a transmitter and broadcast to users' phones and augmented reality systems as proposed by Rium. A pocket-sized radon-thoron detector could be part of a home or building site inspector's kit, and tied into an augmented reality system.

8.9   Augmented Reality—Marker vs. Markerless

A major issue in augmented reality is motion tracking, and geo-locating—knowing where you are. To achieve this task, many sensors have been considered: mechanical devices, ultrasonic devices, magnetic sensors, inertial devices, GPS, compass, and obviously, optical sensors [146]. There was no single solution to solve this problem, which kept augmented reality in a complex laden realm, but as camera sensors got smaller, higher resolution, and less expensive vision-based techniques emerged, once again thanks to the explosion in smartphones sales.

Augmented reality applications are based on accurately computing a camera's position in 3-dimensional space, also known as its "pose". and six-degrees of freedom (6DOF) position. Pose refers to the position and orientation of the camera, and

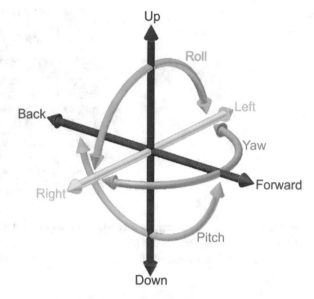

Fig. 8.62 Six-degrees of freedom (Wikipedia)

is needed to help determine where it is and what direction in 3D space it is facing (looking at). Microsoft calls this "inside-outside" tracking.

Six-degrees of freedom refers to the position and orientation of the camera in three-dimensional space: forward/backward (surge), up/down (heave), left/right (sway), combined with changes in orientation through rotation about three perpendicular axes, often termed pitch, yaw, and roll, as shown in Fig. 8.62 (Sect. 8.9).

Pose, or 6DOF as many developers like to refer to it, uses, or can use, inertial sensors (accelerometer, gyroscope) and/or location (compass (magnetometer), GPS, barometric (elevation), and even Wi-Fi) sensor data, and/or mobile phone radio location techniques to establish the viewer's camera's pose with reasonable precision.

The most basic technique uses pre-defined fiducial markers to enable tracking in order to determine a device's pose.

Visual tracking techniques are segmented into methods requiring a priori knowledge (e.g. model-based tracking) and ad hoc methods (e.g. feature tracking).

Ad hoc methods are further sub-divided by the way the environment map is generated: Tracking-only methods, simultaneous localization, and mapping methods (SLAM) and extensible methods. You can further segment Ad hoc marker tracking methods into simple marker tracking, and dynamic marker fields.

A tracking system can save an adhoc created map and use it the next time as a priori information, so the segmentation is not exclusive.

Simple marker-based tracking belongs to ad hoc methods, using a tracking only, predefined marker field to a priori methods and dynamic marker field setups to ad-hoc methods.

Fig. 8.63 Typical
augmented reality marker
patterns

Feature-based tracking methods belong mainly to ad hoc methods, but they often still need some kind of initialization for the scale. A feature tracking method can also use a previously learned feature map of the environment and thus belong to the a priori method category.

8.9.1   Markers and Fiducials

In target-based augmented reality such as used in smart-glasses (and not HUDs), the most common and basic method to determine a camera's pose is a vision-based approach with known fiducial markers (typically square, black and white patterns that encode information about the required graphic overlay). The position of the known marker is used along with camera calibration to accurately overlay the 3D graphics in the display.

Using a marker, such as shown in Fig. 8.63, the tracking function uses the augmented reality device's camera to estimate of the pose of the device in real time based on what it is "seeing."

Markers are a common term in computer vision, defined by Wikipedia as "a piece of information which is relevant for solving the computational task related to a certain application [61].

Because of their predefined shape and pattern, markers are easily detectable and located in or near the item of interest, they are used for quick, and inexpensive pose calculation. The high contrast of black and white squares enables easier detection, so four known marker points enables unambiguous calculation of the camera pose.

Fiducial marker tracking also adds significant robustness to tracking, particularly in poor lighting conditions, or when the camera is far away from the tracked image.

Various approaches to vision-based pose estimation exist, becoming more sophisticated and otherwise evolving over time.

The known object is most commonly a planar object (i.e., the marker), however it can also be a 3D object whose model of geometry and appearance is available to the augmented reality application. Tracking the camera pose in unknown environments can be a challenge. In order to reduce this challenge, a technology known as SLAM (Simultaneous Localization and Mapping), has been developed which enables augmented reality experiences on mobile devices in unknown environments.

8.9.2   Natural Feature Tracking Using Markers

A fiducial marker is an easily detected feature as discussed above, and can be knowingly and intentionally placed, or may naturally exist in a scene. Natural Feature Tracking (NFT) is the idea of recognizing and tracking a scene that is not deliberately using markers. NFT can use items that are embedded in a natural pictorial view to enhance tracking points and regions within the view.; e.g., a known statue, building, or maybe a tree. The result can be seemingly marker-less tracking (since the markers may not be known to the user.

Using the NFT can be less computationally expensive than a full SLAM system, and is more practical for mobile devices. However, there is a practical limit on the number of unique markers that can be distinguished at any one time. Thus, if a large number of images need to be tracked a SLAM or fiducial marker could be more efficient.

8.9.3   SLAM—Markerless Location

A critical component for augmented reality is to know where you are and what's around you. One of the technologies to enable such capabilities is simultaneous localization and mapping (SLAM) a system and process whereby a device creates a map of its surroundings and orients itself within the map in real time.

SLAM starts with an unknown environment where the augmented reality device tries to generate a map and localize itself within the map. Through a series of complex computations and algorithms which use the IMU sensor data to construct a map of the unknown environment while using it at the same time to identify where it is located (Fig. 8.64).

For some outdoor applications, the need for SLAM is almost entirely removed due to high precision differential GPS sensors. From a SLAM perspective, these may be viewed as location sensors whose likelihoods are so sharp that they completely dominate the inference.

However, in order for SLAM to work the system needs to create a pre-existing map of its surroundings and then orient itself within this map to refine it (Fig. 8.65).

There are several algorithms for establishing pose using SLAM. One technique uses a keyframe- solution that assists with building room-sized 3D models of a particular scene. The system runs a computationally intensive non-linear optimization called bundle adjustment to ensure that models with a high-level of accuracy are generated. This optimization is significantly improved using high-performance parallel processors using same-instruction, multiple-data (SIMD) GPU processors to make certain that a smooth operation occurs on mobile devices.

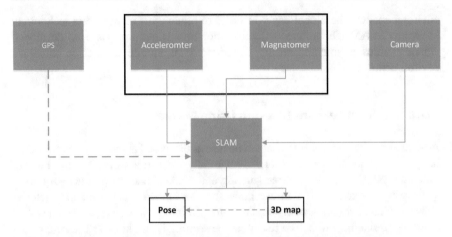

Fig. 8.64 Block diagram of the IMU and SLAM relationship to Pose and the 3D map

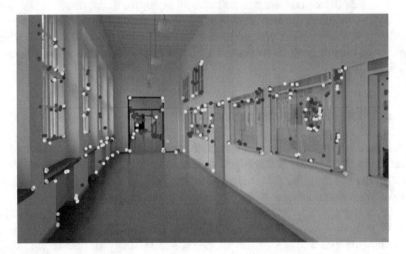

Fig. 8.65 Using SLAM technology the augmented reality device's camera in conjunction with its gyroscope and other location devices assign coordinates to objects in the FoV

During fast motion tracking failures are typically experienced in an augmented reality system. In order to recover from such tracking failures, the system needs a relocalization routine to quickly compute an approximate pose from the camera when images are blurred or otherwise corrupted. The system must also deliver a triangulated 3D mesh of the environment for the application to utilize in order to deliver a realistic augmented experience that is blended with the real scene.

Markerless location mapping is not a new concept and was explored in earlier work by Mann (Video Orbits) [62] for featureless augmented reality tracking [63]. Markerless vision-based tracking was also combined with gyro tracking [64].

In markerless augmented reality, the problem of finding the camera pose requires significant processing capability and more complex and sophisticated image-processing algorithms, such as disparity mapping, feature detection, optical flow, object classification, and real-time high-speed computation.

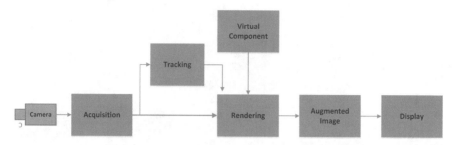

Fig. 8.66 Block diagram for an augmented reality system with tracking

In his report, "Theory and applications of marker-based augmented reality," for VTT Technical Research Center of Finland, Sanni Siltanen [65] generated a block diagram for a simple augmented reality system which has been adopted by the industry, and is presented here slightly redrawn for simplification.

As illustrated in Fig. 8.66, the acquisition module captures the image from the camera sensor. The tracking module calculates the correct location and orientation for virtual overlay. The rendering module combines the original image and the virtual components using the calculated pose and then renders the augmented image on the display.

The tracking module is "the heart" of a non-head-up display augmented reality system; it calculates the relative pose of the camera in real time, and is critical in an augmented reality system with always on vision processing. "Always on vision" is not the same thing as being able to simply take a picture with an augmented reality device. For example, Google glass has no vison processing but can take pictures.

A more detailed view of the tracking system can be seen in the following diagram which is an expanded version of the; Block diagram of a typical augmented reality device diagram shown in Fig. 7.3.

Please note that Figs. 8.66 and 8.67 are labeled in red to illustrate the matching components.

SoCs designed for smartphones with CPUs, GPUs, DSPs, and ISPs are often employed in augmented reality systems and used for doing vision processing. However, they may not be fast enough and so specialized vision processors from companies like CogniVue, Synopsys, or custom devices based on field programmable gate arrays (FPGA) have been developed to speed up the timing and critical algorithm execution.

For the kind of fast updating and image acquisition needed in mission-critical augmented reality systems, there is only 50 ms from sensor to display: the acquisition typically takes 17.7 ms, rendering will use up 23.3 ms, leaving only 10 ms for the tracking section, which really isn't much, or enough.

The specialized vision processors, which handle the tracking problem can process the data in 2 ms typically.

Marker-based systems are less demanding, but unsuitable in many scenarios (e.g. outdoor tracking). Markerless tracking depends on identifying natural features vs. fiducial markers.

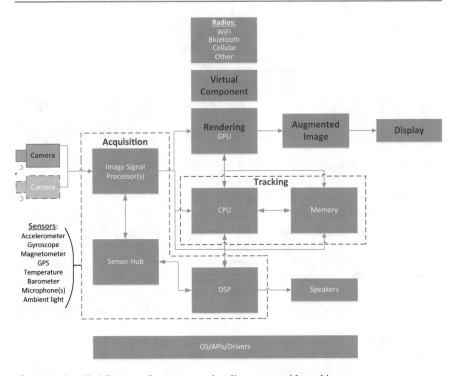

Fig. 8.67   Detailed diagram of an augmented reality system with tracking

Augmented reality systems use sensors for tracking and location (e.g. GPS); or Hybrid; e.g. GPS and MEMs gyroscope for position and visual tracking for orientation.

Mission critical augmented reality systems however, need to use some other tracking method. Visual tracking methods to estimate camera's pose (camera-based tracking, optical tracking, or natural feature tracking) are often the solution.

Tracking and registration becomes more complex with Natural Feature Tracking (NFT).

Markerless augmented reality apps with NFT will ultimately be widely adopted. However, NFT requires a great deal of processing, and it must be done in 50 ms or less.

Different approaches to pose estimation in a markerless application requires feature detection, extraction, and matching

The three fundamental blocks in feature tracking

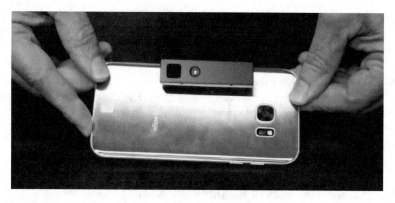

Fig. 8.68 An external 3D sensor attached to an Android phone assembly (Source: Van Gogh Imaging)

NFT involves what is known as Interest Point Detectors (IPD). Before tracking, features or key points must be detected. Typically algorithms found in the OpenCV image-processing library are used, programs such as Harris Corner Detection, GFTT, FAST, etc.

FAST (Features from Accelerated Segment Test) has been preferred for mobile apps as it requires less processor performance, but is not necessarily best for accuracy and precision.

Mobile augmented reality (and robotics) also involves Pose Estimation which uses random sample consensus (RANSAC), an iterative method to estimate parameters of a mathematical model from a set of observed data which contains outliers.

Feature descriptors for matching is where the most processing is required. An example is Scale-Invariant Feature Transform (or SIFT), an algorithm in computer vision to detect and describe local features in images.

SIFT is often used as a benchmark for detection/extraction performance. A CPU by itself typically experiences long processing latency running a SIFT program. Using a GPU for acceleration gives about a 5x to 10x improvement. Specialized tracking processors can often produce a 50 times improvement and are typically 100 times better in terms of performance per power.

Real-time performance is considered 50 ms or less from image acquisition to display (glasses), therefore feature detection, and tracking matching has to be 10 ms (or less), and <5 ms for low power operation.

NFT processing for "always-on" mobile augmented reality needs >100x improvement for always-on performance/power for 1MP sensors.

There are SLAM algorithms which are being carefully tailored to run on mobile devices which require efficient use of processing power, memory, and battery life. The picture above (Fig. 8.68) is an example of a 3D sensor attached to an Android phone. This type of configuration is going to be short-lived since smart tablets and phones are going to have the 3D sensors integrated directly into the hardware.

Wearable augmented reality applications need this performance to make power-efficient always-on augmented reality and vision applications.

So augmented reality smart-glasses manufactures have to weigh the tradeoffs of performance vs the components costs. Adding an extra vision processor may increase the costs and make the device uncompetitive.

8.9.3.1 GPS Markerless Tracking

Markerless augmented reality typically uses the GPS feature of a smartphone to locate and interact with augmented reality resources. Pokémon GO however, doesn't use SLAM, and relies on phone tracking orientation, since the Pokémon GO augmented reality feature doesn't work on devices without a gyroscope.

8.10   User Interfaces in Augmented Reality Systems

There are, as has been mentioned, four basic types of augmented reality displays: (Smart) glasses, helmets, head-up displays, and contact lenses. Each one has a different interactivity modality and interface.

Smart glasses use gesture, tapping on the side of the glasses, voice, and in some cases eye-tracking. Helmets use tapping, voice, and in the case of some experimental military helmets, eye-tracking. Some helmets only have head-up displays and don't require or support interactivity. Head-up displays are generally not as interactive and are used for information mostly such as speedometers in vehicles, or aircraft navigation. If controls are needed they are generally done via a control panel or a touch-screen. Contact lenses are still experimental and will likely use gesture and voice, possibly eye-tracking.

The interactivity used in an augmented reality system is one of the major areas of development and no standards exist, although there are some common concepts such as pinching, or swiping, techniques developed from smartphones. Because of the uniqueness of the various applications it is unlikely that a single common vocabulary can be established, just as the graphics user interfaces (GUIs) of PCs, smartphones, and tablets vary from OS, platform, and browser suppliers.

In addition, an individual's user interface should be able to provide direct interaction with the real world through the use of real physical objects and tools. There are three, non-exclusive possibilities for such interfaces [66]:

- Collaborative augmented reality interfaces which include the use of multiple displays to support remote and co-located activities (also can be thought of as telepresence).
- Hybrid interfaces that combine an assortment of different. But complementary interfaces as well as the possibility to interact through a wide range of interaction devices.
- Multimodal augmented reality interfaces which combine real objects input with naturally occurring forms of language and behaviors such as speech, touch, natural hand gestures, or gaze.

These types natural user-interfaces (NUI). Natural user-interfaces are user interfaces that are effectively invisible, and remains invisible as the user continuously learns increasingly complex interactions. Voice, gesture, and eye-tracking are examples. NUIs are still evolving, as is discussed in the following sections.

Natural user interfaces have been an active discussion since the 1990s and was introduced (and acronymized) as natural user interface. During that period Steve Mann, a pioneer in augmented reality, created several user-interface concepts using what he designated as natural interaction with the real world. He sought an alternative to the command-line interfaces (CLI) of the time, and the emerging GUI. Mann referred to this work as "natural user interfaces", "Direct User Interfaces", and "metaphor-free computing" [67]. Mann's use of the word "Natural" refers to both actions that come naturally to human users, as well as the use of nature itself, i.e. physics (natural philosophy), and the natural environment [68].

8.10.1 Voice Control

The concept of voice control, like augmented and virtual reality, are terms that have been in our vocabulary for so long, many think they know what they are and how they work. The first reference I could find of speech recognition was in Isaac Asimov's (1920–1992) short story, *Little Lost Robot*, published in Astounding Science Fiction, March1947 [69]. In it Gerald Black, a physicist, tells Nestor-10, a robot with a modified first law to "get lost," in strong words, and Nestor-10 takes the order literally and hides among 62 identical looking robots.

The first computer-based speech recognition system was *Audrey*, the "automatic digit recognizer," developed by K. H. Davis, R. Biddulph, and S. Balashek, at Bell labs in 1952 [70]. The system was only capable of understanding only digits (because of the complexity of language), and only by a single speaker. Recognizing numbers to dial a phone is an understandable goal for the research at the phone company of the day.

Ten years later, IBM demonstrated its "Shoebox" machine at the 1962 World' Fair, which could understand 16 words spoken in English [71], which was the inspiration for the two major cultural influences, Gene Roddenberry's, *Star Trek* [72], which first aired on NBC from September 8, 1966, and the HAL 9000 (Heuristically programmed ALgorithmic computer), the artificial intelligence computer in Arthur C. Clarke's *Space Odyssey* film, in 1968 [73].

By that time the idea that computers could (or would) understand humans became ingrained in our common knowledge, even if it wasn't true.

The first significant advances made in the voice recognition software were made by the United States Department of Defense's (DoD) research arm, the Defense Advanced Research Projects Agency (DARPA) in the 1970s. The DoD's DARPA Speech Understanding Research (SUR) program, from 1971 to 1976, was one of the largest of its kind in the history of speech recognition and funded a voice recognition program developed by Carnegie Mellon called 'Harpy' that understood 1000 words, moving from baby talk to the vocabulary of a 3-year-old [74, 75, 76].

Speech recognition took great strides in the mid-2010s, and speaker-independent systems appeared on smartphones and in home appliances. By 2016 speech recognition was considered a solved problem. However, there was still work to be done, and moving the recognition software from the cloud (where the smartphones and alliances got it) to a mobile device in a self-contained (stand-alone) system would prove to be a challenge for a few more years. Nevertheless, the idea of always being connected (through mobile networks and/or Wi-Fi) mitigated the problem and voice recognition was considered an integral part of many augmented reality systems. Still, the issue of a common vocabulary persisted, like the problem with gesture.

Augmented reality smart-glasses with automatic speech recognition (ASR) technologies can be used to help people with disabilities. Studies have been performed in audio-visual speech recognition (AVSR) that combines audio, video, and facial expressions to capture a narrator's voice. Augmented reality and audio-visual speech recognition technologies are being applied to make a new system to help deaf and hard-of-hearing people [77].

Such a system can take a narrator's speech instantly and convert it into a readable text and show the text directly on an augmented reality display aiding deaf people so they read the narrator's speech. In addition, people do not need to learn sign-language to communicate with deaf people.

The results of using AVSR techniques show that the recognition accuracy of the system has been improved in noisy places. Deaf people have indicated they are very interested in using such a system as an assistant in portable devices to communicate with people.

Nonetheless, people may not want to use voice to activate their augmented reality glasses—it's just too public and distracting. However, others ask how would it be any different than what we have now with people walking down the street talking to their smartphone (it used to be only crazy people walked down the street talking to invisible people).

Neil Trevett, president of the Khronos standards organization (and vice president of Nvidia) suggests (tongue-in-cheek) we will need a peripheral for our augmented glasses, a wrist touch pad that you can discretely swipe and tap to work the device. "We could call this new input gadget "Wrist Activator for Touch Commands and Haptics"—or a 'WATCH'".

Trevett also poses the question about the social issues of wearing augmented reality glasses that record your activities. "How," asks Trevett, "Do you act if the person you are talking to could be recording your every move? There may be a red record light—but ubiquitous capture capability will arrive- for better or worse—and society will figure out how to deal with it.

People (smart, tech savvy people) will wear glasses with intense LED lamps and when they see someone with augmented reality glasses they will activate their lamps to screen the other person's glasses' sensor(s). They'll be called Base Limited Input Neutralizing Device with Integrated Non-invasive Graphics- BLINDING".

Fig. 8.69 The Minority Report movie popularized the concept of gesture control (Twentieth Century Fox)

8.10.2 Gesture Control

The use of hand gestures as a means of communicating and controlling the information provided by augmented reality systems provides an attractive alternative to cumbersome interface devices for human-computer interaction (HCI); hand gestures can help in achieving ease and naturalness.

The Minority Report perhaps popularized the concept of gesture control, the movie adaption of Philip K. Dick's short story [78], which featured actor Tom Cruise waving his hands in front of a transparent screen. That design concept was developed by John Underkoffler (1967–) while at the MIT Media Lab in 1999 [79]. (Fig. 8.69)

The first computer-based gesture recognition systems used special gloves called data gloves (or wired glove or cyberglove). The first glove prototypes included the Sayre Glove (1976), the Massachusetts Institute of Technology (MIT)-LED glove, and the Digital Entry Data Glove [80]. The Sayre Glove was developed in 1977 by Thomas de Fanti (1948–) and Daniel Sandin (1942–) based on the idea of Rich Sayre (1942–) [81]. Richard Sayre postulated that a glove that used flexible tubes (not fiber optics), with a light source at one end and a photocell on the other could measure the extent to which a finger is bent (Fig. 8.70).

As the fingers were bent, the amount of light that hit the photocells varied, thus providing a measure of finger flexion.

The first widely recognized device for measuring hand positions, was developed by Dr. Gary Grimes at Bell Labs. Patented in 1983, Grimes' Digital Data Entry Glove had finger flex sensors, tactile sensors at the fingertips, orientation sensing and wrist-positioning sensors. The positions of the sensors themselves were

Fig. 8.70 Sayre glove
(Image courtesy of
Electronic Visualization
Laboratory)

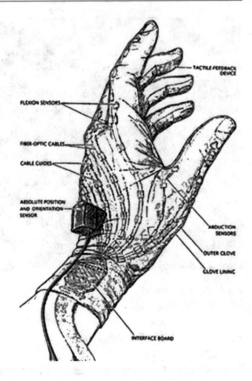

changeable. It was intended for creating "alpha-numeric" characters by examining hand positions. It was primarily designed as an alternative to keyboards, but it also proved to be effective as a tool for allowing non-vocal users to "finger-spell" words using such a system.

This was soon followed by an optical glove, which was later to become the VPL DataGlove. This glove was built by Thomas Zimmerman, who also patented the optical flex sensors used by the gloves.

However, some people credit the first electronic gesture device to Lev Sergeyevich Termen (1896–1993) better known worldwide as Leon Theremin, who invented the Theremin as part of Soviet government-sponsored research into proximity sensors. in October 1920 [82] (Fig. 8.71).

The Theremin produced variable, somewhat eerie sounds as the operator/player waved, or gestured their hands in between its two antennas like rods. The vertical antenna controls the pitch, and the horizontal antenna controls the volume. It proved to be very useful for creating outer space sounds in science fiction movies in the 1950s. The Theremin is the first musical instrument that was played without touching it.

Most researchers classify gesture recognition systems into mainly three steps after acquiring the input image from camera(s), videos or even data glove instrumented devices. These steps are: Extraction Method, features estimation and extraction, and classification or recognition as illustrated in Fig. 8.72.

Expanding gesture recognition to embrace image capture as the sensor (rather than a data glove for instance), shows the gesture capture process [83] (Fig. 8.73).

Fig. 8.71 Leon Theremin demonstrating the instrument before a concert in 1927 (Wikimedia, Brettmann. Corbis)

Fig. 8.72 Gesture recognition system steps

Gesture recognition is recognized as the communication between people and devices through hand gestures and movements.

A taxonomy of hand gestures for human-computer interaction. Meaningful gestures are differentiated from unintentional movements. Gestures used for manipulation (examination) of objects are separated from the gestures which possess inherent communicational character [84] (Fig. 8.74).

For example, volumetric models convey the necessary information required for an elaborate analysis, however they prove to be very intensive in terms of computational power and require further technological developments to be implemented for real-time analysis. On the other hand, appearance-based models are easier to process but usually lack the generality required for human-computer interaction. (*NURBS*—Non-uniform rational Basis spline is a mathematical model commonly used in computer graphics for generating and representing curves and surfaces. It offers great flexibility and precision for handling both analytic (surfaces defined by common mathematical formulae) and modeled shapes. *Primitives* are point and straight line segment, which were all that early vector graphics systems had. In constructive solid geometry, primitives are simple geometric shapes such as a cube, cylinder, sphere, cone, pyramid, torus. *Superquadrics* are a family of geometric

Fig. 8.73 Typical
computer video-based
gesture recognition process

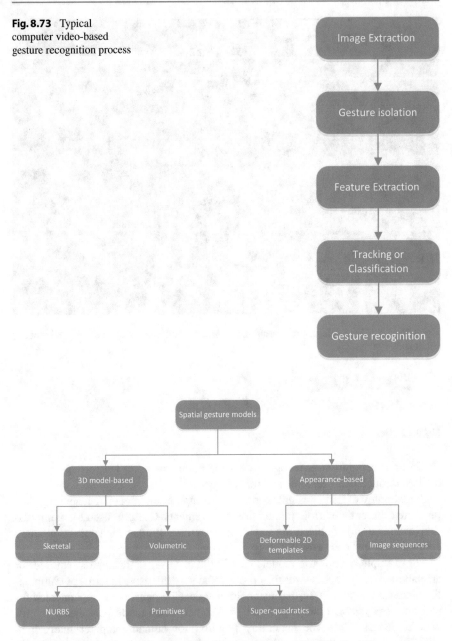

Fig. 8.74 Different ways of tracking and analyzing gestures exist, and the basic layout of steps

shapes defined by formulas that resemble those of ellipsoids and other quadrics,
except that the squaring operations are replaced by arbitrary powers.)

Augmented reality head mounted displays such as smart-glasses and helmets
(and 1 day contact lenses) allow you to use your hands to manipulate and interact

Fig. 8.75 The MIT
ALIVE system, used
computer and video
overlays so users and
virtual agents could
interact (Image: Maes et al.
1995)

with real-world objects, and that in turn creates a challenge of how to interact with the data being presented, sync you no longer have a mouse or keyboard. As mentioned above, voice control is one method of interaction that with a properly trained user can be effective in navigating menus and inputting commands or text. However, it can be inappropriate or inefficient for tasks designed for mouse or touch screens. Also, there are several situations where voice commands are socially awkward or not feasible.

However, there are other means that people can interface with their augmented head-mounted display through gestures. Nintendo surprised and delighted the world when it brought out its Wii game console with wireless handheld controllers (i.e., Nunchuk) that has motion sensing accelerometers. Microsoft came out with an alternative approach using depth sensing (i.e., Kinect), so consumers are aware and familiar in many cases with using gesture control for manipulating things on a display.

Wearing or using hand controllers are not practical in most cases because they are too attention getting in social situations, and in the way of maintenance or assembly operations.

One of, if not the first operational gesture-based systems developed was the ALIVE system developed in 1993 at MIT Media Laboratory. It used computer and video overlays that enabled the user and "virtual agents" to interact in same display space [85] (Fig. 8.75).

One of the first commercial products to use hand gestures was the Sony EyeToy, developed in 2003 It used a 2D camera peripheral device with the Sony Playstation 2 that translated body movements into game controls, predating the popular Nintendo Wii by 3 years.

A gesture-recognition system for augmented reality head-mounted displays consists primarily of the head-mounted display's camera seeing the user's hands, and algorithms to interpret the movement and register the fingers to the appropriate parts of the screen. For example, the navigation of menus which is analogous to the point and click of a mouse, or the manipulation of on-screen content such as selecting, highlighting, scaling, rotating, dragging, etc.

Most augmented reality head-mounted systems have one camera. A few devices have two cameras, or one camera and depth-sensing device (ultrasonic, or IR camera). Two (visible spectrum) cameras can be used to create a depth-map using photogrammetric techniques [86].

However captured, the gestures in such a natural user interface are unfortunately not natural, and the user must be taught the vocabulary of gestures his or her augmented reality headset employs. Each manufacture has their own vocabulary of gestures, and as of writing this book there was no standard or even a proposal for one. Consider the analogies of football referee hand gestures vs a baseball referee or those used by the military, or American sign language. None of them are the same.

In addition to a vocabulary there are technical challenges such as high-speed sensing and fast movement of the hand and motion with translational speeds up to 8 m/s and angular speeds up to 300 degrees/second [87, 88]. Also, there is the issue of occlusion management of the frequent finger/hand occlusions, and most importantly, the sensing resolution. Hands and fingers have a relatively small size compared to the upper and lower limbs and fingers are often clustered. Last but not least, complex gesture semantics: gestures can be either static, dynamic or both; are intrinsically ambiguous, and vary from person to person.

The Association of Computing Machinery (ACM) formed a Special Interest Group on Computer-Human Interaction (SIGCHI) in 1982 to emphasize research directed towards the users, with strong ties to both academia (e.g. UCSD, CMU, U. of Michigan, Virginia Tech) and industry (e.g. Xerox, IBM, Bell Labs, DEC, Apple).

8.10.3 Eye-Tracking

Eye tracking is the process of measuring either the point of gaze (where one is looking) or the motion of an eye relative to the head. Eye-tracking is an old concept developed in 1800s made using direct observations. Keith Rayner (June 20, 1943 – January 21, 2015) was a cognitive psychologist best known for pioneering modern eye-tracking methodology in reading and visual perception [89]. Eye-trackers used to cost tens of thousands of dollars and were precious pieces of equipment at psychology labs. The history of eye-tracking can be found at Wikipedia [90] and EyeSee's web pages [91].

Prior to its adoption in augmented reality and virtual reality, eye-tracking had been primarily used for behavioral studies in real-world environments, and ophthalmology studies.

The simplest use of eye-tracking is as a cursor, similarly to how we use the mouse, where a cursor on a screen follows where your eye is looking. Variations of this include using an eye-tracker to select and place game pieces or characters in a game, or move the weapon cross-hair in a game, as a replacement of the mouse in game play.

When you consider all the sensor input to an augmented reality system's heterogeneous sensor fusion integrated optical, mems, GPS, and other sensors, with

Fig. 8.76 One of the first companies to introduce eye-tracking into an augmented reality smart-glasses device was SensoMotoric Instruments.

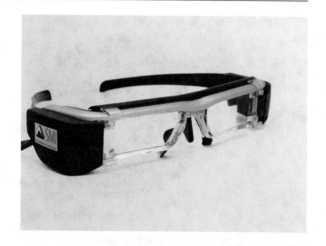

thousands of samples per second, eye tracking becomes a critical technique in these systems. Therefore, being able to track the gaze of the subject and then translate that into how content is being delivered will be a big resource consumer. If all the content that is being delivered (i.e., sensed) had to be collected at its maximum bandwidth, that wouldn't bea very efficient use of the processors or the system's battery. So having the ability to detect, very rapidly, where the eye is looking can help system designers develop architectures that will allow developers to deliver content to the viewer more efficiently.

One of the first to incorporate eye-tracking into smart-glasses was SensoMotoric Instruments (SMI), and it offered the world's first Eye Tracking Integration for Augmented Reality glasses in 2016. It is based on Epson's Moverio BT-200 see-through head mounted display, and on SMI's mobile eye-tracking platform (Fig. 8.76).

Sensor-based eye-trackers typically use corneal reflections known as Purkinje images, and the center of the pupil as features to track over time. The sensors in the headset must be very sensitive and very fast, and able to follow and detect eye movements in less than four-arc minutes (less than a fifth of a degree).

Purkinje images are reflections of objects from the structure of the eye. Four Purkinje images are usually visible. The first (P1) is the reflection from the outer surface of the cornea. The second is the reflection from the inner surface of the cornea. The third is the reflection from the outer (anterior) surface of the lens, and the fourth Purkinje image (P4) is the reflection from the inner (posterior) surface of the lens. Unlike the others, P4 is an inverted image (Fig. 8.77).

The first and fourth Purkinje images are used by some eye trackers to measure the position of an eye. The cornea reflection (P1) is known as glint.

Purkinje-Sanson images are named after Czech anatomist Jan Evangelista Purkyně (1787–1869) and after French physician Louis Joseph Sanson (1790–1841).

A more sensitive type of eye tracker, the dual-Purkinje eye tracker, uses reflections from the front of the cornea (P1) and the back of the lens (P4) as features to

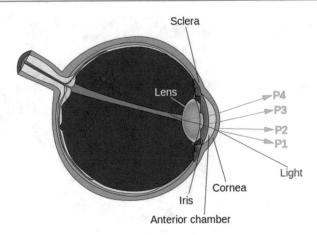

Fig. 8.77 Diagram of light and four Purkinje images (Wikipedia)

track. An additionally sensitive method of tracking is to image features from inside the eye, such as the retinal blood vessels, and follow these features as the eye rotates. Optical methods, particularly those based on video recording, are widely used for gaze tracking and are favored for being non-invasive and inexpensive, as well as security log-in procedures on computers.

Since the 2015s, technology has naturally improved, aided by the reduced size, power consumption, and cost of sensors, largely due to explosion of the smartphone market, and Moore's law. Such developments have made the possibility of putting small, unobtrusive optical sensors into glasses frames or helmets not only possible but practical. The sensors are the same basic CMOS optical sensors used in smartphones, and used in conjunction with very clever software algorithms to recognize the unique characteristics of eyes, and track their movement.

Firms such as, Eyefluence, EyeSpeak, LC Technologies, SensoMotoric Instruments, SteelSeries, The Eye Tribe, Tobii, and others have developed eye-tracking technology that could plug into a range of headsets. (Eye Tribe was acquired by Facebook-Oculus in late 2016.) Other firms are developing their own technology and incorporating it into head-mounted displays they are building. Fove for example has built a VR HMD with integrated eye-tracking.

Eye-tracking is a critical component necesssty to drive augmented reality forward for mass consumer appeal, and a necessity for the success of augmented reality as a whole.

When unobtrusive eye-tracking is available and people can use it for manipulating data and navigation with their augmented reality device, the acceptance, and demand for augmentedreality will be like that of the smartphone. Many people have only had a smartphone for a few years. Before they got one most had no desire to own one. But once they got one, like all other users of smartphones, they will never be without a one again. It was something they didn't know they needed until they had it and now they would never want to live without it.

Augmented reality devices are available and will be available in a variety of configurations driven by application, price, and features. Consumers who experience eye-interaction with an augmented reality device will never want to purchase a device that doesn't have it.

Eye-tracking, like other input techniques has its own vocabulary, the primary two functions being blink activation and dwell time, and a third less developed technique, gaze. Blink activation as the name implies, requires the user to blink some number of times to trigger an event. In some situations, this can be useful, however, it soon becomes annoying, and distracting.

Dwell time requires the user to stare at the same item until the desire event is initiated. The problem using dwell time is the constraint of the eye's saccade. Our eyes are moving all the time, darting left, right, up, down, even while we sleep, but most of the time we aren't aware of it, until you try to overcome it by staring. (see Blind spot, Sect. 8.2.1.)

The saccade of the eye is very fast and the use of a dwell function in an eye-tracking/control function slows the user down significantly. Therefore, the lack of a natural user vocabulary has been one of the things keeping eye-tracking as a major user interface.

Gaze is different from dwell in that the user looks at the general direction of the item of interest (i.e., target), but the period of time is not specified, nor does the user have to stare at the item. However, detecting the gaze has been difficult due to varying ambient light levels. Nonetheless, new developments have greatly reduced the problem [92].

Eyefluence pioneered the technology and concept of letting the eyes behave naturally in conjunction with what the user wants to accomplish, without imposing attention demanding/distracting actions (such as blinking, or staring, known as dwelling). And while most future augmented reality interactions will be a multi-modal combination of using our hands, head, eyes, and voice, natural eye behavior based on interest will most likely become the most common and popular form of interaction.

"The eyes are the windows to the soul," sure but they're also a primary mode of communication. There's a lot more going on when you're looking out as you express delight, contempt, interest, boredom.

Eye tracking and interaction is the sixth natural user interfaceThe first was the keyboard, then the mouse, voice, touch, and then stylus, and maybe the ultimate and final user interface, but it's difficult to do. Traditional eye-tracking companies have tried to translate eye movement into a method for control using the same principles as the standard mouse, requiring users to wait and wink on objects to initiate action. This makes eye-tracking slow, unsatisfying, and straining—and it sacrifices concentration and vision for machine manipulation.

Eyefluence thinks they've mastered the eye tracking user interface, by letting the user do what he or she would normally, and naturally do with their eyes. The company says they have developed a language to transform intent into action through your eyes by letting your eyes do what your eyes naturally do, and claim it takes a typical user 2 min to master their language, at which point it becomes as intuitive and automatic as walking or talking. They call it the language of looking.

Fig. 8.78 "You're always looking at something. And you have the display right in front of your eyes. Why wouldn't you want your eyes to be able to control that?" says David Stiehr, an Eyefluence cofounder

Eyefluence grew out of technology originally developed by a company called Eye-Com that developed some non-commercial eye-tracking technology that had been funded with government grants. Eyefluence acquired the technology and founded Eyefluence in early 2013 in Milpitas CA. The company has advanced the technology for integration with head-mounted displays as a fundamental technological enabler in the next generation of augmented reality and virtual reality products.

The augmented reality, virtual reality, and mixed reality markets are expanding, but one barrier remains—the user interface. The generation of products making their debut this year will be controlled with various combinations of input including touch, hand gestures, head tracking, and voice recognition. These head-mounted displays are limited because they are using interaction models that were developed for the smartphones or controllers for video gaming platforms. But head-mounted displays promise to be the next stage in computing device evolution, requiring a new user interaction model before they can reach their full potential; and Eyefluecne thinks its technology will be one to take advantage of the shortest connection between intent and action—the eyes (Fig. 8.78).

Every future augmented reality product will have eye-tracking and eye-interaction. How could it not? When you are wearing a display on your face, your first instinct is to control the interface with your eyes, whether you realize it or not. Every action begins with your eyes, through purposeful and non-purposeful eye movements.

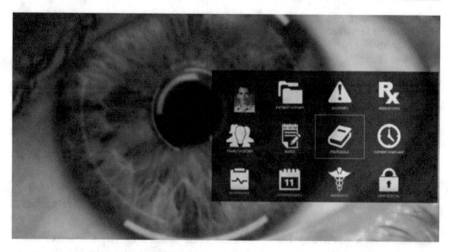

Fig. 8.79 Eyefluence wants you to control devices with your eyes (Image Credit: Eyefluence)

With eye-tracking and monitoring one doesn't interrupt or slow his or her augmented reality experience by swiping, gesturing, waiting, or winking. You don't mire yourself in all the information in the field of view. You simply let your eyes do what they do naturally to access and interact with the specific information you want, when you want it.

Eyefluence has developed a very smart eye-tracking system that does more than just monitor the eye's x-y position. The company built an eye-machine interface that acts on intentional looks and ignores incidental ones.

The Eyefluence iUi is built on the company's 12 Laws of Eye-Interaction and enables users to interact with and control head-mounted displays as fast as their eyes can see. There is a wide range of biometric measurements of the eye (oculometrics), such as pupil constriction rate, pupil size, blink rate, blink duration and others, that can be used to detect physiological states like drowsiness, cognitive load, and even excitement.

They have developed a small flexible circuit that holds a camera, illumination sources, and other tiny bits of hardware. It is meant to fit in and/or around board augmented-reality headsets using high resolution.

The result is a user, any user with normal eyes, can look at an icon (on the screen of the augmented reality device) and without doing anything consciously that icon will be activated. There are action controls for open and close (Fig. 8.79).

• The company claims it can calculate the point of regard, which means that Eyefluence figures out the point in front of you that your eyes are looking at. That's a very important idea in making an interface that is intuitive and easy enough for anyone to learn.

In October 2016, Google acquired Eyefluence.

The ability to look at a device and control it seems like something from science fiction. It is difficult to imagine that this almost superhuman gaze tracking power is a reality. Eyefluence says it's being deployed in not only state-of-the-art computers, tablets, and smartphones, but also the next generation of wearable computers,

Fig. 8.80 Wearing an
EGG headband to control
external devices
(Interaxon)

augmented reality smart-glasses and virtual reality headsets. The science of tracking human eye gaze has experienced a remarkable evolution over the last few years,
not decades, but century.

Eye-Com, is a research company led by neurologist William Torch and funded
by the National Institutes of Health, the Department of Transportation and the
Department of Defense. Torch researched everything from fatigue to blinking and
had accumulated more than a decade's worth of data on eyes as well as built technology to track and analyze the organ. Eyefluence used that foundation to create an
interactive system that uses looks to direct a computer.

8.10.4 Brain Waves

A brain–computer interface (BCI), sometimes called a mind-machine interface
(MMI), direct neural interface (DNI), or brain–machine interface (BMI), is a direct
communication pathway between an enhanced or wired brain and an external
device. BCIs are often directed at researching, a headset or helmet and the wearer's
electroencephalogram (EEG) signals [93].

Research on BCIs began in the 1970s at the University of California, Los Angeles
(UCLA) under a grant from the National Science Foundation, followed by a contract from DARPA. The papers published after this research also mark the first
appearance of the expression brain–computer interface in scientific literature.

The application of BCI will be more applicable to a helmet than smart glasses
(no one wants to go around wearing a hat with wires coming out it. However, there
are design that look like head bands that would be less conspicuous. The Interaxon
company is one supplier. Melon company also made such a device (Fig. 8.80).

In early 2015, augmented reality helmet maker Daqri bought the EEG-tracking
headband company, Melon. According to DAQRI CEO Brian Mullins, "The EEG
space has immediate potential to enhance 4D wearables with safety features, as well
as long term potential to create a game-changing brain-computer interface that will
allow you to control 4D interfaces and objects in the real world."

8.10.5 Summary

If ever the statement, "one size *does not* fit all," was appropriate, it would be in the case of a user interface.

To be truly useful a user interface must seamlessly interconnect diverse sensors, services, and devices so the system becomes perceptive, responsive, and autonomous.

For an augmented reality system to be perceptive, it must sense and understand people, actions and intentions within the view of the user. It needs to understand what actions we need it to take and respond accordingly. Furthermore, to be semi-autonomous, it needs to understand our patterns, anticipate our needs, and proactively deliver experiences and advice, warnings and instruction that fit a situation.

Just as voice commands have been less than satisfying for some people using them on their phone or in their car, or with their TV, they could be (probably will be) just as frustrating for an augmented device user. Also, there is the inappropriateness of using one's voice in a public situation (albeit some people use their phones in such a manner).

Likewise, waving your hands around in space in a public area is going to cause unwanted attention, and possibly social ostracizing and labeling. Tapping on the side of your glasses won't be much better in public, and will make people self-conscious wondering if you are recording them (Google Glass users were physically removed from some places).

Similarly, if eye-tracking and sensing does not work easily and seamlessly, people won't use it. That could be as high as two-thirds of the users, at which time the function becomes what's known as wasteware, software stuck in your device using memory (and maybe power) that you never use.

The last alternative is to use an external control device such as a smartphone, smartwatch, or a dedicated device like a wrist pad or a purpose-built handheld remote/controller. Such a device would be very straightforward to use, highly functional, likely have a short learning curve, and not call too much attention to itself or the user.

And the answer is, all of the above. No single user interface will satisfy all user in all situations, and so combinations of them will be used depending on the disposition of the user and circumstances of the situation.

References

1. Ali, M. A., & Klyne, M. A. (1985). *Vision in vertebrates*. New York: Plenum Press. ISBN:0-306-42065-1.
2. Womelsdorf, T., et al. (2006). Dynamic shifts of visual receptive fields in cortical area MT by spatial attention. *Nature Neuroscience, 9*, 1156–1160. 105.
3. Westheimer, G., & McKee, S. P. (1978). Stereoscopic acuity for moving retinal images. *Journal of the Optical Society of America, 68*(4), 450–455.
4. Optical resolution. https://en.wikipedia.org/wiki/Optical_resolution

5. Prince, S. (2010). Through the looking glass: Philosophical toys and digital visual effects. *Projections, 4.*
6. Wertheimer, M. (1912, April). Experimentelle Studien über das Sehen von Bewegung [Experimental Studies on Motion Vision] (PDF). *Zeitschrift für Psychologie., 61*(1), 161–265.
7. Padmos, P., & Milders, M. V. (1992). Quality criteria for simulator images: A literature review. *Human Factors, 34*(6), 727–748.
8. Pasman, W., van der Schaaf, A., Lagendijk, R. L., & Jansen, F. W. 1999, December 6. Low latency rendering for mobile augmented reality. *Computers & Graphics, 23,* 875–881 (international journal/conference paper), Ubicom-Publication.
9. Amin, M. S., & Meyers, A. D. (2012, February). *Vestibuloocular reflex testing.* http://emedicine.medscape.com/article/1836134-overview
10. Bailey, R. E., Arthur III, J. J. (Trey), & Williams, S. P.. *Latency requirements for head-worn display S/EVS applications*, NASA Langley Research Center, Hampton. https://ntrs.nasa.gov/archive/nasa/casi.ntrs.nasa.gov/20120009198.pdf
11. Lincoln, P., Blate, A., Singh, M., Whitted, T., State, A., Lastra, A., & Fuchs, H. (2016, April). From motion to photons in 80 Microseconds: Towards minimal latency for virtual and augmented reality. *IEEE Transactions on Visualization and Computer Graphics, 22*(4), 1367–1376.
12. Slotten, H. R. (2000). *Radio and television regulation: Broadcast technology in the United States 1920–1960.* JHU Press. ISBN:0-8018-6450-X. "C.B.S. Color Video Starts Nov. 20; Adapters Needed by Present Sets", New York Times, Oct. 12, 1950, p. 1.
13. Hoffman, D. M., Girshick, A. R., Akeley, K., & Banks, M. S. (2008, March). Vergence–accommodation conflicts Hinder visual performance and cause visual fatigue. *Journal of Vision, Research Article, 8,* 33.
14. http://www.kguttag.com/
15. Zheng, F., Whitted, T., Lastra, A., Lincoln, P., State, A., Maimonek, A., & Fuchs, H. 2014. Minimizing latency for augmented reality displays: Frames considered harmful. *IEEE International Symposium on Mixed and Augmented Reality.* p. 195
16. Rolland, J. P., & Fuchs, H. (2000). Optical versus video see-through head mounted displays. *Presence: Teleoperators and Virtual Environments, 9*(3), 287–309.
17. Holloway, R. L. (1997). Registration error analysis for augmented reality. *Presence, 6*(4), 413–432.
18. Barfield, W. (Ed.). (2016). *Fundamentals of wearable computers and augmented reality* (2nd ed.). Boca Raton: CRC Press/Taylor & Francis Group.
19. Karim, M. A. (1992). *Electro-optical displays.* New York: Marcel Dekker, Inc. ISBN:0.8247-8695-5.
20. https://en.wikipedia.org/wiki/Human_eye
21. Murray, W. S.. (2003, August). The eye-movement engine. *Behavioral and Brain Sciences, 26*(04), 446–495. Cambridge University Press.
22. https://en.wikipedia.org/wiki/Cave_automatic_virtual_environment
23. Comeau, C. P., & Bryan, J. S. (1961, November 10). Headsight television system provides remote surveillance. *Electronics, 34,* 86–90.
24. Bionic eye will send images direct to the brain to restore sight. *New Scientist.* https://www.newscientist.com/article/mg22830521-700-bionic-eye-will-send-images-direct-to-the-brain-to-restore-sight/
25. Zrenner, E., et al. (2010). Subretinal electronic chips allow blind patients to read letters and combine them to words. *Proceedings of the Royal Society B.* doi:10.1098/rspb.2010.1747.
26. Brody, T. P. (1997). Birth of the active matrix. *Information Display, 13*(10), 28–32.
27. Armitage, D., et al. (2006). *Introduction to microdisplays.* Chichester: Wiley. ISBN:978-0-470-85-281-1.
28. IBM. (1998). Special session for high-resolution displays. *IBM Journel of Research and Development, 42*(3/4).

29. Clark, N. A., & Sven, T. L. (1980). Submicrosecond bistable electro-optic switching in liquid crystals. Applied Physics Letters 36 (11), 899. Bibcode:1980ApPhL.36.899C. doi:10.1063/1.91359

30. *Display device*, 1986-09-03 (Japanese publication number JP61198892)

31. Tidwell, M., Johnston, R. S., Melville, D., & Furness, T. A. III. (1998). *The virtual retinal display – A retinal scanning imaging system*. Human Interface Technology Laboratory, University of Washington.

32. *Compact head-up display*, US 4711512 A, Dec 8, 1987.

33. Tedesco, J. M., Owen, H., Pallister, D. M., & Morris, M. D. (1993). *Principles and spectroscopic applications of volume holographic optics. Analytical Chemistry, 65*(9), 441A.

34. Mukawa, H., Akutsu, K., Matsumura, L., Nakano, S., Yoshida, T., Kuwahara, M., Aiki, K., & Ogawa, M. (2008). *A full color eyewear display using holographic planar waveguides. SID 08 Digest, 39*, 89–92.

35. Amitai, Y., Reinhorn, S., & Friesem, A. A. (1995). *Visor-display design based on planar holographic optics. Applied Optics, 34*, 1352–1356.

36. Spitzer, C., Ferrell, U., & Ferrell, T. (Eds.). (2014, September 3). *Digital avionics handbook* (3rd ed.). Oxford/New York/Philadelphia: CRC Press.

37. Popovich, M., & Sagan, S. (2000, May). *Application specific integrated lenses for displays. Society for Information Display, 31*, 1060.

38. Cameron, A. A. (2012, May 1). Optical waveguide technology and its application in head-mounted displays. *Proceedings SPIE 8383, Head- and Helmet-Mounted Displays XVII; and Display Technologies and Applications for Defense, Security, and Avionics VI, 83830E*. doi:10.1117/12.923660

39. Bleha, W. P., & Lijuan, A. L.. (2014, June 1–6). *Binocular holographic waveguide visor display* (SID Symposium Digest of Technical Papers, Volume 45). San Diego.

40. Templier, F. (Ed.), (2014, September) *OLED Microdisplays: Technology and Applications*, Section 7.2.2.3.3.4 *Polarized waveguide*, ISBN:978-1-84821-575-7, p. 256, Wiley-ISTE.

41. Kohno, T., Kollin, J., Molnar, D., & Roesner, F.. Display leakage and transparent wearable displays: Investigation of risk, root causes, and defenses. *Microsoft Research*, Tech Report, MSR-TR-2015-18.

42. Bernanose, A., Comte, M., & Vouaux, P. (1953). *A new method of light emission by certain organic compounds. Journal de Chimie Physique, 50*, 64.

43. Mann, S. (2001, January 28), Contact lens for the display of information such as text, graphics, or pictures, Canadian Patent 2280022, filed July 28, 1999. https://www.google.com/patents/CA2280022A1?cl=en

44. Leonardi, M., et al. (2004, September). *First steps toward noninvasive IOP – Monitoring with a sensing contact lens. Investigative Ophthalmology & Visual Science, 45*, 3113–3117.

45. http://www.sammobile.com/2016/04/05/samsung-is-working-on-smart-contact-lenses-patent-filing-reveals/

46. http://appft.uspto.gov/netacgi/nph-Parser?Sect1=PTO2&Sect2=HITOFF&u=/netahtml/PTO/search-adv.html&r=20&p=1&f=G&l=50&d=PG01&S1=(20160407.PD.+AND+(Sony.AS.+OR+Sony.AANM.))&OS=PD/4/7/2016+and+(AN/Sony+or+AANM/Sony)&RS=(PD/20160407+AND+(AN/Sony+OR+AANM/Sony))

47. Lingley, A. R., Ali, M., Liao, Y., Mirjalili, R., Klonner, M., Sopanen, M., Suihkonen, S., Shen, T., Otis, B. P., & Lipsanen, H. (2011, November 22). A single-pixel wireless contact lens display. *Journal of Micromechanics and Microengineering, 21*(12), 125014.

48. Kong, Y. L., Tamargo, I. A., Kim, H., Johnson, B. N., Gupta, M. K., Koh, T.-W., Chin, H.-A., Steingart, D. A., Rand, B. P., & McAlpine, M. C. (2014, October 31). *3D Printed quantum dot light-emitting diode*. Department of Mechanical and Aerospace Engineering, Princeton University, Princeton, New Jersey, Nano Letters, American Chemical Society.

49. Mann, S. (2013, March). *My augmented life*. IEEE Spectrum. http://spectrum.ieee.org/geek-life/profiles/steve-mann-my-augmediated-life

50. https://en.wikipedia.org/wiki/Radio-frequency_identification

51. *Hacking Exposed Linux: Linux Security Secrets & Solutions* (3rd ed.). McGraw-Hill Osborne Media. 2008. p. 298. ISBN:978-0-07-226257-5.

52. Landt, J. (2001). *Shrouds of time: The history of RFID* (PDF). AIM, Inc. Retrieved May 31, 2006.

53. *Lightweight, wearable tech efficiently converts body heat to electricity.* https://news.ncsu.edu/2016/09/wearable-teg-heat-harvesting-2016/#comment-7695881

54. *Sprinkling of neural dust opens door to electroceuticals.* http://news.berkeley.edu/2016/08/03/sprinkling-of-neural-dust-opens-door-to-electroceuticals/

55. *Samsung's AR vision includes smart contact lenses.* http://www.technewsworld.com/story/83354.html

56. *The bionic lens: A new dimension in sight enhancement.* http://ocumetics.com/

57. *Thermal vision: Graphene spans infrared spectrum.* http://www.engin.umich.edu/college/about/news/stories/2014/march/infrared-detector

58. Yu, W. J., et al. (2016). Unusually efficient photocurrent extraction in monolayer van der Waals heterostructure by tunneling through discretized barriers. *Nature Communications.* doi:10.1038/ncomms13278.

59. http://phys.org/news/2015-05-artificial-muscles-graphene-boost.html

60. Kim, G., & Oh, Y. H. (August 2015). A radon-thoron isotope pair as a reliable earthquake precursor. *Scientific Reports, 5,* 13084.

61. https://en.wikipedia.org/wiki/Fiducial_marker

62. Mann, S., & Fung, J. (2002, April). EyeTap devices for augmented, deliberately diminished, or otherwise altered visual perception of rigid planar patches of real-world scenes. *Presence, 11*(2), 158–175. Massachusetts Institute of Technology.

63. Mann, S. (1997, April). Further developments on "HeadCam": Joint estimation of camera rotation + gain group of transformations for wearable bi-foveated cameras. *IEEE Conference on Acoustics, Speech, and Signal Processing, 4,* 2909–2912.

64. Tang, F., Aimone, C., Fung, J., Marjan, A. and Mann, S. (2002, September 30–October 1. Seeing eye to eye: A shared mediated reality using EyeTap devices and the VideoOrbits Gyroscopic Head Tracker. In *Proceedings of the IEEE International Symposium on Mixed and Augmented Reality (ISMAR2002),* (pp. 267–268). Darmstadt, Germany.

65. Siltanen, S. Theory and applications of marker-based augmented reality, Copyright © VTT 2012, Julkaisija – Utgivare – Publisher (ISBN:978-951-38-7449-0).

66. Furht, B. (Ed.). (2011). *Handbook of augmented reality.* New York: Springer.

67. Mann, S. (1998, June 15–19). (Reality User Interface (RUI), in the paper of the Closing Keynote Address, entitled), *Reconfigured Self as Basis for Humanistic Intelligence,* USENIX-98, New Orleans, Published in: ATEC '98 Proceedings of the annual conference on USENIX Annual Technical Conference USENIX Association Berkeley, USA ©1998.

68. Mann, S. (2001). *Intelligent image processing.* San Francisco: Wiley.

69. Asimov, I. (1947, March). *Little Lost Robot,* short story, Astounding Science Fiction, *39*(1), Street & Smith.

70. Davis, K. H., Biddulph, R., & Balashek, S. (1952). *Automatic recognition of spoken digits. Journal of the Acoustical Society of America., 24,* 637–642.

71. http://www-03.ibm.com/ibm/history/exhibits/specialprod1/specialprod1_7.html

72. https://en.wikipedia.org/wiki/Star_Trek

73. https://en.wikipedia.org/wiki/HAL_9000

74. Chen, F., & Jokinen, K. (Eds.). (2010). *Speech technology: Theory and applications.* New York/Dordrecht/Heidelberg/London: Springer.

75. Sturman, D. J., & Zeltzer, D. (1994). A survey of glove-based input. *IEEE Computer Graphics & Applications,* p. 30, http://www.pcworld.com/article/243060/speech_recognition_through_the_decades_how_we_ended_up_with_siri.html

76. Waibel, A., & Lee, K.-F. (Eds.). (1990). *Readings in speech recognition.* San Mateo: Morgan Kaufmann.

77. Mirzaei, M. R., Ghorshi, S., & Mortazavi, M. (2014, March). Audio-visual speech recognition techniques in augmented reality environments. *The Visual Computer, 30*(3), 245–257. doi:10.1007/s00371-013-0841-1

78. Dick, P. K. (2002). *Minority report*. London: Gollancz. (ISBN:1-85798-738-1 or ISBN:0-575-07478-7).
79. Technologies in Minority Report. https://en.wikipedia.org/wiki/Technologies_in_Minority_ Report
80. Premaratne, P.. (2014). *Human computer interaction using hand gestures*. Sinapore/Heidelberg/ New York: Springer.
81. Dipietro, L., Sabatini, A. M., & Dario, P. (2008, July). A survey of glove-based systems and their applications. *IEEE Transactions on Systems, Man, and Cybernetics—part c: Applications and Reviews, 38*(4), 461–482.
82. The London Mercury Vol.XVII No.99 1928.
83. Lyon Branden Transcript of Gesture Recognition. (2013, April 23). 500. https://prezi.com/ piqvjf2g-eec/gesture-recognition/
84. Pavlovic, V. I., Sharma, R., & Huang, T. S. (1997, July). Visual interpretation of hand gestures for human-computer interaction: A review. *IEEE Transactions on Pattern Analysis and Machine Intelligence, 19*(7), 677.
85. Maes, P., Darrell, T., Blumberg, B., & Pentland, A.. 1995, April 19–21. The ALIVE system: full-body interaction with autonomous agents. *Proceeding CA '95 Proceedings of the Computer Animation*, p. 11.
86. Periverzov, F., & Ilies, H. T.. *3D Imaging for hand gesture recognition: Exploring the software-hardware interaction of current technologies*, Department of Mechanical Engineering, University of Connecticut, http://cdl.engr.uconn.edu/publications/pdfs/3dr.pdf
87. Varga, E., Horv'ath, I., Rus'ak, Z., & Broek, J.. (2004). Hand motion processing in applications: A concise survey and analysis of technologies. *Proceedings of the 8th International Design Conference DESIGN 2004* (pp. 811–816).
88. Erol, A., Bebis, G., Nicolescu, M., Boyle, R., & Twombly, X. (2007). *Vision-based hand pose estimation: A review. Computer Vision and Image Understanding, 108*(1–2), 52–73.
89. Rayner, K. (1998). *Eye movements in reading and information processing: 20 years of research. Psychological Bulletin, 134*(3), 372–422. doi:10.1037/0033-2909.124.3.372. Retrieved June 17, 2011.
90. https://en.wikipedia.org/wiki/Eye_tracking
91. http://eyesee-research.com/news/eye-ttacking-through-history/
92. Sigut, J., & Sidha, S. A.. (2011, February). Iris center corneal reflection method for gaze tracking using visible light. *IEEE Transactions on Biomedical Engineering, 58*(2), 411–419. doi:10.1109/TBME.2010.2087330. Epub 2010 Oct 14.
93. David, P. (2012, December 1). 6 Electronic devices you can control with your thoughts. *Scientific American*

Suppliers

9

Abstract

The augmented reality market has attracted interest since the early 1970s and that interest has never stopped. Slowed sometimes by technology limitations, and/or military budgets, in the 2000s with the advent of the smartphone and amazing sensors available for low prices, plus new low cost displays, the market has steadily expanded with new companies. Obviously, that can't go on forever.

9.1   Augmented Reality Devices and Suppliers

At the time of writing this book I identified 80 companies offering, or promising to offer dedicated augmented reality devices (which excludes general purpose devices like smartphones and tablets, contact lenses, and specialized and others such as video viewing glasses). One of the reasons for that is because the augmented reality market is still in development and whenever a new market develops there are a flood of companies seeking to enter it and get in on the ground floor. Typically, when a market matures and becomes established, commoditization sets in and the number of suppliers is driven down to a dozen or less. The same thing will eventually happen to the augmented reality market, but it will take a while, maybe ten or more years. The reason the market will support (some might say tolerate) so many suppliers is because there are no standards (or very few of them), and there are so many vertical (specialized) applications.

And of course, there will be sizing options that will create niche market opportunities for some. You can think of the automotive, TV, or the mobile phone market as examples where commoditization has been established and yet there are enough customers who want something special, or very low cost that one or two suppliers can focus on that segment and make enough profit to stay in business.

© Springer International Publishing AG 2017

J. Peddie, *Augmented Reality*, DOI 10.1007/978-3-319-54502-8_9

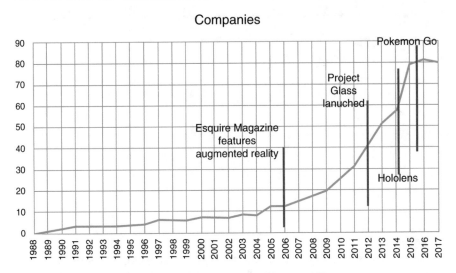

Fig. 9.1 Companies entering the augmented reality market since 1988

I have subdivided the dedicated augmented reality devices into five categories:

- Contact lens—7 suppliers or developers
- Helmet—7+ suppliers
- HUD—10+ suppliers
- Smart-glasses
  - Integrated
    Commercial—26 suppliers
    Consumer—17 suppliers
  - Add-on—14 suppliers
- Projectors (other than HUD) 3
- Specialized and other—6+ developers or suppliers

The companies and developers are listed in the appendix.

9.1.1 Suppliers

The augmented reality market hit a peak of suppliers in 2016, climbing from 15 in 2010 to 80. The market started to stabilize and consolidate as standards were developed and smaller and opportunist companies with little to no real commitment to the industry dropped out or were acquired.

The article in Esquire Magazine in December 2009 got people's attention and new companies started forming thereafter. Since Google announced Project Glass in early 2012, the number of suppliers more than doubled. (Fig. 9.1).

This is typical in the development of a new market or technology. In 1893 there were 102 automobile manufacturers and today (depending on what you include[1]) there are 30. In 1970, almost 100 companies had formed to manufacture minicomputers; today there are none. From 1977 to 1991 there were over 75 manufacturers of PCs, and in 1992 there were 72 suppliers of 3D graphics chips, today six. Do you notice a pattern here?

One such example is Metaio. It was a privately held company founded in Munich in 2003 as an offshoot of a project at Volkswagen. Metaio developed software technology and provided augmented reality solutions. At augmented reality conferences its software could be seen in use everywhere: it was the de facto developer for augmented reality environments by 2015. In May 2015, Apple acquired the company and active cloud subscriptions expired in December 15 and support ended June 30 2016.

In this book alone there are 15 mentions of companies being acquired by others since 2006, and I didn't make any attempt to find them all and know for certain I didn't. The point being the augmented reality industry, even though it can trace its roots back to the early 1960s, is still a very young, dynamic, and evolving field, with enormous opportunities for technological development, and money to be made.

9.1.1.1 Helmet

BAE systems Striker
BMW
Cinoptics
C-Thru
Daqri
Elbit Systems
Intelligent Cranium

9.1.1.2 Smart Glasses—Integrated-Commercial/Industrial

APX Labs
Atheer
Brother Industries
Cannon
Caputer Seer
Coretronic
Epson
Eveno Eyes On (Epson)
Fujitsu
Google Glass
IMMY
Laster Technologies
Meta

---

[1] Passenger cars are motor vehicles with at least four wheels, used for the transport of passengers, and comprising no more than eight seats in addition to the driver's seat.

Microsoft Hololens
Mirage Innovations
Optinvent
Osterhout Design Group
Oxsight
Penny
PhaseSpace
Shenzhen Topsky Digital
Sony
Sulon Cortex
Trivisio
Vrvana
Vuzix

9.1.1.3 Smart Glasses—Integrated-Consummer
Brilliant Service
Dlodlo
GlassUp
Intel Composyt Light Labs
Intel Recon
Kopin Solos
Laforge
LusoVU eyespeak
Luxottica Oakley
Magic Leap
Mirama Brilliant Service
MRK Imagine Mobile Augmented
Murata
QD Laser
RideOn
Solos
Zeiss

9.1.1.4 Smart Glasses—Add-on
Beijing Palo Alto Tech
Chipsip
Coretronic
Eurogiciel
Garmin Varia Vision
Gold Tek Foxconn
Lenovo
Lumus
Mad Gaze
Occipital
Orca m

Seebright
Senth IN1
Telepathy
Vufine

9.1.1.5 HUD
Carrobot
Garmin
Hudway
Iris
Kshioe
Mygoflight
Navdy
Pioneer
Springteq
WayRay

9.1.1.6 Projection
CastAR
Hololamp
Realview

9.1.1.7 Contact Lens
EPGL
Ghent University
Google
Gunnar
Innovega
Ocumetics
Samsung
Sony

Conclusions and Future Possibilities

10

Abstract

Augmented reality will touch all parts of our lives, our society, and the subsequent rules we live by. As we adapt to the new capabilities and power that augmented reality bestows on us, we will have to think about things differently and give up some cherished ideas and fantasies. It will change social mores and rules, and challenge those who hold power arbitrarily.

As suggested by Raimo van der Klein, augmented reality is our seventh media experience or vehicle (Sect. 1.7.2).

Having an inconspicuous and personal augmented reality display, much like having a watch or a smartphone, that presents data in the wearer's field of view will be the biggest step forward in how we play, work, learn and communicate since the internet and mobile phones. Augmented reality devices will enhance and expand our memory as well as become our guide, teacher, and backup record in case of, or durin emergencies.

10.1 Privacy—Is There Such a Thing Today?

As consumers embrace augmented reality, and I can't emphasize that too much, that it won't happen until the devices are inconspicuous and don't call attention to themselves or the wearer, society must come to grips with a new understanding of the concept of privacy. Protesting about being photographed when in a public environment will not be defendable. We have been photographed in airports, department stores, casinos, taxi cabs, and other common places for over a decade. There is no privacy in public. Therefore, the use of augmented reality glasses that record everything you see (and everyone you see) cannot be considered violating someone's privacy. However, the concept changes when the wearer enters what might be considered a private domain such as a private club, a home, or maybe someone's automobile. And yet if you were in any of those places you have no assurance you are not being recorded. This is Mann's classic philosophic argument about surveillance and sousveillance [1].

Mann argues, and correctly so in my opinion, that another person or agency can't legitimately prevent you from recording them, if they in turn are recording you.

The issue extends to the use of facial recognition and the collection of associated information about the person whose face has been identified. People concerned about such things should remember that all that information obtained in such a way came from profiles created by the person expressing the concern. As Avram Piltch said, "You're the one violating your own privacy" [2]. If one has a criminal record, that too is public information and available, as is your driver's license and any other publicly issued license you might have. In many parts of the U.S., a person's tax records can be found as well as high school and college records.

10.2 Social Issues

Privacy is one issue, another is self-isolation and lack of interaction. We've all seen people walking, head down, looking at a smartphone, and maybe it's even been us once or twice. We've seen the vacant look of people on public transportation with earphones on, or lost in a game on their phone. Parents and educators, as well as sociologists and anthropologists worry that we may be building (or already have built) a generation of detached children that don't know how to interact, who are not socialized and therefore don't know how to act, and worst, maybe become sociopaths.

Brendan Scully, of Metaio, one of the pioneers in augmented reality and acquired by Apple in 2015, said: "The dream of augmented reality is to prevent the dream of virtual reality," He also said: "We're going to walk outside, see where our friends are and interact with virtual objects. We're going to use the Internet, which we do right now for hours and hours in our rooms, but [now we'll use it] as we walk around and take part as citizens." Let's hope his vision is correct.

To that point, The New Zealand Auckland Council ran a trial of outdoor games for children using augmented reality (see section "Geo AR games").

Regardless of the side-effects of augmented reality, and remember, all new technological developments bring unexpected, and sometimes unwanted side-effects, augmented reality is going to have such a significant and overall positive impact on our lives we truly will wonder how we managed to get along with it.

10.3 Nano-Scale Technology

And we will owe much, if not all of it to microminiaturization, the shrinking of parts while expanding the technology.

As the world of semiconductors has shrunk to nano and microscopic our lives have got better. Whereas the steam and gasoline engines gave us a better standard of living by scaling up in size, the third industrial revolution benefits us by getting smaller. So small we can't see it but can feel its benefits, soon to be coursing through organs and veins, our eyes and brains.

As I like to point out, the technology works when its invisible. Your two proudest possessions, your automobile and your smart phone work flawlessly and very few people, even most of the Technorati[1] don't fully understand the internal workings of these essential tools, status symbols, and entertainment devices. And that's the good news. We don't really understand how our bodies work, and like our wondrous machines only become aware of them when they don't work.

And it's only going to get better. Better at such a rate some of us will not be able to absorb it and go into a Luddite-like counter-reaction and try to thwart the inevitable march of technology with superstition and violence. But for those who embrace it, life is going to be so rich, so exciting, enlightening, and entertaining we will consider plastic surgery to get the perpetual smile off our faces.

It's not just semiconductors, although semiconductor manufacturing techniques have been the catalyst for most of the miniaturization. Nano-scale transistors, smaller than a virus, approaching the size of atoms, and be packed together by the billions, approaching the population of the earth, and fit in a package the size of a U.S. silver dollar. All those transistors can be hooked up to make the most powerful computers imagined, and run on thin batteries in our pockets, all day long.

But the transistors are not alone, and couldn't work their magic if they were. They, and we, rely on the tiny electro-mechanical devices, smaller than a grain of rice that sense our movements, the earth's magnetic poles, the local temperature and atmosphere's pressure, the photons immersing us with energy transfer elements that convert them to electrons, and the nano-scale micromachined capacitors that can detect sound waves surrounding us. Only neutrinos, and gravity waves are being ignored—today. After the wondrously tiny processors manipulate the data from the nano-sensors, it is sent places. Through equally miniscule radios to the world at large, to localized devices stuck in our ears, to internal storage devices, and most importantly to displays.

Some of the displays are in the device, others are in devices near us, and still others are in things mounted on our heads; glasses, helmets, and one day, contact lens. As amazing as it is to contemplate a panel the size of small note book containing 8.3 million light emitting crystals, it's even more astounding to think about 2 million such crystals occupying a space smaller than the diameter of pencil, embedded in our glasses.

The tiny radios can receive as well as transmit, and provide us with geo-spatial reference data from dozens of orbiting satellites, nearby radio towers and local nodes in shops or other people. All of that to help us know where we are, exactly, almost any place on the earth. Not just where we are, but where we are looking, the tilt of our head, and the velocity, if any, of our movement.

With that precision positioning information, we can receive, and send critical information about our immediate environment. We can receive information about the geography, history, construction above and below the ground, and the proximity of others. Likewise, we can provide that same level of information about what we are seeing and experiencing, making us the archivers of life, and dispelling once and for all misrepresentation of the facts. And if truth and information are not the

---

[1] Technorati is a portmanteau of the words technology and literati, which invokes the notion of technological intelligence or intellectualism.

greatest gifts our tiny technology can give us, I'm at a loss to imagine what else it might be other than pseudo physical sensations from haptic devices. Our teeny tiny technology has augmented our lives on our bodies, the next phase will be to augment it inside our bodies. Already being experimented with for the blind and partially blind, for insulin delivery, and seizure maintenance.

And the teeny tiny devise not only augment us, they augment the things around us, our lights, TVs, automobiles, and even our refrigerators. Like the ants and mites that clean up after us, our tiny things make our lives richer than could be imagined just a half decade ago. Small is wonderful.

10.4 What the Future May Hold

A common assumption held by many, but not me, is that augmented reality and virtual reality will merge, possibly through light field display and become what is called mixed reality.

The concept of modality driving such a forecast is that people will spend most of their day in augmented reality and occasionally switch to virtual reality for entertainment or specific job-related tasks in design, training, medicine, travel, and real estate, and possibly shopping. That makes a lot of sense, but doesn't require an all-encompassing tight-fitting face covering device. I have seen prototypes of augmented reality headsets (e.g., Phase Space's Smoke HMD [3]) with pull down visors that obscure most of the wearer's vision of his or her immediate environment, and that is more than adequate. Being able to still maintain some sense of connection to the real world while watching a virtual reality video, or playing a game is highly appealing to many people. There are dedicated viewing devices like Adant's Glyph, which are specifically designed that way, and they give a very comfortable and non-claustrophobic experience, one that you can enjoy for an extended period, which is not something one can say about virtual reality in general.

But we live in a Darwinian world of technology where almost every possibility will be tried and tested. And like some creatures which survive without any understandable reason for their survival, obscure and esoteric products too will survive. It seems in technology nothing ever really goes away.

The vision of the future will not be a giant screen that one waves their hands in front of as Tom Cruise did in the movie Minority Report, based on the Philip K. Dick story (Fig. 10.1).

We will all the information we need right in front of us in space, or associated with some physical thing. Our augmented reality glasses will make large screens obsolete for most of us.

Predicting the future is easy, getting the dates right is difficult. So, I won't pick any dates for when things might happen. But you are just as good at predicting the future as anybody. Just let your imagination wander and extend the possibilities of what could happen. More than not, what you imagine will come true. Science-fiction writers do that for a living (and amusement), you're just not getting paid for your vison—other than being able to say, "I told you so."

Fig. 10.1 A person reads from a futuristic wraparound display screen. (Wikipedia) This is NOT how the future will look, augmented reality will make large screens obsolete

I am getting paid for my vision, and my "I told you so," is that we will be using augmented reality sooner, and more frequently than you and I can imagine. It will make us smarter, possibly kinder, governments fairer, and helpers more capable and faster.

Augmented reality is where we all will live.

References

1. *Wearable Computing and the Veillance Contract*: Steve Mann at TEDxToronto. https://www.youtube.com/watch?v=z82Zavh-NhI
2. Piltch, Avram. (2014, July 2) *Augmented reality makes us more human, not less*. http://www.tomsguide.com/us/augmented-reality-future,news-19099.html
3. http://smokevr.net/

Appendix

The Appendix has all the reference material such as the Index, Glossary, information on standards, and a bit of whimsy.

This section contains supplementary material, explanatory, definitional, and information for reference use, as well as the index of terms, people, some products, and organizations.

Prototype WWI Augmented Reality Glasses?

Were the Germans ahead of the times

I found this photo in a collection of old photos sent to us by our friend and former (now retired) collogue, Pat Meier. Knowing my interest in augmented reality I assumed that was her motivation for forwarding it. The concept, developed by Germany in 1917, was quite advanced (Fig. A1).

Upon further investigation, I discovered they are actually directional sound finders used to detect incoming enemy planes in 1917. A junior officer and NCO from an unidentified Feldartillerie regiment modelling what appears some kind of portable sound locating apparatus. The goggles were binoculars set to focus on infinity so when they found the source of the sound by turning their head, they could see the aircraft creating that sound.

Drake Goodman, who collects old photo and memorabilia of the era commented, "One can't help but automatically jump to the conclusion that these fellows must belong to an anti-aircraft battery, which would explain the sound-detection gear, but the AA role was performed by the Air Service, not the artillery. Another mystery for the files." https://www.flickr.com/photos/drakegoodman/5612308131/

Standards

Augmented reality brings computer-generated graphics and information to the user. By superimposing all types of information, and lifelike, digital images on what a person is seeing in the real world.

© Springer International Publishing AG 2017
J. Peddie, *Augmented Reality*, DOI 10.1007/978-3-319-54502-8

Fig. A1   Is this an early augmented reality system (Photo credit Drake Goodman)

Various technologies, and therefore standards organizations are associated with augmented reality, there is no augmented reality standards body (yet).

The International Electrical and Electronics Engineers (IEEE) standards association published dozens of standards pertaining to augmented reality, and they can be found at: http://standards.ieee.org/innovate/ar/stds.html

Specifically, the IEEE Digital Senses Initiative [1] (DSI) was launched in 2015 by the IEEE Future Directions Committee, the organization's R&D arm.

"The DSI is dedicated to advancing technologies that capture and reproduce the real world or synthesize the virtual world, and add the stimuli of human senses," said Yu Yuan, the initiative's chair. "Our scope includes combining reproduced or synthesized stimuli with natural stimuli and helping humans or machines to perceive and respond to them."

Augmented and virtual reality, and human augmentation technologies are all growing fields, he notes, but the lack of collaboration among participating entities has become a barrier to development and widespread adoption.

All three technologies have been around for decades, but early applications were lacking, according to Yuan, because their virtual stimuli did not feel real enough and the overall experience was not rich enough.

The initiative has been sponsoring several IEEE Standards Association Industry Connections groups to propose technical standards in the three areas.

The Augmented Reality in the Oil/Gas/Electric Industry Group is exploring how head-mounted displays, head-up displays, and other applications might benefit the three fields. The Smart Glasses Roadmap Group is working to overcome hurdles blocking the adoption of smartglasses in a number of markets and applications.

The 3-D Body Processing Group is devising standards for the capture, processing, and use of 3-D data on various devices so they can communicate with one another and transfer information. The group also plans to tackle security, privacy, metrics, communications and sharing protocols, and methods for assessing results.

The DSI is also working with the Industry Connections program to form a Digital Senses Alliance, which would foster cross-industry and cross-disciplinary collaborations to identify gaps in technologies and standards.

Several publications are available. One is a yearly report covering upcoming advances. Another highlights best practices for filmmakers and game developers.

Because augmented reality allows for a mix of real and virtual objects, Yuan predicts we'll see new types of services and business models in retail, transportation, manufacturing, construction, and other industries.

"augmented reality will change how we interact with the environment and the services around us," said Yuan.

The Association of Computing Machinery (ACM) has several papers on augmented reality and some discussions on standards at: http://dl.acm.org/citation.cfm?id=2534379&CFID=867791712&CFTOKEN=83157534

Reference

1. http://digitalsenses.ieee.org/

Glossary

The following is a list of terms and acronyms used in this book, and a brief explanation.

360 video There is a difference between augmented reality and 360-degree video. The latter is less immersive and typically keeps the viewer in a fixed point surrounded by roughly 360 degrees of video that was captured by someone else usually. However, augmented reality glasses and helmets can also capture 360-video if the user stands still and slowly turns in a circle while the camera is recording.

6DOF Six-degrees of freedom, see below.

Accelerometer An accelerometer measures linear acceleration of movement Accelerometers in mobile phones are used to detect the orientation of the phone, they measure rate of change.

ACM The Association of Computing Machinery.

Addressable occlusion where the image from the GPU/IG has a geometric and synchronous correlation to a segmented part (or parts) of the image on the display (screen) which blocks out light directly behind the augmented imagery.

Adjustable depth of field is the ability to correct the augmented reality image focal point to correlate to the real world. If that isn't done there will be an accommodation-convergence conflict which causes viewer discomfort and fatigue because of the vergence accommodation. Visual fatigue and discomfort occur as the viewer attempts to adjust vergence and accommodation appropriately.

AP/FP Application processor/function processor, fixed function engines, task-specific.

API application program interface.. A series of functions (located in a specialized programming library), which allow an application to perform certain specialized tasks. In computer graphics, APIs are used to expose or access graphics hardware functionality in a uniform way (i.e. for a variety of graphics hardware devices) so that applications can be written to take advantage of that functionality without needing to completely understand the underlying graphics hardware, while maintaining some level of portability across diverse graphics hardware. Examples of these types of APIs include OpenGL, and Microsoft's Direct3D.

ASR Augmented reality smart-glasses with automatic speech recognition.

AVSR Audio-visual speech recognition.

© Springer International Publishing AG 2017
J. Peddie, *Augmented Reality*, DOI 10.1007/978-3-319-54502-8

BCI A brain–computer interface, sometimes called a mind-machine interface (MMI), direct neural interface (DNI), or brain–machine interface (BMI), is a direct communication pathway between a headset or helmet and the wearer's EEG signals.

Birdbath A combination of a beam-splitter and a curved combiner. Google Glass might be considered a "modified birdbath."

BTLE Bluetooth low energy.

Candela The candela per square meter (cd/m2) is the derived SI unit of luminance. The unit is based on the candela, the SI unit of luminous intensity, and the square meter, the SI unit of area.

CAVE Cave Automatic Virtual Environments.

CCFL cold cathode fluorescent lamps, a LCD back-panel lighting technology.

CMOS Complementary metal–oxide–semiconductor, a technology for constructing integrated circuits.

Combiner The optical combiner works to combine light from the external world and from the image generator into a single presentation of visual data to the imaging optics and eyes.

COTS commercial off-the-shelf, an adjective that describes software or hardware products that are ready-made and available for sale to the general public. For example, Qualcomm's Snapdragon is a COTS product that is a heterogenous processor designed for mobile devices.

DARPA Defense Advanced Research Projects Agency.

Depth of field The distance between the nearest and the furthest objects that give an image judged to be in focus of the viewer.

DERP Design eye reference point, where a pilot is at the optimum location for visibility, inside and outside the cockpit, as well as the correct position for access to the cockpit switches and knobs.

DL Dynamic digitized light field Signal, or digital light field for short.

D-ILA JVC's Digital Direct Drive Image Light Amplifier (like LCoS).

DLP digital Light Processing device, same as DMD.

DMD Digital micromirror device, a micro-opto-electromechanical system (MOEMS) that is the core of the trademarked DLP projection technology from Texas Instruments.

DNI See BCI.

DSP Digital signal processor (for cameras, mic, range finders, and radio).

ERP Eye reference point.

Exit pupil A virtual aperture in the optical system.

Eye-box The eye-box is the volume of space within which an effectively viewable image is formed by a lens system or visual display, representing a combination of exit pupil size and eye relief distance.

Eye relief distance The distance between the vertex of the last optic and the exit pupil.

Eye tracking Eye tracking is similar to head tracking, but instead reads the position of the users' eyes versus their head.

EVS Enhanced vision systems.

FSC Field sequential color in which the primary color information is transmitted in successive images, and which relies on the human vision system to fuse the successive images into a color picture.

Field of view (FoV) Field of view is the angle of degrees in a visual field. Having a higher field of view is important because it contributes to the user having a feeling of immersion in a VR experience. The viewing angle for a healthy human eye is about 200 degrees. So, the bigger that angle is, the more immersive it feels.

FPS frames per second, the refresh rate of the display.

GPU Graphics processing unit.

Gyroscope The gyroscope, or gyro for short, tracks the angular rotational velocity or twist of the augmented reality device. Both accelerometers and gyro sensors measure rate of change.

GUI Graphical user interface.

Haptics tactile feedback in the form of vibration is the common meaning for haptic feedback in an augmented reality or virtual reality system. It means users feeling like they're touching something that's not really there.

Heterogeneous processors heterogeneous computing refers to systems that use more than one kind of processor or cores. These systems gain performance or energy efficiency not just by adding the same type of processors, but by adding dissimilar coprocessors, usually incorporating specialized processing capabilities to handle particular tasks.

HCI Human-computer interaction.

Head mounted display or HMD typically goggles or a helmet of some type, the kind one straps to the face or puts on the head. Also called a headset.

Head tracking this term refers to the sensors that keep up with the movement of the user's head and move the images being displayed so that they match the position of the head. If one is wearing a HMD, head tracking is what lets the user look to the left, right, up, or down, and see the world that's been built in those directions.

Headset see head mounted display.

HIT Human Interface Technology lab at the University of Washington.

HWD Head-worn display.

ICT Information-and-communications-technology.

IEEE International Electrical and Electronics Engineers.

ILED Inorganic LED, also referred to as MicroLED.

IMU Inertial measurement unit, used as a gyroscope.

Inside-outside Six-axis of freedom, see below.

IoT The Internet of Things.

ISA Image signal processor (for camera output).

Jitter jitter is the result of electromagnetic interference (EMI) and crosstalk with other signals. Jitter can cause a display monitor to flicker.

Judder judder is the unsmooth, jerky movement of the visual (due to insufficient display updating or refresh speed). It is a combination of smearing and strobing that's especially pronounced on virtual reality/augmented reality HMDs. Judder is not the same as jitter.

Lag lag is defined as the time it takes an instruction in a GPU to ask (or command) a drawing operation until the image actually appears on the screen or display.

LCD Liquid-crystal display, a flat-panel display that uses the light-modulating properties of liquid crystals. Liquid crystals do not emit light directly.

LCoS Liquid crystal on silicon (LCoS or LCoS) a miniaturized reflective active-matrix liquid-crystal display or "micro-display" using a liquid crystal layer on top of a silicon backplane.

Latency is in an augmented reality or virtual reality experience when the user turns his or her head and the visuals don't keep up. It can be unpleasant, because that's not something that happens in the real world. That lag is a complaint about virtual reality, and to a lesser extent augmented reality, experiences.

Magnetometer The magnetometer in an augmented reality device utilizing modern solid state technology to create a miniature magnetic field sensor (called a Hall-effect sensor) that detects the Earth's magnetic field along three perpendicular axes X, Y and Z. The Hall-effect sensor produces a signal proportional to the strength and polarity of the magnetic field along the axis each sensor is directed to.

MEMs Micro Electro Mechanical systems used for miniature gyroscope-like sensors.

Metaverse the science-fiction idealized vision of what virtual reality and augmented reality are. The term came from Neal Stephenson's 1992 science fiction novel *Snow Crash*, where humans, as avatars, interact with each other and software agents, in a three-dimensional space that uses the metaphor of the real world. Broadly, it's a bit of a philosophical underpinning of virtual reality; Forbes defines it as a "collective virtual reality," but there's plenty of debate about what that applies to and really, what exactly that is.

MicroLED microLED, also known as microLED, mLED or μLED, is a flat panel display technology that consists of arrays of microscopic LEDs forming the individual pixel elements.

MMI see BCI.

NED Near to eye display. (Also called near eye display.)

Nit (nt) is a unit of luminance. It is a non-SI name used for candela per square meter (1 nt = 1 cd/m2). See candela.

NFT Natural Feature Tracking is the idea of recognizing and tracking a scene that is not deliberately using markers.

NUI Natural user-interface a user interface that is effectively invisible, and remains invisible as the user continuously learns increasingly complex interactions. Voice, gesture, and eye-tracking are examples.

NURBS Non-uniform rational Basis spline is a mathematical model commonly used in computer graphics for generating and representing curves and surfaces. It offers great flexibility and precision for handling both analytic (surfaces defined by common mathematical formulae) and modeled shapes.

OLED An organic light-emitting diode in which the emissive electroluminescent layer is a film of organic compound that emits light in response to an electric current. An OLED does not use a black light (and so can be on transparent film, and can achieve a higher contrast ratio than an LCD.

OS Operating system. An operating system is system software that manages computer hardware and software resources and provides common services for computer programs. All computer programs require an operating system to function.

PBS Polarization beam-splitter.

PMD Personal media devices are head-mounted displays that are direct-view devices. They obscure the user's immediate (front-facing) view, but not the bottom or top. They are used primarily for entertainment such as movies, 360-videos, games, and remote viewing—such as a drone camera.

PPI Pixels per inch.

Presence presence, a term derived from the shortening of the original "telepresence." It is a phenomenon enabling people to interact with, and feel connected to, the environment outside their physical bodies via technology. It is defined as a person's subjective sensation of being there in a scene depicted by a medium, augmented or virtual in nature (Barfield et al. [2]).

Primitives are point and straight line segment, which were all that early vector graphics systems had. In constructive solid geometry, primitives are simple geometric shapes such as a cube, cylinder, sphere, cone, pyramid, torus.

Projected reality the use of a structured light projector and some type of viewing device to see 3D objects in a local space. Used indoors, and in a confined space. Also considered mixed reality.

Refresh rate refresh rate is how fast images get updated on the screen or display. Higher refresh rates cut down on lag, and cutting down on lag reduces the possibility of getting simulation sickness. The refresh rate is the number of times a display's image is repainted or refreshed per second. The refresh rate is expressed in hertz so a refresh rate of 75 Hz means the image is refreshed 75 times in one second.

RID Retinal imaging display, same as a retinal projector.

RP Retinal projector (RP), projects a raster display (like a television) directly onto the retina of the eye.

RSD Retinal scan display, same as a retinal projector.

RTOS Real-time operating system.

S3D Stereoscopic 3D viewing using two screens (or a split screen) to create a quasi 3D image. Glasses used for stereo 3D (S3D) viewing can be used in theaters, with TV, and PCs, and in CAVEs. They are not a display device but rather a modulator of a display, causing an alternate view of the image to be presented to each eye.

SAR Spatially augmented reality.

SIMD Same Instruction Multiple Data describes computers with multiple processing elements that perform the same operation on multiple data points simultaneously. Such machines exploit data level parallelism, but not concurrency: there are simultaneous (parallel) computations, but only a single process (instruction) at a given moment. SIMD is particularly applicable to common tasks like adjusting the contrast and colors in a digital image.

Simulator sickness Simulator sickness is the conflict between what the user's brain and body register, and what their eyes are seeing (see Latency). Science Magazine suggests that this disparity is interpreted as a toxin, and the human body does what it can to get that toxin out, e.g., vomiting. However, everyone has different thresholds, not everyone gets sick, or as sick as someone else might.

Six-degrees of freedom 6DOF position, refers to the position and orientation of the camera. Microsoft calls this "inside-outside" tracking 6DOF refers to the freedom of movement of a rigid body in three-dimensional space: forward/backward (surge), up/down (heave), left/right (sway), combined with changes in orientation through rotation about three perpendicular axes, often termed pitch, yaw, and roll.

SLAM Simultaneous Localization and Mapping (SLAM) is a computer vision technology. SLAM allows an entity to track its location while simultaneously mapping its surroundings. The computational problem of constructing or updating a map of an unknown environment.

SME Subject matter experts.

SoC system on a chip processors used in mobile phones and tablets contain a CPU, GPU, ISA, AP/FP, and usually a sensor multiplexor.

Social AR This term refers to a type of application that aims to create a shared augmented reality space where users can interact with each other and even participate in activities.

SDK Software Development Kit or "devkit." A software development kit is a set of software tools for the creation of applications for a particular device and/or OS.

Special augmented reality Special augmented reality (SAR) is a branch of augmented reality based on projectors that delivers a glasses-free and hands-free augmented reality experience.

Stitching Stitching is the process of taking video or photos from the camera(s), and combining those images into either a very wide photo or a spherical video. The process uses specialty software that orients the video or photos, eliminating seams, and general editing so it looks like one continuous view rather than a patchwork.

Structured light A technique used for depth sensing. A projector sends out an infrared dot pattern to illuminate the environment (a point cloud). As the dots get further away they become larger. The size of all the dots are measured by a camera algorithm to determine the relative distance from the user.

Superquadrics are a family of geometric shapes defined by formulas that resemble those of ellipsoids and other quadrics, except that the squaring operations are replaced by arbitrary powers.

SXRD Sony's Silicon X-tal Reflective Display (like LCoS).

Telepresence see Presence.

TIR total internal reflection principal.

ToF Time-of-flight. A depth measuring technique like RADA that measure the time it takes for an emitted pulse of light from the headset to strike an object and return to the camera sensor.

UI User interface.

Vergence The simultaneous movement of both eyes in opposite directions to obtain or maintain single binocular vision.

Visual discovery the technology or technique that fulfills a user's curiosity about the world around them by giving them information and relevant content when objects and images in the field of view are selected.

Visual marketing the practice of using images and objects to enhance brand communications and utility via image recognition, augmented reality and visual discovery.

VR/augmented reality sickness see Simulator sickness.

VRD Virtual retinal display, same as a retinal projector.

Reference

1. Barfield, W., & Hendrix, C. (1995). *Virtual Reality, 1*, 3. doi:10.1007/BF02009709.

Index

Printed in the United States
By Bookmasters